The Church Amid Revolution

A Selection of the Essays Prepared for
the World Council of Churches
Geneva Conference on Church and Society

Edited by HARVEY G. COX

ASSOCIATION PRESS · NEW YORK

The Church Amid Revolution

Association Press, 291 Broadway, New York, N. Y. 10007

Publisher's stock number: 1652p

Library of Congress catalog card number: 67–21140

 72

PRINTED IN THE UNITED STATES OF AMERICA

PREFACE

by Paul Abrecht *

The World Council of Churches Conference on Church and Society continues to arouse discussion. It is therefore fortunate that this selection of chapters from the four study volumes published for the conference makes some of the preparatory material available to the great number of laymen and pastors who may never have time to wade through the fifteen hundred pages of those books. Not only is the conference itself more understandable when seen against the background of the preparatory volumes, but also the books stand as an ecumenical study project of value in their own right, apart from the conference. Indeed one of the criticisms made by those attending the conference was that it did not take sufficiently into account the thinking in the volumes. Perhaps the idea that four substantial study volumes could be digested by the participants in the three months before the conference was an illusion. But whatever the merits of that argument, the volumes will provide,

---

* Mr. Abrecht, who is Executive Secretary of the Department on Church and Society of the World Council of Churches, was responsible for planning and administering the WCC Geneva Conference on Church and Society. —*Editor*.

along with the report of the conference, basic material for discussion in our churches for some years to come.

I sympathize with Professor Harvey Cox in his effort to make a selection of twelve chapters from the more than eighty possibilities. The reader of these essays must remember that much of the balance and perspective of the original volumes had inevitably to be sacrificed in the selection. It is not suggested that these are the best or the most important essays of the entire lot. They were chosen to give the reader a sample of the range of opinion in the original volumes and a taste of the diverse points of view that must somehow be reconciled in the development of a universal Christian perspective.

With this in mind, Professor Cox has rightly emphasized the new Christian thinkers of Africa, Asia and Latin America, and it is good that six of the twelve essays come from these areas. He has also selected contributions from theologians and laymen under fifty years of age! The fact that in his selection Professor Cox favors the theologians slightly may be attributed to what our French friends call *une deformation professionelle*. I am glad that he has selected at least one of the Roman Catholic contributions to the volumes, for the theologians and laymen from that church made an enormous contribution to the study volumes and in several joint Roman Catholic–WCC consultations prior to the conference, to the program of the conference as well. The presence of the highly qualified group of observers from the Vatican, of the official Roman Catholic guests and of the large and highly competent Roman Catholic press corps was one of the striking features of the 1966 conference. Indeed it can be said that the quality and intensity of the post-conference discussion in Roman Catholic journals has equaled that of our own ecumenical debate in quality and intensity of interest. We have yet to assess the full meaning of the new possibilities of World Council–Roman Catholic collaboration in social thought and action which the World Conference has apparently opened up.

It should be evident, therefore, from this selection of essays that ecumenical study and discussion of social questions has entered a new and dynamic period. I foresee that the wide-ranging debate on church and society will continue for some years to come;

and these essays offer little hope of an easy or rapid solution to some of the most acute differences. If the western reader is offended by some of the non-western challenges to his accustomed ways of thinking, let him remember that these are his Christian friends writing. He has yet to hear the even sharper words of his friends from other religions.

CONTRIBUTORS

Rev. Emilio Castro Pastor of the Central Methodist Church in Montevideo, Uruguay; licentiate in theology of the Evangelical Theological Seminary; postgraduate studies in Basel, Switzerland; secretary of the recently formed Commission for Evangelical Unity in Latin America.

Monsieur A. Delobelle Assistant to Professor A. E. Collard, Faculté Sciences Economiques Sociales, Université Catholique, Louvain. (Roman Catholic Church)

André Dumas Professor of ethics at the Faculty of Theology in Paris. Author of *Der Krieg in Algerien; Le contrôle des naissances; Opinions protestantes; La soumission chrétienne* (L'éthique interhumaine des épitres du Nouveau Testament et notre temps); *Une théologie de la reconciliation: Dietrich Bonhoeffer;* co-author of *L'homme marxiste et l'homme chrétien.* (Église Reformée de France)

Mr. Cesar Espiritu Vice-president of the Credit Corporation of the Philippines. Vice-president of the Executive Committee of the World Student Christian Federation. (United Church of Christ in the Philippines)

ABBÉ FRANÇOIS HOUTART Professor of sociology at the University of Louvain and Director of the Centre de Recherches Socio-Religieuses, Louvain; general secretary of FERES. Author of many studies of the sociology of development, especially in Latin America; his recent books include *The Challenge to Change: The Church Confronts the Future*, 1964; *El Cambio Social en America Latina*, 1964; and, with E. Pin, *L'Eglise à l'heure de l'Amérique Latine*, 1965. (Roman Catholic Church)

DR. JOHN KAREFA-SMART Professor at the School of Public Health and Administration, Columbia University; formerly Minister of External Affairs of Sierra Leone; coauthor of *The Halting Kingdom—Christianity and the African Revolution* (with Mrs. Rena Karefa-Smart); consultant to World Council of Churches Assembly, Amsterdam, 1948, and Africa consultant to World Council of Churches Rapid Social Change Study 1956–57. (Evangelical United Brethren)

PROFESSOR J. M. LOCHMAN Professor of systematic theology and philosophy at the Comenius-Faculty, Prague. Author of several publications, including *Religious Thought of the Czech Enlightenment* (2 volumes); *Theology and Philosophy; Theology and History of Religion;* and *Importance of Historical Events for Ethical Decisions*. (Evangelical Church of Czech Brethren)

PROF. MAURICIO LOPEZ Secretary of the Department on Church and Society of the World Council of Churches; formerly the Latin American secretary of the World Student Christian Federation; leader in many Latin American student conferences and consultations; articles and lectures on the church and the Latin American social revolution: coauthor of *Race, a Signal* (1961) and *Witness in Six Continents* (1964). (Evangelical Church of Argentina)

PROFESSOR RICHARD SHAULL Professor of ecumenics, Princeton Theological Seminary; pioneer in Church and Society studies in Latin America; a younger theologian appealing especially to the new student generation. Author of *Encounter with Revolution* and many articles and essays. (United Presbyterian Church)

PROFESSOR ROGER L. SHINN William E. Dodge, Jr., professor of applied Christianity and dean of instruction, Union Theological Seminary, New York City. His writings include *Christianity and the Problem of History* and *Life, Death and Destiny;* editor of *The Search for Identity: Essays on the American Character;* a leader in Christian social action movements sponsored by the National Council of Churches, U. S. A., and his own church. (United Church of Christ)

MASAO TAKENAKA Professor, Christian social ethics and sociology of religion, and dean of school of Theology, Doshisha University; chairman of the Committee of the Witness of Laity of the EACC; chairman of Political Commission of WSCF. (United Church of Christ)

MR. M. M. THOMAS Director of the Christian Institute for the Study of Religion and Society, Bangalore, India; chairman of the Working Committee for the Department on Church and Society of the World Council of Churches; secretary of East Asia Christian Conference; author of many books on the church and problems of nation-building: *Mud Huts and Steel Mills* (with R. Taylor); *Christian Participation in Nation Building* (with C. Devanandan); *Political Outlook in India Today* (with R. Chandran); *Problems of Indian Democracy* (with C. Devanandan); *Christian in the World Struggle* (with D. McCaughney). (Mar Thoma Church)

CHARLES C. WEST Professor of Christian ethics, Princeton Theological Seminary; formerly assistant director of the Ecumenical Institute at Céligny, Switzerland. Author of *Communism and the Theologians; Outside the Camp,* a study of the church in mission; co-editor with Robert Mackie of *The Sufficiency of God: Essays in Honor of Dr. W. A. Visser't Hooft;* and, with David Paton, of *The Missionary Church in East and West.* (Presbyterian)

CONTENTS

INTRODUCTION

by Harvey G. Cox

FEW try to deny anymore that churches everywhere in the world are going through a tumultuous new reformation, one that will certainly leave them more significantly altered than did the reformation of the sixteenth century. But there is an important difference between what is happening to us today and what occurred then. While the reformation of the sixteenth century had important social consequences, it represented in the first instance a change in the life of the church itself. The implications for the church's role in society were secondary. In our time, on the other hand, the main debate centers on the question of what is the church's proper role in society. Only after this question is settled will we be able to see how the internal life of the churches should be changed and renewed.

During the next few years the issue of church and society will become increasingly prominent. On nearly every continent of the globe churchmen will come together in a series of conferences on this question. Following up a world conference sponsored by the World Council of Churches in Geneva in July, 1966, they will grapple with the issue of how the churches, both as institutions and as the People of God dispersed in the world, should meet the major challenges confronting world society today. The American conference is scheduled for October, 1967, in Detroit, Michigan. This book is especially prepared in conjunction with that conference and for the lively discussion that is sure to follow it all over the country and the world.

In preparation for that historic assembly in Geneva fully eighty different preliminary papers were written. They were published in four volumes by the Association Press early in 1966. Taken together they cover a vast range of theological, political and ethical issues. These selected examples from those preparatory essays in no way pretend to be representative. These may not be the best or even the most important essays. They have been selected to bridge the gap between the kind of thinking that went into the preparation for the Geneva conference and the kind of action that will have to emerge after the American conference in the fall of 1967. Let me now say something about the essays I have selected for this volume and why I selected them.

It has been widely noticed that the word "revolution" was central in the lexicon of disputed terms and central ideas at Geneva. This came as a surprise to many of the American delegates, but not to Richard Shaull, an American with wide experience in Latin America. His essay on revolutionary change in theological perspective leads off our collection. Shaull is clearly committed to Christian participation in revolutionary change, and writes lucidly about the theological implications of this kind of participation. He knows that a theological understanding of revolution is based not so much on a doctrine of man as it is on our understanding of human history, where God is at work, and of what he is doing in that history. Shaull argues that what Christians need most in a revolutionary situation is not so much an ecumenically defined view of the good society but a theologically sound understanding of the process of revolutionary change.

From a "western" voice we move to a man from the "East." Professor J. M. Lochman, who contributes the essay "The Service of the Church in a Socialist Society," teaches at the Comenius Protestant Faculty at the Charles University in Prague, Czechoslovakia. It is important that his essay be included in this collection,

especially since the United States is now basically reevaluating its
relationship to Eastern European countries and countries with
communist and socialist governments. Professor Lochman does
not bewail the state of the church in his country; he believes, in
fact, that when the church is shorn of the privileges it acquired
during the long Constantinian period of church history, it may be
freer than it has ever been to witness to the gospel. Lochman believes this will require what he calls "civil interpretation," by
which he means something close to the secret discipleship that
Dietrich Bonhoeffer once discussed. He believes that the Christian
community in socialist countries can serve to keep those nations
open to the continuing need for the humanization of their societies.

We can learn much from Lochman and his peers, not just about
Eastern Europe but about our own situation, since the spiritual
environment he describes, one of accelerating secularization, ob-
tains not only in communist countries but in our own country as
well.

Roger Shinn speaks as an American theologian about the ethical
dilemmas of American society, especially its enormous affluence.
He describes the characteristics of the affluent society and then
tries to trace out alternative ways of understanding wealth which
come to us from our Christian history. He finds that we have not
yet developed an adequate theological understanding of what it
means to be Christians in an era of affluence. He then calls the
church to learn something about the meaning of the affluent society, and to use the opportunity it presents. Should the church
call other institutions to responsibility in the midst of affluence, and
should it even *use* its own affluence in an exemplary way? Shinn
says Yes. He also points out that the church is an international
community and believes this should remind us of our deep inter-
relation with people around the world, most of whom do not yet
share this affluence. His article obviously calls for a further thinking about how we can live in the midst of riches and wealth,
neither flagellating ourselves for our violation of the call to apostolic
poverty nor simply reveling in the swill of prosperity, but bringing to bear the power which wealth gives us to the upbuilding of
the whole world community.

In Latin America the problems faced by the church are not affluence and cybernation but poverty, hunger, political oppression and neocolonial control from the outside. These conditions have made it clear to many Latin Americans, including the Reverend Emilio Castro, that God calls the church to participate in the task of social transformation. As a Methodist and a real Evangelical, however, Castro asks the question many people have asked: How does individual conversion relate to the calling of social transformation? His essay suggests the beginning of an answer to this question but it is certainly one which will require further discussion. Castro's article also serves to inform us that below the Rio Grande there is a vast continent of ferment and unrest, and also a continent where a new, highly biblical and politically radical form of theological ethics is being born. Emilio Castro is one of its midwives.

The next four essays take us around the world to the problems of man, church and society in four different regions of the so-called "third world." M. M. Thomas, an Indian Christian who served as chairman of the Geneva conference, surveys this entire scene for us and points out the crucial importance of the newly awakened and developing nations for world politics. Mauricio Lopez pencils in the piping hot political particulars of Latin American society today. Mr. Lopez is himself an Argentinian. One wonders after reading his article whether North American Christians ought not be more concerned about the policies of our government and of our private corporations south of the Rio Grande and, if so, how this concern should be expressed. Next we turn to Africa. John Karefa-Smart writes about African nationalism in the exceedingly difficult stage after political liberation has been won, but before really effective national governments have emerged. Mr. A. C. Espiritu, a citizen of the Philippines, writes about economic development in Southeast Asia and its relationship to foreign aid, regional trade and the structure of world trade. His is an article of high technical competence, and he is a native of the section of the world about which he writes and with which Americans have recently become painfully familiar. Espiritu helps us to realize that underlying much of the ideological rhetoric and military argument about that troubled region there remains the basic

hallenge of economic development. This is an issue which will
remain whenever and however the war in Vietnam is ended.

The increasingly warm relations between the World Council of
Churches and the Roman Catholic Church were particularly
evident in Geneva. Among the Roman Catholic observers present
were Abbé François Houtart, professor of sociology at the University of Louvain, and Monsieur A. Delobelle, who is at the Catholic University in Louvain. In this collection Houtart surveys the
attitude of the Roman Catholic Church toward economic planning
at the national and international level. It is good that he does so
because it is becoming increasingly evident that since the churches
form one of the largest nongovernmental agencies working in the
field of economic development, the combined contribution of the
Vatican and the World Council of Churches might be considerable
in tipping the story of development away from exploitation and in-
equity and toward the emergence of a real world community.

The final essays in this collection come from the fourth of the
preparatory volumes, entitled *Man in Community*. Masao Takenaka
writes about Asia between the old and the new worlds. As a
Japanese Christian who is deeply involved in industrial mission
as well as teaching, Takenaka describes the transformation of his
society from a vertical plane to a horizontal one. He then examines
the increase in patterns of conformity, but also sees that the
Christian church, though a tiny minority in Japan, can still play
a significant role in calling people to a common interest in the
whole society rather than into individual fulfillment. André Dumas,
a French Protestant theologian, contributes a brilliant essay on the
ideological and psychological tensions in advanced industrial society, such as his own in France. Mr. Dumas is particularly sensitive to the high price we all pay in complex industrial societies in
which one must sacrifice the spontaneous, the intimate and the af-
fective in the interest of efficiency and complex organization.
Finally, Charles West, an American theologian, issues a singularly
clear and unavoidable call for the church to take seriously the
secular society in which we live and to speak to it in terms which
it can understand. He does not bewail the emergence of secularization but feels we need a new style of secular theology in order to
present the gospel to it. Mr. West also believes, I think rightly,

that a secular future is hastening not only toward the United States
or Western Europe but toward the entire world, especially as it is
caught up in technical change, population growth and industrialization.

As American Christians gather for the Church and Society Conference it should quickly become evident to us that although we
have a host of domestic issues to think about, surely the most
pressing issue we will have to face is that of the enormous power our
nation wields in the world community. How will this issue shape
up? I hope it will not take the form of a continuing pursuit of the
sterile and obsolete division between the so-called "free" and the
so-called "communist" worlds. At Geneva this outdated definition of the issue was left behind. Participants from those countries where some form of communism is established had no reason
to feel they were outsiders. The conference nowhere condemned
communism. Rather it suggested that Christians should work within
their various societies to help communist countries move toward
just and humane goals. In fact, not only were the East Europeans
not condemned by the West, but the two often found themselves
drawn closer to each other in response to the stinging criticisms of
Africans and Asians. This "attack from the South" made the old
East–West dichotomy almost irrelevant.

Here denominational labels counted for nothing. Methodists
from Uruguay argued stridently with Methodists from the United
States but agreed with Catholics and Presbyterians from south
of the Rio Grande.

But while Geneva showed that a North–South breach does
exist, it also revealed that communication across it is not impossible. Robert Theobald, the controversial economist and social
critic, had told the conference that Geneva might mark the last
church conference in which the rich, white nations of the North
and the poor, colored nations of the South would even try to
communicate with each other. He had said he doubted whether
the rich were ready or able to listen to the poor. The conference
demonstrated, however, that this kind of communication, though
difficult, is by no means impossible. Not yet anyway.

The question that remains is whether the churches are now ready
to address themselves to the main issue dividing the two camps.

That issue is not communism. It is not even revolution or colonialism but the question of what is to be done about the wretchedly
unjust system of international structures which regulate and control
the flow of trade and wealth among the nations. It was the nearly
unanimous opinion of all the Christians at Geneva who were from
the poor nations that these structures would have to be altered
radically if a real world community were to become possible.

Most westerners and northerners were caught off guard by the
intensity of the feeling on this subject among people from developing nations. The third-worlders are convinced that the rules under
which the game of trade and development is now played are cruelly
stacked to their disadvantage. They believe the widening gap between developed and developing nations comes from the fact that
the developed nations treat the other nations merely as sources
of raw materials (whose prices are set outside the third world)
and as markets for manufactured goods. They resent being objects
of charity, and their experience with western theories of economic
development in the past decade has not been a very happy one.
Only a few have reached anything like the magical "takeoff stage."
The rest see the chasm between themselves and the North widening. In their rejection of "development" talk and their demands for
more radical policies they sound very much like American Negroes
spurning all gradualism and demanding "Freedom Now" or even
the international equivalent of "Black Power."

This "international class gap" in the church should remind us
that our euphoria about our ecumenical togetherness may be a
trifle premature. However pleasant it is to converse with our opposite numbers in other wealthy churches, the world church includes people whose hunger and anger we must recognize. These
people are also a part of *oikoumene*. To live in separation from
them is also to perpetuate the sin of disunity.

The Geneva conference set an example of candor and liveliness
that will be hard to emulate. The spirited essays in this book convey
the volatile and refreshing atmosphere Geneva helped to create.
Will the American churches be able to do as well? Will American
Christians be ready to rethink their xenophobic attitudes toward
communism, to look again at the questionable role of American
capital in Latin America and American military power in South-

east Asia? Will they be able to discuss "Black Power" rationally or think about China without hysteria?

Geneva 1966 may have marked a turning point in ecumenical social thinking and social action. But unless its impulses are absorbed into the lives of the churches themselves, it could turn out to have been just another high-flown ecumenical talkfest.

This book provides a set of essays that should help our discussion in America become concrete. Still, much is missing that Christians ought to think about in order to live faithfully within modern society. For example, we need discussions on political participation, on what is happening to family life, on the emergence of alienated subcultures, on youth, on the escalation of defense spending, on the racial crisis in America and around the world, on what technology portends and promises for the years ahead. All these subjects were covered and covered well in essays contained in the preparatory volumes. Some of them are alluded to briefly in the articles appearing in this book; but the very fact that this book is not a complete one, that it has deficiencies and chasms in its coverage, may be useful. It suggests that the real work of thinking through the meaning of the gospel in our time is not a job that books can do for us. They can stimulate, prod, anger and inspire us, but finally we must do the thinking ourselves. We must sit down with those with whom we share responsibilities in God's world and with those with whom we share life in the church. We must search out what God is doing in our world and what he is asking us to be and to do and then we must write our own response, not simply in essay form but in the way we live our individual and corporate lives.

The Church Amid Revolution

I

REVOLUTIONARY CHANGE IN THEOLOGICAL PERSPECTIVE

by RICHARD SHAULL (United States)

As we have become increasingly aware of the dynamic nature of society today, ecumenical social thinking has focused on *rapid social change*. Technology has emerged as the central factor, in a close and unusual relationship with other elements. The technological revolution developed in the West as a consequence of a fundamental change in man's understanding of reality and of the social order. At the same time, the spread of technology seems to accelerate this shift to a functional and secular attitude and to make imperative the development of new and more flexible forms of institutional life. In *Christianity in World History,*[1] Professor A. Van Leeuwen insists that this is part of an irresistible historical process in which traditional "ontocratic"[2] patterns of life are being shattered. All orders of society are losing their sacral character and are now open toward the future, to be shaped as man wills. At the same time, the author discerns a growing tendency toward the emergence of messianic movements dedicated to the liberation of man from all that enslaves and dehumanizes him.

---

[1] London: Edinburgh House Press, 1964.
[2] By "ontocratic," PROFESSOR VAN LEEUWEN means having an understanding of reality in terms of a total order of harmony between the eternal and the temporal, the divine and the human. The divine order is identified with nature and society, especially with the state conceived of as the "embodiment of cosmic totality." All structures of society are given a sacred character; they dare not be tampered with or changed.

Given the fluidity of a dynamic society, we should now be witnessing gradual progress toward the shaping of new social structures, which would offer a greater degree of justice and well-being to the depressed classes of the world. Thus far, however, this has not happened to any significant extent. Over against the discovery that society can be changed stands the fact that those who most benefit from the present situation have tremendous economic and political power and are willing to go to almost any length to preserve it. Entire classes and races of people have discovered that their suffering is not inevitable and have thus awakened to a new hope for a better life. But this hope has not been fulfilled. Institutions structured for a stable society have failed to adjust to the new order and are in crisis. Economic development, industrialization and the rapid growth of large cities, the population explosion and other factors have raised new problems, which they are unable to meet creatively; especially in the developing nations, this technological progress has often tended to increase the misery and insecurity of the poor, provide even greater opportunities for the few to profit, and leave the masses in greater insecurity than before. The process of secularization has undercut traditional concepts of authority, but new patterns of relationships have not yet evolved. In the midst of rapid social change, the uprooted masses discover the extent to which society has deprived them of their selfhood and left them in a state of alienation. In these circumstances, mass movements become the way by which they acquire a new identity as they participate in a struggle to shape a new society.[3]

We are thus confronted by a new and unprecedented polarization between those who have enjoyed the benefits of the status quo and those who are most anxious to change it. Our world is divided sharply between the rich and the poor nations; and in each country, a struggle is taking shape between those groups, races and classes who have awakened to their inferior position and those who are reluctant to make way for a new order. Consequently, it would seem that *social revolution* is the primary fact with which our generation will have to come to terms.

---

[3] ERIC HOFFER, commenting on the Negro revolution in the United States, writes: "Mass movements are often the means by which a population undergoing drastic change acquires a sense of rebirth and a new identity." *New York Times Magazine,* Nov. 29, 1964, p. 109.

Except in Latin America, the anticolonial struggle has now passed its peak; but the struggle of the poor and weak nations for an opportunity to participate more fully in international life and to have a more equitable share of the wealth of an interdependent world has only just begun. In developing and developed nations, the revolution of the dispossessed is still in its early stages. The Negro revolution in the United States now occupies the center of attention; it may well trigger similar upheavals among other under-privileged racial and economic groups, especially in large urban centers. The tremendous concentration of economic and political power in a few hands, which has occurred in our modern tech-nological society, will sooner or later lead to revolutionary de-mands for greater participation on the part of many groups of people. There are signs that this is already taking place in some of the communist countries; it may not long delay in western Europe and America. All around the world, a sort of revolution is brewing among young people, which may take on increasing significance in the years ahead.

If the analysis above is correct, it will be on the frontiers of revolution that many of the major issues of humanization and dehumanization will be decided in our modern world; it will be on these frontiers that those most concerned for the well-being and for the future of man will find themselves involved. This will be true not only for those young people—from both the privileged and underprivileged classes—who discover that their responsibility for their fellowmen leads them to participation in revolution, but it will also be true for those in positions of power in the established order who understand the world in which they are living and feel com-pelled to work for change. If we hope to preserve the most impor-tant elements of our cultural, moral and religious heritage and to contribute to the shaping of the future, we cannot remain outside the revolutionary struggle or withdraw from it. The only path of responsibility is the one that passes through it toward whatever may lie ahead.

For most of us, this will not be easy. Our past experience and training have not prepared us for this type of struggle. Many of us are too closely identified with the status quo to understand or participate freely in a revolution against it. Moreover, we are sur-

rounded by evidences that revolution is a highly ambiguous phenomenon. It represents a passion for justice and for the liberation
of the oppressed, but it also releases great forces of destruction and
leads to new forms of injustice. Vast numbers of men and women
have struggled and sacrificed their lives for the sake of a new society; all too often, the order that is established after the revolution
has spent itself is not very different from the previous one. Movements that succeed in awakening the masses and invite them to
participate in the use of public power often lead to destructive
fanaticism and end up by depriving them of power. New centers
of power are indispensable if change is to be brought about, but, in
a revolutionary situation, it is impossible to predict how this power
will eventually be used. The unselfish commitment of the young
revolutionary to the service of his people is one of the most hopeful developments in the modern world, but this very attitude may
lead him to exaggerate the rightness of his cause, as well as the
injustices on the other side, and to close his eyes to aspects of
reality that must be taken into account if the revolution is to
achieve its goals.

If revolution is to be our destiny, we are challenged to find new
categories of thought about social and political questions, and a
new perspective on the relationship between stability and change.
We are confronted by the need to develop communities of thought
and action, on both sides of the major revolutionary struggles, that
will search for solutions and work for reconciliation in the midst
of tension and conflict.

Our major political movements do not offer much ground
for hope. Conservative ideologies cannot understand the problem,
much less meet its challenge; liberal ways of thinking do not seem
to fare much better. The liberal, who works for *orderly* change in
a world in which he can perceive signs of continued progress toward a better society, may be quite at a loss when confronted with
the reality of a revolutionary upheaval. Marxism stands alone in
its attempt to understand revolution as essential to the creation
of a more stable and just society, and, in some parts of the world,
it is the supreme symbol of hope for those who long for a new
day. Yet after it comes to power, alters the structures of society
and institutionalizes a new order, the situation changes. Then, the

very ideology that provided the dynamic for revolution gets in the way of a creative response to the problem of order and change.

In this situation, has Christianity any contribution to make? Religion has traditionally given a sacral character to the institutions of the status quo and has thus been a major factor in preserving them against the forces of revolution. In the West, Christianity has been so closely identified with the established order of Christendom that it has tended to play the same role. In the face of revolutionary upheavals, the great temptation for the church is to become the rallying point of all who fear change.

At the same time, the breakdown of Christendom and the process of secularization have undercut the authority of the church, transferred this task of saving the status quo to new secular ideologies and movements and thus set the church free to be once again a revolutionary force.[4]

Moreover, as small groups of Christians become involved in revolutionary struggles, they discover in the Christian heritage resources for thought and action of which they were not previously aware. If these resources are available, we should give a certain priority to the type of study and research that will work them out and put them at the disposal of those who are now moving toward involvement in these areas. We indicate below some lines which may deserve further investigation.

Toward a Theological Perspective on Revolution

If we look at our history in the light of biblical history, we may feel quite at home in the midst of revolution. There are several strands of biblical thought that may justify such an affirmation:

1. *The fact that God is both the Creator and Ruler of all spheres of nature and of society.* These are temporal realities ex-

---

[4] For an interesting discussion of this thesis, see the paper by B. MOREL: "L'Avenir du ministère de l'Eglise dans un monde en voie de sécularisation," *Bulletin du Centre Protestant d'Etudes,* Geneva, XIV, 4, June, 1962. Taking as his starting point a recent discussion, in anthropology, of the role of *interdit* and *transgression* in the social sphere, he suggests that the task of preserving certain *interdits,* formerly exercised by the church, has now passed to secular institutions, and that the church is now called to be a force of *transgression* against the limitations imposed by such restrictions.

isting to serve God's purpose for *man;* therefore, they can and must be used and changed in line with that purpose. Throughout the Bible, there is a strong eschatological emphasis, which stresses the dynamic nature of God and the fact that his action in history is moving toward a goal. It is this which has led Professor Van Leeuwen to conclude that the biblical attitude toward the world has made our modern revolution both possible and inevitable. It has desacralized all institutions and awakened a concern for the reshaping of human life.

2. *The revolutionary character of biblical messianism.* From the first pages of the Old Testament, it is evident that God's rule over the nations and over Israel constantly runs into difficulties. His redemptive action means judgment, which is, at the same time, a new beginning. The scattering of the nations at Babel (Genesis 11) is followed by the calling of Abraham (Genesis 12), who will be the instrument for their restoration. In Israel, those most sensitive to the divine activity are convinced that he is tearing down in order to build up (Jeremiah 1 : 10), that he breaks the power of the oppressor in order to establish his justice.[5] As H. Berkhof puts it, "The Gospel introduced . . . a revolutionary God, whose 'righteousness,' according to the Psalms and the prophets, means that he lifts up those who are bowed down and humiliates the oppressors." [6]

In this atmosphere of revolution, the Messiah is the central figure. He arises after the house of David has been destroyed, as a shoot out of an apparently dead trunk. In Isaiah especially, central attention is given to his role as a political revolutionary, an emphasis that breaks forth in the New Testament in the Magnificat (Luke 1 : 50–53). In the life, death and resurrection of Jesus, the messianic theme of destruction and restoration finds new meaning and focus.

3. *The dynamic historical character of God's action.* Israel meets and knows God in the midst of her history, in her involvements in political crises and complex social and cultural problems. In the Incarnation, this God relates himself once and for all to man within a dynamic process. As God's action in the world aims at its

---

[5] See I Sam. 2 : 1–10; Ps. 9, 72, 146.
[6] *The Doctrine of the Holy Spirit.* Richmond, Va.: John Knox Press, 1964, p. 102.

transformation, the coming of Christ and the work of the Holy Spirit release new and disturbing forces in history that affect the process itself. As the influence of Christ grows, old stabilities are swept away, and the struggle for humanization moves to new frontiers; at the same time, new threats appear, and the forces that resist Christ become stronger and more manifest. Along this road, there can be no turning back; those who would participate in God's work cannot seek refuge in old ways nor draw back from the front lines because the situation is becoming increasingly dangerous. For it is in this struggle that the battle for the future of man is being waged; it is in the midst of apocalyptic events that we perceive signs of imminent victory (Luke 21 : 28).

The Augustinian View of Social Change

The history of Christian thought does not provide us with many theologians of revolution. Augustine stands out across the centuries. Living as he did at the time of the collapse of the Roman Empire, much of his thought, especially in *The City of God,* deals with questions similar to those which face us today. As Professor Charles Cochrane has shown,[7] the trinitarian dogma provided him with a foundation for thought and action precisely at those points where classical culture had failed. Taking as his starting point a "principle" *beyond* nature and history, which was nevertheless at work *in* nature and history and which was capable of being apprehended there, he was able to take account of "being and movement in the universe"[8] in a new way. Trusting in a divine sovereignty at work in and through an "order of causes," Augustine was able to admit the impossibility of finding a satisfactory rational relationship of these causes to each other. And, at the same time, he sought new clues to an order, which, though not fully perceived, was nonetheless present. Convinced that the Logos of Christ, revealed in Scripture, was the ultimate reality in human life and history, he could think and act on the conviction that "each and every occurrence in the manifold of events bears wit-

---

[7] *Christianity and Classical Culture.* New York: Oxford University Press, 1940.
[8] *Ibid.,* p. 456.

ness to the activity of God." [9] It was this "principle of intelligibility," according to Professor Cochrane, which was capable of "saving the reason as well as the will," [10] for, in the working out of it, the rich diversity of human experience was pulled together in a meaningful configuration, and the historical process was seen as full of meaning and purpose.

Those who looked at the world in the perspective of the Logos of Christ as its "creating and moving principle," perceived that personality was as central in the historical process; crisis and change became meaningful. Historical events were seen as occurring along a line set by the dynamic reality of God's Providence, his bringing in of his Kingdom, the work of the Holy Spirit in the world and the movement of history toward its final goal. Along this road, two cities coexist. In constant conflict with each other, they are also "inextricably intermingled . . . in the concrete reality of history." [11] Both these cities are striving after one thing only, *peace,* which Augustine defined as "the tranquillity of order." [12] The peace of the eternal city, which is constantly permeating and transforming the city of man, is that of a "perfectly ordered and harmonious communion of those who find their joy in God and in one another in God." [13] But the peace of the earthly city, which is an attempt to develop some sort of order among men motivated by self-love, is a temporary, partial and unstable peace. It is an order that is always being established in the midst of conflict, in which men must often wage war for the sake of peace, and in which the divine judgment upon human pride and self-centeredness means that, from time to time, certain structures of society must be reformed and, in some cases, must collapse. [14]

This Augustinian perspective, with its wealth of insight into the meaning of events and the nature of responsible action in a revo-

---

[9] *Ibid.,* p. 480.
[10] *Ibid.,* p. 384.
[11] *The City of God,* X, 2.
[12] *Ibid.,* XIX, 13.
[13] *Ibid.*
[14] Speaking of the Romans who were upset by the crisis of the empire, Augustine says, "If they only had sense, they would see that the hardships and cruelties they suffered from the enemy came from that Divine Providence who makes use of war to reform the corrupt lives of men." *The City of God,* I, 1.

lutionary world, provides a basis for political realism that recognizes both the importance and the ambiguity of political action. The political struggle forms an essential part of the life of the earthly city and contributes to the renovation and reconstruction of human life in community, but not to its regeneration. For the Christian, the vortex of the social struggle has a very definite attraction. It is there, at the heart of the commingling of the two cities, that both the inevitable destructiveness of human self-love and new possibilities for social reform and for new structures of human relationships are exposed. Thus, the decline and collapse of the old order is not necessarily a disaster; it may well be the one way by which the divine purpose for a more just human order can move forward.

Among the theologians, Professor Paul L. Lehmann seems to have gone furthest in exploring Augustine's thought about the action of the triune God in history and has provided a number of theological categories for dealing with revolution; and, not surprisingly, there is, among those who are involved in revolutionary struggles, a certain interest in his thought. Professor Lehmann contends that it is only in Christianity that history is understood as a compound of stability and change, decay and fulfillment, in such a way that change is seen as the prelude to authentic stability, and decay as the occasion for fulfillment. This unusual perspective is the result of God's revelation of himself as "I will be who I will be," the God whose "moving strength" is at the heart of events and whose action must be understood by looking to the future, more than to the past.[15] But, for Professor Lehmann, it is primarily the messianic tradition and imagery of the Bible that provide the real clue to what is going on in the world. Here the focus is on the "political character" of God's activity, by which he is creating the conditions for human fulfillment in interrelatedness in the world.[16] The Messiah is the bearer of God's new deliverance where all human possibilities are played out; his purpose goes forward as he tears down in order to rebuild (Jeremiah 1 : 10; Luke 1 : 46–55).

---

[15] See his development of this theme in "The Dynamics of Reformation Ethics," *Princeton Seminary Bulletin*, XLIII, 4, Spring, 1950, pp. 17–22.
[16] See his *Ethics in a Christian Context*. New York: Harper & Row, 1963. Especially Ch. 3.

He is the Incarnate Son of God, "the humanization of God for the sake of the humanization of man." [17]

The Messiah was also crucified: It is only God's program, not man's, that offers the road to human fulfillment, a fulfillment that comes through judgment and reconciliation. The church is a sign and foretaste of this possibility present in the midst of life. When it is faithful to its Lord, the church incarnates this "passion for and vision of human deliverance and fulfilment"; [18] its disobedience contributes to the creation of a messianic vacuum, such as is evident today.

For Lehmann, revolution must be understood theologically, for it is set firmly in the context of God's humanizing activity in history. As a political form of change, revolution represents the cutting edge of humanization. We must therefore look to the revolutionary process if we hope to understand the dynamics and direction of change. But, in this context, revolution is the bearer both of signs of fulfillment and of symptoms of decay. The Christian looks for stability on the other side of change; he is therefore free to be fully involved in the revolution. At the same time, his understanding of what is going on there obliges him to work constantly for reconciliation.

The Role of the Christian Koinonia in the Revolutionary Process

As a consequence of the self-invalidation of Christianity and the increasing dominance of a secular mentality, especially among revolutionaries, Christians cannot speak to the revolution by means of systematic theological treatises on the nature of the divine activity. What is now called for is rather the presence on the frontiers of revolution of communities dynamically involved in the struggle for humanization and engaged in a constant running conversation with their biblical and theological heritage. Such *koinonias* will find it easier to raise questions than to provide answers, and their voice may sound weak over against that of political ideologies. To the degree that they are faithful to their heritage, they will live in sharp

---

[17] PAUL L. LEHMANN, *Ideology and Incarnation.* Geneva: John Knox House, 1962, p. 24.
[18] *Ibid.*

tension with the revolutionary movements in which they participate or with the established order of which they are a part. And yet it is precisely this type of existence that may contribute something to the deepening of insight, the recovery of purpose, the rebirth of courage and the work of reconciliation among Christians and non-Christians alike. Certain concrete issues reveal that the possibilities are these:

1. *The dynamics of the revolutionary process.* Christians, and many others, especially of the middle class, are upset and confused when confronted with the reality of revolution. Although identified with the status quo, they see certain injustices around them and want to work for reasonable and gradual changes in society. They may even be enthusiastic about revolution in its early stages. But they find themselves confronted by a dynamic process which they cannot understand, and which leads those on each side to assume more radical positions. As attitudes become more extreme and actions more excessive, the Christian may find himself attempting to expose the exaggerations of both groups but unable to identify with either of them. Thus he soon finds himself far from the front lines of the struggle and ignored by all.

At this point, a radical theological reorientation would seem to be called for. The God who is tearing down old structures in order to create the conditions for a more human existence is himself in the midst of the struggle. It is his presence in the world and his pressure upon those structures which stand in his way that constitute the dynamics of this process. God has taken human form in the concreteness of historical life and has called us to follow this path if we are to be the salt of the earth and the light of the world (Matthew 5 : 13–14). In this context, the Christian is called to be fully involved in the revolution as it develops. It is only at its center that we can perceive what God is doing, understand how the struggle for humanization is being defined and serve as agents of reconciliation. From within this struggle we discover that we do not bear witness in revolution by preserving our purity in line with certain moral principles, but rather by freedom to be *for man* at every moment. It is also in the midst of this situation that we who have been silent and inactive in the face of suffering and injustice are made to see our guilt and accept the judgment that has come upon us. If our failure to act in the past is responsible for this radicalization of the revolutionary process, we can accept our guilt and work for reconciliation only as we are free to participate in movements in which we have lost the right to be heard and in which our sincerity may now be called into question.

Here we also face *the nature of the revolutionary process itself.* The forces of reaction often tend to ignore or underestimate the dynamics of this process; the revolutionaries consider it as an inevitable law of historic necessity. Especially since the time of the French Revolution, revolution has been understood as a series of tremendous events following a destined course beyond human control. Hegel's philosophy of history may well have been greatly influenced by his reflection upon these events, and Marx gave definitive formulation to this deterministic view.

In a Christian perspective, the revolutionary process is a reality that we dare not ignore, but it loses its character of determinism and inevitability. As Augustine interpreted history in the light of God's sovereignty over an order of causes, so the Christian understands events in a revolutionary situation. He is free to attempt to understand what is happening by analyzing the concrete social, economic and political realities, while remaining sensitive to the direction in which things seem to be moving. The dynamics of the process is determined not by some inevitable law of history, but by the interworking of God's pressure for change and man's response to it—by trying to stop it, or by absolutizing the revolutionary struggle or by taking concrete steps toward a more just society. The development of the revolution will thus be determined by the way in which those on each side of the struggle respond to the pressures for a more human society, as it takes shape in the "providence of God and the confusion of men."

2. *Stability and change.* In the Christian perspective, order is the order of humanization as it is made visible in the *koinonia;* it can be established only in and through the renewal and transformation of structures, even though such changes bring with them also new possibilities of dehumanization. A crisis in any social structure does not necessarily endanger the well-being of those who live in it; it is more likely to be a new opportunity for a richer life, espe-

cially for those groups whose well-being has been ignored. In a world that operates this way, the past can be preserved only as it is constantly being transformed. Efforts to save our heritage by enclosing it in rigid institutional forms of a former era can lead only to its repudiation.

In this context, men and women discover new possibilities for creative thought and action in the midst of revolution. Those who are closely identified with the established order may be free to recognize the judgment upon their way of life, accept the loss of privileges in the interest of their neighbor and look for new opportunities of fulfillment, even for themselves, as the new order takes shape around them. They may be able to take initiatives in bringing about changes in their society, thus opening the way to a more gradual and less violent transition.

Likewise, the revolutionary may discover that he should not make an idol of revolution. The overthrow of the old order will not automatically bring about a more just society. That can come only as the result of an intensive effort that works toward the shaping of the new out of the concrete material given in a specific situation. Moreover, in the long run, the new order will be an instrument of humanization only if it, too, is open to change. A revolution will be able to move toward an approximate realization of its objectives only if it develops a type of institution in which self-criticism and sensitivity to dissatisfaction are built into its very structures. It is this fact that modern revolutionaries, dominated as they have been by a mistaken understanding of the historical process, seem singularly unable to comprehend. It is hard to find examples that match Thomas Jefferson's reaction to the news of Shays' uprising: "God forbid that we should ever be twenty years without such a rebellion."

Moreover, in the Christian community, we have certain clues to the type of structure that is most clearly in line with God's work of humanization. Revolutions today are basically struggles for justice. But, in God's world, justice and reconciliation belong together. The enemy must be taken seriously. This does not necessarily imply that a two-party political system must be preserved in all circumstances nor does it imply that the nerve of revolutionary action must be cut by endless and fruitless search for an agreement on a program that satisfies all groups in society. It does mean openness toward those whose criticisms expose our rationalizations and our mistakes, and constant efforts toward reconciliation of conflicting interests and restoration of broken relationships. In the *koinonia,* human fulfillment comes through growth to maturity in interrelatedness. Thus, only as a person has the opportunity to participate in the life of his community and in the decisions that shape his destiny, can he be fully human.

3. *The new revolutionary order and the kingdom of God.* The conservative of the established order may be aware of its limitations, and even of its injustices; what he tends to ignore is the dynamics of history. The revolutionary, on the other hand, is sensitive to the dynamics of the historical process; his temptation is to trust in the power of man to build a completely new order and to solve all problems that may arise.

The kingdom of God always stands over against every social and political order, thus exposing its dehumanizing elements and judging it. At the same time, the Kingdom is a dynamic reality; it is "coming" through the work of him who is restoring the nations (II Isaiah) and in whose good time the kingdom of this world shall become the kingdom of our Lord and of his Christ (Revelations 11 : 15). Thus, a particular crisis of structures may be the result of God's relentless pressure; and the Christian may perceive, in certain situations, a relative coincidence of direction of the revolutionary struggle with God's humanizing action in the world.

When this occurs, we are confronted with forces that will shape the future, and in relation to which our obedience must be defined. Guidance for such discernment cannot come from a philosophy of history or a political ideology, but only from participation in a community that, orientated by God's revelation, is also involved in the world where he is at work. For those who have eyes to see, this coincidence of direction will be found not only in the crisis of structures of a feudal or bourgeois society but also in the struggle for humanization in those orders established by revolutions today. In the perspective of the Kingdom, involvement in revolution means living in a state of tension that can become a creative force. The new order of society is a "gift." It comes in the midst of, and in spite of, our limitations and failures. What is of ultimate significance is the fulfillment of human life in a new context of relationships. For this new order, a change of structures in society is essential, but it is only one element in a larger process of humanization. Thus, we can participate fully in the political struggle at the same time as we recognize its limitations. We can be open to unexpected possibilities of meaning and fulfillment, which may come at any moment, even when our most strenuous political efforts seem to suffer complete defeat. Each new experience of community points to the Kingdom toward which we are moving, but in which, even now, we participate in a partial way.

4. *Thought and action orientated toward the future.* In our dynamic society, the categories of thought on which we rely for understanding are soon outmoded, the shape of the problems we confront is constantly changing, and our methods of dealing with them can become inadequate almost overnight. Those who are bound to the past become victims of fear and frustration, and men who have offered creative leadership at one moment may discover that they are suddenly unable to meet the new challenge before them. Even those who contribute to the establishment of a new society may betray their cause because they are not free to think and act in the new situation, which their own revolution has created.

In spite of our traditional ways of thinking, Christian faith does look at the present in the light of the future; and the future, brought into the present, provides a unique perspective of understanding and becomes an explosive force. As we respond to the God who is moving ahead, we find ourselves directed toward "the shape of things to come." This action of God is hidden to a certain extent, but we need not, for this reason, formulate a world view that affirms the absence of God or the absurdity of history. Trusting that every moment of history is shaped by the divine activity, we can await the manifestations of God's action along the road toward the future. This understanding of reality saves the reason by freeing it from the tendency to absolutize its systems of thought and from the pretension to omniscience and infallibility. At the same time, it grounds our efforts at understanding upon an order of truth which is not necessarily logical, but which is determined by the providential ordering of God, partially apprehended by faith in the midst of concrete historical reality. Along this road, the reason is free to seek new patterns of society not according to some social dogma or utopian dream, but by a realistic apprehension of the possibilities of change and development that open up as we move from one stage to another in the revolutionary struggle. What matters at each stage is not the success or failure of a specific project, but the way in which, in success or failure, the struggle for humanization moves to a new level.[19] To the degree that we participate in a community that is present on the frontier and lives by this hope, we shall be able to meet the breakdown of present structures without fear and act in a way that points to the shape of things to come.

Orientation for Ethical Decisions

The Christian in a revolutionary movement finds himself surrounded by a variety of groups and ideologies, each of which has specific proposals for the creation of a new society. Has Christian faith anything to say about the shape of the new structures that are to be established after the collapse of the old? This question, central in all Christian ethical reflection today, takes on new importance in a revolutionary situation for at least two reasons:

1. The revolutionary finds himself caught up in an accelerated process in which he is confronted, at every moment, with a new configuration of facts and events. All schematic definitions of ethical responsibility tend to hinder him from dealing with concrete reality. In fact, it is in the revolutionary struggle that the attempt of modern secular man to formulate a new conception of reality and find a new basis for ethical decisions has a special appeal.

2. In the midst of revolution, life is insecure, the shape of the future is unclear. The struggle for a new order takes place in the

---

[19] Interesting examples of this are provided by the civil-rights struggle in the United States. A small group of Negro and white students organizes a sit-in at a few lunch counters in an Alabama city. They do not accomplish their immediate objective, yet they spark off a movement that affects the entire country. Other similar efforts fail, but they do lead to the adoption of civil-rights legislation by Congress, which changes the pattern of race relations at many points.

midst of opposition, repeated failures and the constant appearance
of new threats of dehumanization. For the revolutionary, the ethical question is not merely that of a logical definition of a new order; what he most needs is an understanding of the revolutionary
process that orientates his struggle for change in the direction of
the future and provides a context of hope and trust in which he
can make wise decisions.

In the face of these demands, it is not surprising that the natural-
law tradition, with its rational definition of cosmic order and its
attempt to formulate general principles for an ideal society, breaks
down. What may not yet be so evident is that our ecumenical studies, to the degree that they depend upon this tradition, may prove
irrelevant. To speak only of the situation I know most directly, in
Brazil, the rapid social change studies were widely used until we
confronted a revolutionary situation. Then we discovered that those
most involved were turning elsewhere for orientation.

Professor Hendrik Van Oyen, in his paper on "Fundamental
Problems of Evangelical Social Ethics," [20] suggests why this was so.
He finds that our ecumenical studies have preserved the unresolved
tension in Anglo-Saxon Christian social thought between "the Cal-
vinistic ideal of the rule of the Kingdom of God over the whole
creation" and "the claim of natural law as a cosmic order of life,
in other words, the ideal of reason." [21] Many of our more specifically theological statements have followed the first line; our definitions of structure, the second. Useful as the latter has been, it is
questionable whether this logical enterprise can deal effectively
with the concreteness of the revolutionary process or with the increasing demands to give sufficient attention to the knowledge of
the specialist in the formulation of ethical goals.[22]

---

[20] *Background Information,* World Council of Churches: No. 32. Feb.,
1964, pp. 1–9.

[21] *Ibid.,* p. 3.

[22] This unresolved tension, with its consequences, is evident especially in
the Evanston Report. The introductory statement ends thus: "Our hope in
Christ does not offer technical answers or specific solutions which statesmen
and experts have not found. But in the context of Christian faith, we gain
new insights into our dilemmas and ways to overcome them." Rather than
pursuing this line, the report then moves into anthropology and natural law,
defining a responsible society, which provides "a criterion by which we
judge all existing orders and at the same time a standard to guide us in
the specific choices we have to make."

Where, then, can we seek answer to the question regarding the shaping of structures in a revolutionary situation? In Brazil, among certain groups, there has been a decisive shift toward a contextual ethic, the starting point of which is a "theology of messianism" rather than a theological anthropology together with a modified natural-law theory. As Professor Lehmann describes it, a theology of messianism focuses on what God is doing in the world to make and keep human life human. This divine action follows a line indicated by the doctrines of providence, the kingdom of God, and eschatology, as well as by the third article of the Creed, regarding the activity of the Holy Spirit in the church and in the world. Along this road, every situation in which the Christian finds himself called upon to live and act is an expressionn of the commingling of the two cities, which continues throughout history. In this process, the pressures of the redemptive God upon the earthly city and the constant encounter and conflict between the two constitute the context in which men strive for order and peace in the world. In Lehmann's words:

The complexity of the actual human situation . . . is always compounded of an intricate network of circumstance and human interrelationships bracketed by the dynamics of God's political activity on the one hand and God's forgiveness on the other.[23]

If this is the nature of the reality with which we are dealing, the proximate good for which Christians or non-Christians strive cannot be defined in terms of principles and precepts; it is, rather, a question of relationships and acts that point to the opportunities for human fulfillment, which God opens up at a particular time and place, on the road to the future. Guidance for the shaping of structures cannot be provided primarily by any general, rational set of values, but by participation in the *koinonia,* where—through word, sacrament and interrelatedness—the concrete shape of God's humanizing work in the world is becoming visible.

The basic issue is not whether the Christian can formulate certain values with which the non-Christian can agree as a basis for common action. It is, rather, whether or not the Christian is able

---

[23] *Ethics in a Christian Context,* p. 141.

to perceive and respond to fundamental dimensions of reality, which Christian and non-Christian alike should take into account in making ethical decisions. In every situation, there are certain aspects of worldly reality that can be understood and analyzed only by the sociologist, the political scientist or the economist. But none of these disciplines is able to capture the full dimensions of this reality. This real world, in its concreteness, has been accepted, is judged and is being reconciled to God. In the midst of the full complexity of this situation, God is creating the conditions for the fulfillment of human life. Only as these elements of reality receive attention, alongside the technical, can proximate goals be realistically defined; only in the light of the ultimate toward which it is moving can the penultimate be properly understood.

The Christian Contribution to Revolutionary Goals

What, specifically, are the elements at the center of God's humanizing activity in the world? One of them is the fact of forgiveness, which sets us free to act for our neighbor; free to see the ambiguities of the situation, as well as of our own motivation, and still move ahead; free to participate fully in a struggle involving conflict and the risk of violence, injustice and the power of self-interest, and there know that the power of sin is broken; free to perceive that when the human situation is falling apart, God is picking up the pieces and putting them together again. Another basic element is justice, the recognition that God's order is being established on the other side of change, as structures are shaped that defend those classes and groups in society that have no power and can count on no one to defend them. A third is reconciliation, which occurs in the midst of struggle and hostility as all perspectives are transformed through the encounter and reconciliation of differences.

If Christians are able to deal competently with reality in full openness to these dimensions, their presence could make a significant difference in the definition of proximate goals. Their participation will be a constant reminder that, at every point, the crucial issue is what is happening and what is likely to happen in human relationships. They will recognize that revolutionary structures can contribute to this goal only as they provide all classes and groups in society with an opportunity for increasing participation in the shaping of the life of the community, the economic order and the nation. They will make evident that the most adequate goals are those which are worked out in dialogue with the widest variety of ideologies and with those technically competent in many different aspects of the problem. They will recognize that only those structures open to change and renewal can serve the well-being of man in a dynamic society such as ours today. Most important of all, they should bring into the situation a basic attitude of trust and hope and a creative imagination for handling the facts, which are manifest because the absoluteness of the technical has been broken and each situation is seen in the light of the goal toward which it is moving.

In the revolution confronting us, the real test of any theological and ethical perspective will be its ability to recognize fully the importance of the insights of the expert and to contribute something in the dialogue with him. Recent writings of Professor Denys Munby provide a basis for further reflection on this question. In his book, *The Idea of a Secular Society*,[24] and in an essay, "The Importance of Technical Competence," [25] he contends that the size of our society, the wide variety of situations in it and the fact of rapid social change make it impossible to find much help in any set of principles or values. We live in a world in which there is no longer any image that reflects generally accepted common ideals. If we want to get anywhere in solving our problems, we must study the diverse aspects of reality with the tools provided by the various scientific disciplines: "It is only possible to discover the truth about men in society by the patient application of complicated techniques to the empirical facts." [26]

Has a Christian ethic, then, anything to contribute to the definition of goals? Professor Munby would urge caution at this point: "Men do not always act according to facts, but it remains, nevertheless, surprisingly true that, in a large number of cases, once the

---

[24] London: Oxford University Press, 1963.
[25] In *Essays in Anglican Self Criticism,* D. M. PATON, ed. London: SCM Press, 1958.
[26] *Ibid.,* p. 47.

facts have been elucidated, the appropriate action almost inevitably follows." [27] This may be true as far as it goes. But the technical mind all too easily acquires a very restricted idea of just what the "facts" are and forgets that the technical is ethically ambiguous. As a phenomenon of the commingling of the two cities, it points toward the ethical and contributes to the dehumanization of man. The technical is concerned with knowledge and power, and power is both "gracious" and demonic. Unless the technical analysis of reality is confronted constantly with a witness to the dimensions of that reality, which may escape the technician, we face a very dangerous situation in the society.

Professor Munby is always dealing with the technical in the context of Christian faith. His deep concern for the well-being of man, his relative optimism about the human enterprise and his confidence in the redemptive activity of God in the world all have a decisive influence. He is an economist, but he looks upon worldly reality in terms of an Anglican sacramental theology.[28] But, if a creative dialogue is to develop between the expert and the theologian, our reflection on these problems in ecumenical circles must give more attention to the terms of the discussion and explore further the lines suggested both directly and indirectly by Professor Munby.

It is our contention that a contextual theology and ethic offer creative possibilities at this point. When technical insight is set in the context of the humanizing activity of God, it makes sense to affirm that once the full facts are known, the appropriate action will follow. Along this road, it may be possible for theology to move into the center of the current struggle—rather than being, as is so often the case, a burden or an irrelevant factor for those who are involved in the secular world—and thus "assume its servant-critical function through which all the sciences may be summoned once again to their authentic humanistic occasion and promise." [29]

[27] *The Idea of a Secular Society,* p. 26.
[28] *Ibid.,* pp. 89–91.
[29] PAUL L. LEHMANN: "The Formative Power of Particularity," *Union Seminary Quarterly Review,* XVIII, 3, ii, March, 1963, p. 318.

2

THE SERVICE OF THE CHURCH
IN A SOCIALIST SOCIETY

by J. M. LOCHMAN (Czechoslovakia)

THE world has changed: This is a universal experience that—in the face of a progressive secularization—is being felt and expressed by Christians in almost the whole ecumenical world, but that applies in a more radical sense to the churches in the socialist countries. In recent decades our churches have gone through a radical change of the temporal order. The changes are far-reaching and almost unprecedented. Their main emphasis has naturally been in the economic and social fields; their aim is reconstruction toward the socialist society. But they affect other levels too, for example, the sphere of the church. This reconstruction is based on the sharply defined presuppositions of an ideology that claims to be the sole authority in all essential social spheres. It is the ideology of Marxism-Leninism, consciously materialistic, which has never had a positive relationship to religion. Consequently the life of the church, too, finds itself in a changed situation. We may formulate that change by using an almost notorious slogan: We have come to the end of the "Constantinian epoch."

By the "Constantinian epoch" we mean the era of the powerful *corpus christianum,* of the political and cultural power of Christianity, of "Christian civilization," the epoch of concordats between state and church, an arrangement whereby the church is either patronized by the state or at least protected, and where the state is regarded by the church as *"defensor fidei"* and exalted by her. For centuries Christendom in Europe belonged to this epoch and received its distinctive character—even in the depths and heights of its theological and ecclesiastical existence—through all the typical facets of this epoch. Christendom built its historical "house" in this epoch, dwelt in it and got accustomed to it. The churches of the Reformation did indeed fundamentally rebuild it—but nothing more. They too—apart from the radical movements which have always remained a small minority—firmly maintained its foundations.

As far as men can judge, this era, which covered nearly the whole of church history until now, is at an end for us. The residue of the "Constantinian order" still survives into the socialist epoch— the weight of a thousand years of European history still makes itself felt in it—for example, in the fact that in the CSSR (Czechoslovakian Socialist Republic) the church still receives financial support from the Marxist state, or in the cultural and historical context, when certain decidedly Christian movements and traditions of the past—as, for example, the Hussite movement—are maintained by public opinion even in a society that is avowedly atheist. In all essentials, however, the Constantinian solution for the relationship between church and society is over. The church is no longer one of the official pillars of society. The opposite, rather, is true: in the context of the fundamental aspirations of this society the church is ultimately regarded as a relic of a past epoch, which for pragmatic political reasons is to be tolerated but which (at least in its original, religious form) is intrinsically foreign to the future of a socialist society. To the individual Christian this means that he is no longer protected and privileged by his society, that his public prestige is not increased on account of his being a Christian, that he no longer conforms to a desirable rule, but that he is an exception, not the "householder" but, rather, "a stranger and sojourner."

At this point the urgent question arises: how is the church to react to this deep change in the temporal order? This is the question that has confronted our congregations most urgently in recent decades—both in the context of the problem of a fundamental theological orientation, and in respect of the important practical question of the proper function of the church in the new society. How is this question to be answered?

If we attempt shortcuts in responding to this situation, we shall, I believe, risk entering two *culs-de-sac* on this road:

1. There is the danger that faced with this change, we shall be overcome by a spell of "theological giddiness." By this I mean that we shall lose theological independence, that the gospel will simply become adapted to the new situation and ideology. Confronted with this temptation we should not be too ready to assume a self-righteous attitude. This, after all, has been the notorious danger to the church throughout the whole course of its history. It has always been tempted to adapt itself to its surroundings. One look at the history of the church shows that fact. Consider the extent to which Christianity in the feudal age became feudalized—even to the most subtle problems of theology! And in the bourgeois epoch Christianity became simply—bourgeois! Why, then, in a socialist epoch should a "socialist Christianity" not come into being? Why do people only then, as so frequently happens, get frightened and sound the alarm? Yet it is, and remains, a temptation.

2. But there is the opposite danger: the temptation to say a clear-cut "no" to this development, to see the threat to the Constantinian era simply as a threat to the cause of Jesus Christ, and consequently to oppose this development to a greater or lesser degree. This temptation is, so to speak, "natural," particularly so for the Roman Catholic Church, or at least for her conservative wing, for whom rejection of the Christian (and this generally means the medieval-feudal) civilization is identical with rejection of Jesus Christ. But the other Christian churches—including the churches of the Reformation—are equally faced with this temptation, especially where a form of society as clearly defined as in the socialist society is replacing the "Constantinian society."

Two Temptations Confronting the Church

Both these possible positions are theologically false—and for a faithful church they are indeed "impossible." The error of the former position is obvious: using the important formulation of the Confession of Barmen which, in its marvelous actuality, proved to be a prophetically testing and strengthening word in our situation too—the "one Word of God" is made a relative entity with which other historical entities are associated. The Word of God loses its sovereignty, it is made to conform. The error of the other position is less obvious, yet it is—in spite of the opposed practical attitude—surprisingly like the error of the former position: for here, too, the one Word of God is in a similar way associated with a historical entity, this time perhaps an ecclesiastical one, yet, even so, an entity which is no less human and historical. This is the temptation to identify "Christian civilization" with the cause of Jesus Christ, and this means in our case the negative attitude in the face of the threat of the "Constantinian epoch." Here, too, one becomes a victim to human and historical prejudices. Here, too, God's Word loses its sovereignty and becomes conformable.

Both these positions are therefore equally impossible. Both these ways lead astray. Both are to be avoided. Yet as soon as we leave principles behind and turn toward factual Christian existence, it is necessary to add that these temptations are not equally real or equally dangerous. The first of them is relatively less so, both in the ecumenical world and with us. The temptation to assimilate the church to the "post-Constantinian order," particularly in its most pronounced form of a "socialist Christianity," of an ideological blending of Marxism with the gospel, is only slight. Neither the church nor the Marxist state encourages it. We may say, perhaps, that the changed climate of post-Constantinian society in regard of religion—for example, the atheism of Marxist ideology—in a way benefits Christian existence in the socialist system. The danger of an ideological assimilation on the part of the church is undoubtedly less than if it were confronted by a religious or idealist ideology of the state.

The second temptation, on the other hand, is much greater—and for the same reason: faced with atheism the church is being tempted by its own presuppositions and on principle to assume a hostile attitude and to extend this hostility to other components of the *Weltanschauung* (or the system), especially if they are not to the taste of its traditional bourgeois position.

It has been the task of our theological work to withstand precisely this second "reactionary" temptation—without losing sight of the first. This has been done mainly through the pioneering work of J. L. Hromadka. His creative "one-sidedness"—frequently misunderstood and criticized in the ecumenical world—must be understood precisely in this connection: as the attempt to defend the freedom of the church against the temptation of an unfruitful negativism in the light of the revolutionary breakup of the Constantinian order. We attempted this—in the context of the ecumenical biblical theological renewal chiefly represented by the theology of Karl Barth—by a return to the foundations of the biblical message. Is not the gospel of the kingship of Christ the center of that message? But if Jesus is lord—lord of the church and lord of the world—then the church is neither simply forsaken nor lost in any historical change. On the contrary, it may confidently set out on unknown and hitherto unexplored paths. And, according to the New Testament, is not the community of the disciples, obediently following this lord who was nothing but a servant, sent into the world as a servant church? If so, then its mission can never come to an end at the moment when it is losing its privileges. On the contrary, again, such a moment may well offer a genuine opportunity of seeking new ways of service. And does not solidarity with, and understanding of, the poor and oppressed correspond to the impulse of the prophetic and apostolic message? Should not the church, then, be showing understanding for socialism which, in its social experiment, is taking the part of the oppressed and underprivileged?

All these questions and the biblical answers to them offer a fundamental assurance for the church's way into the post-Constantinian society: *this way is open*. The mission continues. The service is being done. It is not superfluous to stress this statement, for it is not an obvious truth which faith is stating here. Even in our congregations, faced with an estranged and secularized environment, people are often heard asking: has the church any future at all? And in our ecumenical relationships we are obliged to listen to the questions so frequently raised by Christians who live under different and still largely "Constantinian" conditions: can the church exist at all in a fundamentally atheist society? And can it discharge its commission in that society?

One slogan emerges frequently in this connection: the slogan of *totalitarianism*. The doubts concerning the possibilities of the socialist society, and especially the possibilities of the Christian witness in it, are often justified by referring to its "totalitarian tendencies." We cannot discuss the full problem of totalitarianism in this context. Sometimes, this term has been used simply as a tool of the cold-war propaganda to support the argument that communism and fascism are only two branches of the same totalitarian tree. We emphatically reject this argument. There is a basic difference between communism, with its constructive and humanistic possibilities and destructive and nihilistic fascism. Yet the term totalitarian can be used in a more sober and less biased way, in denoting the tendency of a society to proclaim one ideology— and possibly one political party—as the only legitimate power within that society. We cannot deny that there is such a tendency in our society and that it poses serious human problems, especially for those people who do not profess that ideology—for example, for Christians within a Marxist society. Still the problem should not be exaggerated and "metaphysically absolutized." There are two basic reasons for this warning: (1) An ideology is never the whole of human reality. It is an important and influential—therefore by no means indifferent—element of social life. But the real life of men is always much richer and more complicated than its ideological pattern. Concretely, an atheistic ideological program does not create an atheistic society, just as a Christian program does not create a "Christian society." (2) A socialist society is by no means a static but, rather, a dynamic society. It may have had its days of rigidity, but those days are gone and the creative changes are not only a possibility, but a decisive reality, and bring with them a growing range of responsible participation and effective social action. To see the basic situation of man—and the situation of the church—in this society as captured within a "totalitarian structure" is totally inadequate.

From this pragmatic point of view, the skeptical doubts about the possibility of a Christian existence and mission in a socialist society are not justified; and, from the *theological* point of view, they must be dismissed, recalling the fundamental biblical assurance: The way is open. In the light of this promise, such doubts may frequently manifest a spiritual inertia that, consciously or unconsciously, links the cause of Christ with a historical "Constantinian" opportunity which is incapable of thinking imaginatively of the creative possibilities of the Holy Spirit, or even with a latent "atheism," which does not take seriously the sovereign freedom of God. That is why, in answering these well-meant but sometimes slightly petulant questions, we say emphatically, as Christians in a socialist society: The way remains open, the mission continues, the service is being fulfilled. No false cares—the cares of unbelief! Rather, the true care of faith. How, in fact, are we to go this way and walk in it straight and upright? How may the church in our society serve in obedience, and what is it to do? To this question we now turn.

A Worldly Interpretation of the Function of the Church in Society

I shall try to consider some of the thinking and reasoning on the problems of the church's witness in the post-Constantinian society, which in our actual situation is a Marxist-socialist one, under the motto "worldly proclamation" (*zivile Verkündigung*). This motto has been coined in our congregations during recent years of intensive inquiry into a more credible and effective way of service for our church. In English it sounds slightly enigmatic. It points in a similar direction as the ecumenically inspiring program of "nonreligious interpretation" of Dietrich Bonhoeffer, with the difference that with us the ethical-social component rather than the hermeneutical is in the foreground. We try to denote by it the search for new ways of the church's witness in a world that, on account of the general secularization and of its official ideological basis, has to a large extent become estranged from the church, so that the customary "Constantinian" opportunities—like the customary media of mass-evangelization—have become spiritually as well as technically inadequate. The motto itself is of no importance. We use it merely because it contains many shades of meaning and thus brings out clearly some of the implications with which we have been concerned.

We are concerned with these assertions, particularly as regards the consequences for the church's function in society: (1) Proving the freedom of the gospel: reducing traditional "uniforms" (rules of life); (2) serving the movement of the church toward the world:

an ex-centric congregation; (3) witnessing the interhuman relations: an unconditional humanism.

1. We begin with an external, almost banal, aspect of "civilian witness" which, however, has a certain significance, because it is the presupposition of Christian service in a society where traditional ecclesiastical forms and institutions are no longer socially relevant. There is, first, a *civilian mode of life* for Christians—a *witness without religious uniform,* "without long robes," without the traditional solemn ecclesiastical "dress." In many people's minds Christianity—as one looks back to the Constantinian form of the church—is at first related to a certain "dress," a "uniform" in the sense of a distinct mode of life. Thus, Christianity may be understood, for example, as an institute for cultivating religious-liturgical or ascetic laws and customs. To be a Christian, then, implies to take part in religious ceremonies, liturgical actions, pious usages or self-denying exercises. Or one interprets Christian faith in a moralistic, puritanical sense: the Christian "does not smoke, or drink, or dance. . . ." Or, again, Christianity is assigned to cultural-political categories: to be a Christian is to belong to a certain party, generally a "party of the pious against the 'godless'."

The Christian church bears a large part of the guilt for these misinterpretations. In the course of its history it has seen itself in these "uniforms" and shown itself in them to Christians and non-Christians alike. How often has the church succumbed to the temptation to understand itself—or to let itself be understood—as a religious institute, as a society for the cultivation of a religious style of life! In this way all kinds of prejudices were implanted and developed, so that the gospel became identified with religion both in the minds of its friends and then, consequently, in the minds of its foes. This, above all, may have been the danger of the Roman Catholic Church. But the Evangelical church too, for its part, has cultivated distinct, if perhaps different, prejudices. We may think, for instance, of the "puritanical uniform" so dear to the Reformed (Calvinist) or the pietistic type of the Reformation. Allegiance to Jesus Christ was frequently mistaken for allegiance to a puritanical-moralistic style of life. And do not large numbers of Christians today—both Roman Catholic and Protestant—fall victims to the third form of misunderstanding by linking Christianity with the cause of a distinct civilization—that, for instance, of the "Christian Occident"?

In all these "uniforms" a terrible temptation assails the church: the gospel of the free grace of God becomes a law; the redemption of the whole of life a fragment of life; salvation for all becomes salvation only for those who are near, which in turn is all too easily misunderstood as disaster for those who are far off. All this results in a separation that is bad because it is superficial, self-chosen, not justified by the gospel. Thus, the gospel is considerably reduced. There are, admittedly, many and diverse laws of human behavior and style. Many of these laws also apply to Christians and control their lives. But the gospel must on no account be confused with these laws, for it is not they that characterize and distinguish the Christian. The distinctiveness of the Christian is not a program which could be realized through these outward means; it goes much deeper: it is rooted not in a style of life but in faith itself.

"Civilian proclamation" attempts to withstand these temptations to legalize or to make wrong distinctions. It tries to lead the congregations away from cultivating a certain style, a "Christian manner," a code of conduct, from being different on principle, and to lead them to what is simply human, natural, even worldly. The Christian is first and foremost simply a man, a man of his age, a man among men. And this means today: a modern man. He is not fundamentally different from others. "To the Jews he is like a Jew and to the Greeks like a Greek." He is not living a deliberately distinct existence. In his "dress," that is, in his style of life (in the outward forms of his demeanor, in his interests) he is a man of his time. He is not a keeper of ancient monuments, not an exponent of the Middle Ages. He is not a person who on principle always draws lines and guards them—one who is always different, a man whose heart beats to a different rhythm from that of his fellowmen. On the contrary, he is, in the full meaning of the phrase, a "*con*temporary," a man among men—a *civilian*.

This civilian state of the Christian is certainly not an end in itself and not the last word. It is not in itself the testimony, but a means of promoting it: this civilian man is now being called to bear witness to Jesus Christ. He stands where his neighbors stand. But he stands there as one who tries to remain faithful to his lord. Here, then, begins the way of the Christian—in following Jesus, in believing, hoping and loving. In the midst of unbelief—faith. In the midst of despair—hope. In the midst of hatred—love. Where this is happening, the true distinction and the real witness come to pass, yet not through any self-chosen differentiation, but through the fundamental direction of existence. To guard this direction, to defend it from shallow legal limitations, and to distinguish the true witness to Jesus Christ from the substitute wares of a religious style of life, this is the intention of the "civilian proclamation" as implied in our motto.

At a time of social change, when a certain social order (a "law") is being replaced by another, this proclamation may be of particular significance. At such a moment there looms the danger of the church being identified with the "old law." It appears to be the exponent of the past order, and the gospel is seen as the ideology of the former society. And even worse: the church is tempted to understand itself within these categories. This is attractive because at first it seems promising: some people are joining the church for cryptopolitical reasons and out of resentment. And yet, every step in this direction is fateful, for it endangers the true witness of the gospel—and makes it particularly inaccessible to the representatives of the new society. This is the point at which, for example, the theology of "anticommunism" becomes disastrous: it turns the free gospel—which must also be understood as the gospel for atheists—into a law of bondage. Thus, in striving after a "civilian proclamation" we seek to maintain the freedom of the gospel in the very age of social change.

2. Here the second dimension of the worldly testimony becomes evident: evangelical service within a worldly, social and therefore civilian life. We understand this service not merely as a demand for decent behavior as a citizen. This, too, is important. But more is at stake in our aspect of civilian proclamation: it is the understanding of and witnessing to the gospel in its movement "from the church to the world"; it is the direction of the Christian life which corresponds to this encounter.

Movement from church to world: from the point of view of the church this may of course seem dubious. Do not these words sum up precisely the program of secularization, eliminating the influence of the church from one department of public life after another? Of course we have to distinguish: there is a theologically exaggerated version of the movement "from the church to the world"—If this is understood to mean, with R. Rothe, the "merging of the church into the state," or if a thoroughly justified criticism of eccelesiastical institutions is magnified into a desire to destroy these institutions. This almost looks like a manichaean attitude. The historical burden—and the historical guilt—of ecclesiastical institutions is immense. But the institutional aspect of church life is not only a menace but also a need and a necessity: life in the flesh—in history—also needs this support of spiritual life.

And yet the movement from the church to the world is a legitimate way for the church—and its duty. Perhaps that process of secularization "from the church to the world" is but a response to the guilt which the church itself has committed by notoriously curtailing its movement toward the world. Church history is full of evidence: Again and again the church has yielded to the temptation to replace the legitimate movement of its service—and this is what matters in this movement—by one in the opposite direction: from the world to the church. This assumed different forms: the form of a domineering clericalism in its Roman-medieval version, or in the Protestant-modern version of a "purple church." This tendency was also at work in much more subtle, more spiritual guises—even within the structure of the church's work. We see it, for example, in the customary superiority of "Sunday" over the "working day" (that is, the unquestioning concentration of attention almost exclusively on solemn, festal, religious occasions); in the superiority of the priest over the layman, which, in spite of Reformed principles, keeps its ground even in the Evangelical churches—at least in the form of a questionable sovereignty of the religious "professional" over the "amateur" (or in the minister's one-sided claim on the interest of the laity without, as a rule, any real interest on his part in questions which occupy the laity). This is in line with typically religious attitudes: a hierarchical movement in worship, in theology, in social structure. The priest likes to be at the head of the community: *Ecclesia praecedit*. The movement of the gospel is diametrically opposed to this typical movement of religion: According to Philippians 2 : 5–11 it is service, sacrifice, umanity that matter. In this movement the church is being constituted, not as an autocratic institution but as an ex-centric community, a community, that is, which does not have its center within itself. Here is the paradigm of its discipleship: from the church to the world.

A "civilian interpretation" tries to do justice to this movement. It stresses the theological honor of the "working day." This does not detract from the true sovereignty of "Sunday"—the lord's day. But this day is indissolubly linked with the "working days": "The sabbath was made for man and not man for the sabbath" (Mark 2 : 27). A church which remains true to its constitutive movement can therefore never be content to be the church of a single day. It will always claim the "whole week." The theme of the weekday must also be taken much more seriously in the liturgical activity of the church, so that the worship of the church does not become a sacred reserve, but is offered in dedication to the world, to the actual joys and sorrows, labor and suffering of man. And this applies also to the scope of parochial life. It is the purpose of the Christian congregation—particularly of the churches of the Reformation to which it was committed as a special *charisma* and a special obligation—to grow not merely into a ghetto-like community centered on a cult, but into a community of all life, into a fellowship that prays, works and suffers together. This implies a much more serious participation of the laity in the work, for where the church understands itself in this way, it becomes obvious that the church is maintained not only by the clergy but by every member. Indeed, where the movement "from the church to the world" is taken seriously, there it is precisely the layman who becomes the true exponent of this legitimate movement of the church. It is precisely the revolutionary changes of the Constantinian order which make it unambiguously clear that the laity constitutes the proper "apostolic existence" of the church of Jesus Christ in the post-Constantinian world.

And it is not only the layman: The atheist, estranged from the church is caught up within the true movement "from the church to the world." In a certain sense even those who perhaps have never set foot on the floor of the church belong to its sphere—namely the sphere of its prayer and its work. They, too, should be its

concern, even in their absence—and perhaps for that very reason
They, too, have the right to have their say even as regards the ser
mon—they, too, should be included in its message, and not merely
as the "dark background" of the lost from whom those present i
church are so nicely set apart as children of light from the childre
of darkness (how often the church has preached in this way—an
still does!), but as those with whom we are united in sin and i
hope through Jesus Christ. Thus the world becomes present in th
church—and the church in the world.

This "civilian testimony" has not only a human and individua
dimension, but also a social and collective one. Ultimately our serv
ice is concerned with real persons. But the development of moder
society has shown with absolute clarity that there are no real per
sons without wider social relations. These relations—in particula
the economic and the political—therefore concern the church. I
cannot practice political abstinence and offer as a reason for it tha
"the political song is a nasty song." It has to join in singing it—
with a genuine and pure intention in the light of the gospel, with
out any opportunism or resentment of the prevailing fashion. Wher
this is done, this song—care for better justice, truer freedom and
really just peace of the world—is part of divine service. And in
versely, divine service—the perspective of the gospel—belongs t
the center of the life of society in the civilian expression of faith

This civilian participation of the church in the life of the worl
forms an important basis for a credible witness. It seems that it i
only from this serving presence in the world, from an undemandin
engagement of Christians in the burning problems of the time, tha
a witness is evolving which makes their neighbors prick up thei
ears. At a time of immense inflation of all words through the mas
media of advertising and propaganda, the mere religious word i
more powerless than ever. And the same may well apply to th
customary means of mass evangelization and mission, even if from
time to time their success—apparent or real?—is great. "Mature,
"worldly" men will hardly be reached by these methods. A credibl
testimony will be developed only from out of the depth of rea
life, not hastily and superficially. It is in this sense that a tru
civilian mode is a presupposition of Christian witness in the mod
ern world.

And it is not only a presupposition. In a sense this civilian pres-
nce in the world is already the witness—even if it is not yet con-
idered or labeled as such. Dedication to the world in following
5od's way to men is meaningful in itself—quite apart from any
esults achieved by the church's standards. "Results," "successes"
n the church's activity are, of course, by no means a matter for
ndifference. The missionary point of view in the church is justi-
ied. But it is not the only point of view—not even the first or the
ast one. Only service itself ranks so high. We do well to remember
his in regard to the church's activity—also in regard to new ways
of this activity, in regard, for example, to the attempts at a "civil-
an proclamation." These experiments might also be understood
s another "new strategy," "method," as a clerical "gimmick"—
s the last attempt of the church to conquer the world. Some of the
ew ways of the church's work could be so interpreted. But this
s ultimately a misunderstanding—and no true help for the church
r for the world. For the promise of Jesus Christ to the church
s given only in the way of guileless, simple service. A genuine
urning of the church to the world will be based not on clever
alculations, but on following the way of Jesus. Only by following
im can the true dimension of a civilian witness be perceived and
aith be tested in the world.

3. We come now to the third "level" of the civilian service of
he church in our society: witnessing to the gospel in interhuman
elations, striving after an evangelical proexistence. It was mainly
n this sense that our congregations understood the concept of
civilian interpretation" as one of the most urgent tasks and as
ne of the opportunities for Christian service in our society. And
ightly so, for the quest for the neighbor is one of the most burning
uestions of our time. Indeed, this question is an ancient human
uestion, one of the few basic questions of man. Today, however,
t is being asked with particular urgency. This urgency is implicit
n the structure of modern life: in the rise of "technical civiliza-
ion," of "mass society" in the world. The Christian need not de-
lore this development. He knows in sober fact that it has unlocked
nheard-of possibilities and realities for man. Foundations have
een laid for effectively overcoming some of the fundamental evils
of past epochs: we cannot sufficiently stress what it means that

from large parts of the world hunger, epidemics, unemployment have disappeared and are still disappearing. We have much reason to be proud of our present age. Yet it, too, has its dangers and troubles. And one of its deepest needs is the need of man for his fellowman. Amid the incalculable entities and numbers of this technical civilization and its mass society, man is always in danger of becoming a cog in a vast machine, of representing a function rather than a person. He is easily ignored as a personality. Lonely people in the human masses of great cities, men forsaken by the welfare state, neighbors in close physical proximity unknown to one another—these problems are well known. In this situation man is in danger of losing much that is essential: personal relations, mutual understanding and interest, individual assistance. Men's hunger for personal humanity, for their fellowmen, is not being stilled.

Here, then, is an important opening for the "civilian testimony" of a Christian in the modern world. It is precisely here that he is being called and demanded with particular urgency. The gospel itself sends him on this way, the way of fellow humanity; for ultimately the gospel is God's search for man. We need but to recall the hymnological summary of the way of Jesus Christ in Philippians 2, with its key sentence "and was made in the likeness of men," or the saying in Titus of the appearing of the "love of God toward man" (3 : 4). And we may remember Matthew 25 : 40 where, following this "divine humanism," men's turning toward their neighbors is made the touchstone of their Christian faith: "Inasmuch as ye have done it unto one of the least of these my brethren, ye have done it unto me." Here the scope of the Christian witness is indicated: proexistence, existence for others. Only in this movement toward one's neighbor can Jesus Christ be obediently followed; only in this movement can we tread the Christian way.

This way, then, leads to an unconditional humanity. I emphasize the "unconditional" of man's turning to his neighbor, for it is here that Christian humanism is distinguished from general philanthropy. We appreciate secular forms of solidarity with men in the numerous humanist efforts of our days. We gratefully share part of the way in common with these efforts. At times we are pu shame by the resolve and willingness, on the part of non-Christians, to make sacrifices in this cause. We do not separate from them prematurely and rashly. And yet—there is a legitimate parting of the ways. Current humanism is all too fond of drawing lines. Its first and often exclusive concern is for the "neighbor" in the literal sense of the word: for him who is "nigh," for those who belong to the same nation, race, class or religion. Sooner or later the open windows are shut. But the Christian is called to his fellowman even when every natural or ideological sympathy has ceased; when he can no longer see any natural or historical reason for it; where only walls or chasms of traditional enmity may be distinguished. It is difficult indeed to demonstrate true humanity in such conditions. But this, precisely, is the mission of the Christian: to seek and to see the face of Jesus Christ over every man. There is a beautiful saying by Luther: "to receive Jesus Christ in every man and to be Jesus Christ to every man." This means that for the sake of Jesus Christ none may ever be excluded from our common humanity. To look for our common humanity even when we are defending ourselves, when we are contradicting, when we are facing the opponent—and to love even the enemy—this is the witness of the Christian.

Let us finally mention two examples and results of this unconditional Christian service within the framework of human relations. Right from the start Christian solidarity has tended with particular devotion those for whom nobody cares, the poor and the sick, the forgotten and oppressed, those who from a utilitarian point of view are considered unproductive and superfluous. Let us remember the place of honor in the Old Testament for the "orphans and widows" or in the gospel for those who "labor and are heavy laden"! Here is the point at which both the temptation and the honor of Christian philanthropy arise. I speak of the temptation of philanthropy, namely, of the temptation for the church to express its responsibility for man, for the neighbor, exclusively in categories of personal welfare, of charity. This is a harmful limitation of Christian brotherly love. It is a judgment on our faithfulness that a movement outside the church—in particular, socialism—has recognized this state of things more clearly than the majority of Christians. To help a person effectively demands a purposeful, organized and planned system of welfare for the whole sphere of men's social life, a reconstruction of society, not only the dealing with crying individual needs. Here is the reason, based on the gospel, for our saying "yes" to socialist reconstruction, to its principle and to many of its results, such as the generous provisions of our health services. Yet precisely here where the church gratefully acknowledges this national welfare, it will underline again the honor of philanthropy in the sense of turning to those who need personal understanding, personal care, personal interest, in particular the "orphans and widows" of the modern age—people who are lonely and half-forgotten. Philanthropy in the church—which becomes a stumbling block when it claims to do everything—thus acquires a new meaning where a broad framework of solutions and opportunities has been realized, but where the personal turning of man to man is still necessary. "The poor ye have always with you"—this sentence (which in the history of the church did much harm because it was understood as a general doctrine of the impossibility and ineffectiveness of social reconstruction)—is true here It is here that there is scope for our congregations and for every Christian, scope for our "civilian interpretation" of the gospel.

The task of a civilian interpretation in the sphere of human relations does not, however, end at the level of personal, individual relations. The light of the unconditional philanthropy of God (Titus 3 : 4) also shines on international relations, that is on the search for a peaceful order of a world threatened by atomic annihilation. How often has the church at this point hidden its light under a bushel? How often has it strengthened the barriers between nations and power blocs rather than destroyed them? Often it has spiritually justified or even kindled the spirit of the "cold war," instead of energetically opposing it. Here is the sphere where Christianity has failed again and again. Yet here there is still an almost unlimited opportunity for new service. Never before, i seems, have we been shown as clearly, now that we are faced with the atomic danger to mankind, that the gospel of God's unconditional will for peace is of direct actuality even in the sphere of "high politics": There is no other way for the future of mankind than the will for reconciliation and peace. In our present situation this means the unconditional will for peace in the world. This is the point at which those who are aware of this will and of its grounding bear an immense responsibility. The witness of brotherly solidarity in a restless and divided world—for instance in the work of the ecumenical movement or of our Christian Peace Conference—is gaining great importance amid the rising tension of these days. It belongs to the most precious experience of our ecumenical relations in these recent years, especially at meetings of Christians from East and West, that again and again we have been able to discover: notwithstanding all our weaknesses and all our helplessness, the pure service of reconciliation, the service of peace is being accomplished in some small part through our ecumenical work. Thus, the witness of the gospel for this world is being borne through its "civilian interpretation" in the modern world.

Wherever this is done, wherever in torn human relations—of a wider or narrower range—a little island of genuine humanity becomes visible within our churches, there witness is being borne to Jesus Christ, even where his name has not yet been expressly named. Witness to Jesus Christ is not borne only where he is named. This witness is already borne where the thirsty are given a "cup of cold water" in his name. His witness is not at work only where he is acknowledged and named as such, where he stands his ground, where he is successful. We are learning afresh that in the biblical term for witness, "martyr," an abiding undertone is clearly discernible. The testimony of Jesus Christ gives light even where its witness seems to be failing, where he is not standing his ground, where he is not being recognized and acknowledged, but where he is serving in simple faithfulness to man and thereby to his lord. Here is "civilian interpretation" in the deepest meaning of this phrase.

Renewing the Credibility of the Christian Witness

We have outlined a pattern of Christian witness for a post-Constantinian society. It is a narrow way: the church as an institution is of no decisive significance for the public life of society. The opportunities for a direct, organized, institutionalized claim on society are few and isolated. In this sense too the church—compared with its possibilities in an unbroken Constantinian order

—has become poor. Therefore, the way is narrow. And yet—
remains open. And it does not remain without promise. Our Chris
tian witness is, on this narrow way, given the chance of a ne
credibility.

It cannot be denied that the credibility of the Christian church i
the world today—in East and West alike—has been largely ur
dermined. The history of modern secularization is also a history c
the shrinking credibility of Christianity. And Constantinian Chris
tianity is not without blame. The interpenetration of ecclesiastica
institutions with the institutions of the society of the day, whic
was particularly obvious in the various forms of the union c
"throne and altar," provided not only an opportunity to exert
dominating influence but for an unevangelical capitulation—an
this unfortunately even more so. How often did the Constantinia
church stand in its own way—fettered by false considerations of it
own interests as an institution of the given order! And so the gospe
was frequently hidden under the bushel—hidden from those ver
people who, travailing under a heavy social load, had been waitin
for the justice of the kingdom of God by word and deed. Notwith
standing some outstanding achievements of a christianly inspire
philanthropy, the church and its message lost all credibility, espe
cially through its failure to meet the social needs of modern indus
trial society. How many then arrived at the bitter conclusion: th
church speaks of God—but it means its privileges and those of it
society. It is a community of conscious or unconscious hypocrites

The burden of this failure lies on us all. Yet now that the Con
stantinian opportunities have been lost we may be offered a nev
chance. It may be that a church which has no longer any privileges
and therefore need no longer defend itself, need no longer stanc
in its own way or in that of others: for in the post-Constantinia
society the Christian has nothing more to gain by being a Chris
tian. The one ground for becoming and remaining a Christian ir
that situation is the ground of faith. Thus the shadow of hypocris
grows less. And here is the chance of credibility. The mere ex
istence of the Christian church can then already be true witness
A community of pilgrims, of civilian men who do not seek to pre
serve any social privileges or to maintain any political "anti"
conceptions; who consciously live in the new society and take i

seriously—but who try to do so unequivocally as Christians: is not this already—this presence of the Christian community within the Marxist-Socialist world—a basic witness to this society?

There were times when it seemed that this presence was the only possibility of action left to the churches—because of the deep distrust of the revolutionary society toward the church and because of a certain ideological and administrative rigidity of the system. I think of the "Stalinist era." Yet there was nothing passive in this presence: the patience and the loyalty of the church—loyalty to Jesus Christ and loyalty to the people of our society—helped to shape the spiritual basis for a new and fresh service. And when the rigidity lessened, melting away, the Christians received a new chance to participate in the spiritual ferment of their country. A new relevance of the anthropological and ethical quest made many of our countrymen—including the Marxists—more attentive to the possible relevance of a Christian contribution. What is man—can he be understood and explained in economic categories only? Where is the final criterion of his humanity? The history of the past years and the role of Christians in the socialist society has proved that Christians cannot be dismissed simply as reactionary partisans of the past system, and a new dialogue became possible. As Professor Hromadka says, we are "at the threshold of the dialogue," nothing more. But we hope it will go on. We participate in it not as the "ideological masters" of our society, but as real servants. We try, by way of "civilian interpretation," to open the perspective of the gospel of God's way to man for the issues of our lives and of our society. We try to do so through a type of "Socratic evangelism," in which the evangelist is "midwife rather than preacher," to use an illuminating expression of Dr. Visser 't Hooft's. Even in this sense our way is and will be a narrow one—and there is no guarantee of success. But this may be the right way for the Christian church in the post-Constantinian era and may offer a real chance of credible and hopeful service for men in our society.

* * * * *

Postscript: Comments
by Professor WOLFGANG SCHWEITZER (Germany)

1. What is the relation between gospel and law in Professor Lochman's paper? Certainly it is theologically unsound if the gospel simply becomes a law. It must remain the gospel of God's grace, the gospel which makes man free and opens new ways in every situation. But as the Word becomes flesh, so the gospel, when it reaches man, and especially when it is accepted by man, affects his behavior toward his fellowman and toward society. In the second half of his chapter, Lochman himself gives many examples under the heading "civilian proclamation" (or testimony) of the gospel. In the second half of the paper he speaks about this in a very concrete way, and I should like to subscribe to what he has said there. I would hesitate to call this a new Christian law. Non-Christians are often very good humanist "philanthropists" too. But should we not say that the gospel—and the faith of the Christian who accepts the gospel—gives existing humanistic aspirations a certain definite direction? This includes its influence upon the "laws," the moral standards, the conduct of a given society. If that is true, the trouble with the Constantinian period was not that Christians had such influence, but that they were unable to move forward with the history of man; the church became a relic of the past. I agree that the Constantinian period has ended, and this has many consequences for all of us, not only for those who live in socialist countries. Our social teaching must be radically transformed. But we should not pretend to be able ever to preach the gospel alone. We should accept the fact that Christians at least to some extent can be recognized by a certain attitude or behavior—namely in the direction which Professor Lochman himself has described under another heading.

2. Biblical ethics is always an ethic of concrete decisions in concrete situations; the main question is always: Which way of conduct is in harmony with my faith in Jesus Christ—and which is not? To accept Christ as lord surely implies following him into the world, and I fully support Professor Lochman's concern at this point. But should he not indicate where Christians may be forced to say "no" under certain circumstances?

In this connection it should be made clear that there is indeed a remarkable difference between a church "showing understanding for socialism" and the assimilation, which Lochman so well describes in the early pages of the essay. It is very important, though very difficult, to make this difference as clear as possible.

3

THE CHURCH IN AN AFFLUENT SOCIETY

by Roger L. Shinn (United States)

A momentous economic revolution is at work in the world today, loaded with promise and with portent. A new technology has increased fantastically the possibilities of economic productivity. The revolution shatters the patterns expected by traditional capitalism and Marxism. It faces men with ethical opportunities and challenges never before anticipated. It reorganizes the institutions of production and of government, changes man's relation to nature and to his fellowmen, transforms the hopes and fears of vast populations and among its many consequences is "the affluent society."

A significant part of mankind and of the Christian church lives in this new kind of society. It is most evident in the United States of America and parts of western Europe. The Soviet Union is acquiring some of its characteristics. Japan, with the most phenomenal record of economic growth in the current world, is moving toward affluence. In this chapter, the American experience will furnish the primary example of the affluent society.

Although some social historians think that Christianity has been one of the several forces that have brought this new society into being, it is unanticipated in the Bible and in most of the theological tradition. Hence it calls for a rethinking of ethics, even of some aspects of theology.

The Christian church, in its centuries of history, has lived through many revolutionary eras. It has learned, or should have learned, not to ally itself too closely with any specific social environment. St.

Augustine, referring to the many types of human societies, wrote of the city of God: "It therefore is so far from rescinding and abolishing these diversities, that it even preserves and adapts them, so long only as no hindrance to the worship of the one supreme and true God is thus introduced." [1]

However, the church obviously does not remain a static community in the midst of a shifting landscape; the changing environment inevitably affects it. Its people are part of their society. They talk the language, make their livings, dwell in buildings, communicate and travel, use social institutions—all in ways provided by society. If the church is to serve a living God who reveals himself in history, then it must become even more attentive to change in that society. Its task is to respond to the leading of a God who often calls a pilgrim people to get up and move, as he surely calls today.

Characteristics of the Affluent Society

The affluent society is an exceedingly complex social organization, often misunderstood by those who live in its confusion and by those who look at it from outside. We must avoid being deceived by terminology: it is certainly not a society in which everybody has all he wants, because human wants are insatiable. It is possible to raise the standard of living so that everybody participates in the general prosperity. But human nature craves more than a share—most people want greater wealth and status than their neighbors. Since it is impossible for everybody to live in the upper tenth or even the upper half of society, many are bound to feel that they are not affluent.

Furthermore, the affluent society creates poverty as it creates wealth, because it develops ways of living in which luxuries become necessities. It brings a metropolitan style of life in which high production and consumption become requirements for survival. Consider a few typical attainments of the affluent society: electric refrigeration, elaborate plumbing, central heating, elevators, automobiles and intricate road networks, telephones. Through-

---

[1] *The City of God*, XIX, 17.

out most of history mankind has lived without these symbols of wealth. Now cities are built that would strangle without them. They have become necessities for many, many people.

Another side of the story is that some of the common gifts of life, once available to everybody, have become expensive luxuries. As the affluent society offers electricity to everybody, it makes unpolluted air a rarity. Green grass and flowing brooks become costly. People make frantic efforts to enjoy quiet, to escape from the tyranny of the telephone, or to enjoy a simple stroll in the countryside.

For a variety of reasons, therefore, the economic strain upon the family in the affluent society is often as great as the strain upon its ancestors in impoverished societies. To enjoy mammon without serving mammon is not easy for the society or its members.

The affluent society can be defined in terms of several characteristics, some of which are important to its self-understanding and to its ethics:

1. The most obvious characteristic of the affluent society is its high production and widespread distribution of goods. It has learned to use technology to produce huge quantities of commodities which are distributed among the majority of the members of society. The economy is able to produce an abundance of the traditional necessities of mankind—food, clothing and shelter; and there is certainly no economic need for anyone to die of starvation or exposure.

2. Instead of persuading men to restrict consumption in order that limited goods may go farther, society works to stimulate consumption in order to sustain economic activity. In the new culture-ethic, the man who does not spend is not doing his duty to the system. Poverty becomes a social offense, not simply because of compassion for the poor, but because they cannot do their part in maintaining a market for commodities and employment for other poor people. The affluent society may come to the point of valuing man-the-consumer above man-the-producer. Some of its members enjoy good incomes, but never find the satisfaction of contributing anything to the society. The results for human dignity and morale are crushing.

3. The nature of work changes significantly. Fewer and fewer

people earn their living by the sweat of the brow.[2] Perhaps more and more make their income by strain on the nerves. The affluent society needs more white-collar workers than blue-collar workers —that is, more people to work in offices and sell products than to manufacture and transport them. The most obvious change is in agriculture: fewer and fewer farmers raise greater and greater crops. The distinguished economist, Kenneth Boulding, estimates that at the height of the Roman Empire seventy-five per cent of the population engaged in farming. Now in the United States of America only a small minority farm—and produce agricultural surpluses. Boulding continues:

It is by no means impossible to suppose a world at the end of this process in which we can produce our whole food supply with one per cent of the population; in which we can produce all basic commodities such as clothing, housing and so on with perhaps another two or three per cent or perhaps even at most ten per cent.[3]

Obviously the traditional definitions of work and social usefulness must change.

4. The change in work means a change in the role of persons. High productivity requires a high degree of specialization of labor. Even Marxist societies recognize this fact, despite Marx's own polemics against the division of labor. In modern industry persons become as interchangeable as parts of a machine. The affluent society is possible only because of the interdependence of millions of people who do not know each other. The meal on the table, the auto in the garage, the utilities that serve the home—all these involve the work of vast numbers of people whom the consumer never sees. He usually becomes aware of them only if something goes wrong. The result is that society is tempted to value its members more as *functions* than as persons. It does not care whether the person finds meaning in his work or even whether he disappears, so long as the function continues.

5. The affluent society gives man a seeming mastery of his environment. He tends to become less grateful to nature and to

---

[2] Gen. 3 : 19. This is only one of many examples in which the affluent society robs biblical language of its power.

[3] KENNETH BOULDING, "The Death of the City: A Frightened Look at Post-Civilization." *Ekistics,* Jan., 1962.

God than to the human systems in which he lives. He is more aware of what he can buy than of what he is given. Although he knows vaguely that all energy comes from the sun and that water comes from clouds and oceans, he deals more directly with electrical switches and faucets. His dominion over nature is a valid achievement—the fulfillment of a biblical command beyond biblical expectations. But it sometimes deceives man as to his real powers and limitations. Often it tempts him to substitute self-congratulation for gratitude.

Two Christian Traditions Concerning Wealth [4]

The Christian church is confused about how it should approach the affluent society. It can adapt itself uncritically to the norms of the new culture, abandoning its prophetic ministry. Or it can indulge in caustic condemnation, as though it were somehow superior to the culture. Both answers are common among churchmen, but neither is an authentic service of God or men. The fact is that the church has no preconceived set of solutions for problems never before experienced by mankind. Its ignorance is no reason for shame. It should confess its guilt for its share in the injustices and idolatries of the affluent society, but its uncertainties are not shameful. The church's confidence is in God's gospel, not in its own wisdom for every situation.

Christian faith brings to the affluent society certain traditional teachings and attitudes that arose out of quite different situations. Old injunctions, woodenly applied to new circumstances, are often irrelevant and unrealistic. Neither the pastoral-agricultural practices of the Bible nor the tradition of natural law nor the casuistries of Catholicism and Puritanism tell us precisely how to live faithfully in the new world. Yet the church can too easily write off the past without appreciating the faith that lived in it. As we look at two inherited traditions, we need both to recognize the authentic elements in them and to see how our time requires its own formulations.

---

[4] A few paragraphs in this section are adapted from an earlier study that I prepared for the Department of Church and Economic Life of the National Council of Churches of Christ in the U.S.A.

The first tradition, with its deep rootage in prophetic faith and in the Christian gospel, shows a deep distrust of wealth and a glorification of poverty. Amos and Isaiah criticized the predatory rich, not only for their injustice toward the poor but also because of their deluded self-sufficiency and pride. Jesus Christ came to preach "good news to the poor." [5] He upset the normal attitudes toward wealth and poverty: "Blessed are you poor, for yours is the kingdom of God. . . . But woe to you that are rich, for you have received your consolation." [6] For centuries the church has puzzled over one of his warnings and tried to take the sting out of it: "It is easier for a camel to go through the eye of a needle than for a rich man to enter into the kingdom of God." [7]

In the early church most Christians were poor. But gradually men of affluence joined the church, and reinterpretations of Jesus' teachings seemed advisable. Within two centuries, Clement of Alexandria wrote his rather cheerful essay on the question, "Who is the rich man that shall be saved?" Much of it is clearly valid: it is not the quantity of wealth that is important, but the attitude toward it and its use that are important, says Clement. But Clement misses the point of Scripture when he says that since the rich man need not worry about his livelihood, he may be less greedy than the poor man, and therefore closer to salvation. [8]

As the church grew, wealth looked increasingly good to many Christians. But there were always those who worried about easy accommodation to the world. The monastic movement protested against dilution of the Christian ethic and re-emphasized the ideal of poverty. The Benedictine Rule ordered the "vice of private ownership" to be "cut off . . . by the roots" and prescribed utmost simplicity in food and dress. [9] But monasteries too grew wealthy. Although monks took vows of poverty, the orders acquired lands and money. In resistance to this movement St. Francis of Assisi again renounced luxury. "Married to Lady Poverty," as he put it, he demanded complete rejection of wealth in his mendicant

---

[5] Luke 4 : 18.
[6] Luke 6 : 20, 24.
[7] Matt. 19 : 24.
[8] *The Ante-Nicene Fathers*, Vol. II.
[9] *The Rule of St. Benedict*, Ch. 33.

order—an ideal that future generations of Franciscans quickly compromised.

The modern world, including both affluent societies and those striving to become affluent, is uncomfortable with this traditional praise of poverty. It sees the Manichean heresy that lurks in much asceticism, and prefers to emphasize the goodness of God's creation and man's right to subdue and enjoy it.

The vocation of voluntary poverty persists today in occasional impressive forms, less as a deliberate rejection of wealth than as part of a ministry to the poor. Most Christians, however, are unlikely to seek poverty. If they moralize about the temptations of wealth, usually they set the boundary of dangerous wealth somewhere beyond their own resources.

A second, more recent, Christian tradition has given higher regard to productive work. Although the Weber-Tawney thesis [10] on the relation between Calvinism and capitalism is strenuously debated, it is at least clear that Protestantism has often supported the virtues that had a useful function in the period of an expanding economy. If feudalism was occasionally romantic and usually paternalistic toward the poor, the Calvinists were more likely to ask, "Are you poor because you are lazy?" The question did not prejudge the answer. Calvin knew that men were poor for many reasons, but when laziness was the cause, Calvinists were not eager to say, "Blessed are you poor," or to offer alms.

An expanding industrializing economy—whether within a capitalist or a socialist framework—requires that considerable effort be directed to producing capital equipment (such as factories or machinery) rather than consumer goods. The society, or at least some within it, must accept the discipline of deferred enjoyment. The Puritan heirs of Calvin were willing to do that. For religious and moral reasons, they praised the virtues of diligence, frugality, honesty and thrift. Since such virtues frequently led to accumulation of wealth, the Puritans could often provide the capital needed for developing industry. Some of them happily accepted their wealth

---

[10] See MAX WEBER: *The Protestant Ethic and the Spirit of Capitalism,* translated by TALCOTT PARSONS. New York: Charles Scribner's Sons, 1930. Also R. H. TAWNEY: *Religion and the Rise of Capitalism.* New York: Harcourt, Brace and Co., 1926.

as evidence of God's approval, although Calvin had warned against such attempts to fathom the mysteries of providence.

Puritan moral injunctions have been preserved throughout American history even though their basis has shifted from religious to economic grounds. Benjamin Franklin, for example, poked fun at Cotton Mather, but turned many of Mather's moralisms into witty aphorisms. To this day some Americans are not sure whether their favorite sayings come from the Bible or from *Poor Richard's Almanack*.

At about the same time John Wesley was teaching his followers to "gain all you can, save all you can, give all you can." [11] This exhortation did not mean to England's impoverished workers what it did to later generations; but some of Wesley's followers distinguished themselves by following the first two-thirds of his advice. Wesley himself remembered the biblical warnings against wealth and frequently worried over the results of his own movement.

Puritan and Methodist piety have been highly important in shaping some of the societies that eventually attained affluence. In the process, Protestantism sometimes came to stand for middle-class respectability, for reliability and for a confusion of bourgeois with Christian virtues. The "pillars of the church" have often been the "pillars of the community." To this day, any political appeal for economy in government, the balanced budget and practice of the old-fashioned economic virtues is likely to stir deep responses among churchmen.

These two traditions of Christian economic ethics clearly differ from each other. The one praises poverty; the other inculcates habits that often lead to wealth. Nevertheless the two agree on a central contention: they condemn extravagance. Spending for display or for luxurious living is regarded as sinful, and waste is a religious offense.

Thus traditional Christian ethical formulations clash with the spirit of the affluent society. Frugality, once a religious virtue, has become a social threat. Debt for the sake of indulgence, once sinful, is now the basis of prosperity. Where once greed was regarded as detrimental to human welfare, we now hear that it contributes

---

[11] JOHN WESLEY: "The Use of Money," *The Standard Sermons of John Wesley,* E. H. SUGDEN, ed. London: The Epworth Press, 1921, Vol. II.

to public good. Jesus taught, "You cannot serve God and mammon"; [12] propagandists today tell us, "You serve society best by serving mammon." The New Testament said, "The love of money is the root of all evil"; [13] popular doctrine today announces, "The love of money is the root of prosperity for all."

Seeing this clash, the Christian church must ask once again the meaning of its faith. It cannot simply succumb to the blandishments of the affluent society, forget its heritage and get on with the enjoyments of reckless consumption. It may—and on rare occasions does—resist the current economic changes, attack affluence as a snare and seek ways to adhere literally to one or another of its traditions. Such attempts are usually halfhearted, and are likely to substitute the culture-ethic of a past generation for the prevailing culture-ethic of the present.

Surely our era calls for a more daring answer. D. L. Munby, the British economist and lay theologian, has written: "God is in process of transforming our economic order. . . . We can, and should, participate in that activity." [14] We can, in the spirit of Dietrich Bonhoeffer, seek a Christian worldliness for our time. These enterprises are not easy. Forces opposed to God and indifferent to him are at work in modern economies, and the church must learn to distinguish these. Talk of Christian worldliness easily becomes the pretext for pagan worldliness. Yet, recognizing the dangers, the church knows that it must answer to its vocation in the modern economy. This does not mean adapting in all respects to the affluent society. It means serving the God of Jesus Christ in the present age.

Christian Responsibility in the Affluent Society

If the church is to maintain a faithful witness in the affluent society, it must carry out four tasks. These will call both for theological understanding and for sensitivity to the needs of the society.

---

[12] Matt. 6 : 24.
[13] I Tim. 6 : 10.
[14] D. L. MUNBY: *God and the Rich Society*. London: Oxford University Press, 1961, p. 179.

1. *The church needs to understand the affluent society and to appreciate the opportunities it offers.*

At first glance such appreciation may seem easy. Who does not enjoy wealth? Yet men often resent change, and Christians resist the passing of the culture in which they have been at home. Protestants have frequently found their affinities in rural culture, have made a fetish of work and have nourished a false piety that disdained economic processes. Some Christian criticisms of the affluent society arise more out of nostalgia than out of faith. It is easy —and not very helpful—to deplore the materialism of modern society. Christians should know from their Scriptures that God is concerned for the whole life of man and that no spirituality can release the church from material concerns. They should realize also that the material gains of the affluent society make possible the liberation of the human spirit from many forms of bondage.

Education is an example. Throughout most of human history education has inevitably been a luxury. Most children had to become wage earners as early as possible. Most adults had to work long hours with little access to the information and ideas that are basic to education. The affluent society makes it economically possible—even advantageous—to prolong the years of education for youth. The laborer on a thirty-five to forty-hour week has time for learning. Books, periodicals, television and educational institutions provide the means. Where there is a will to learn, the opportunities are there.

Leisure is another example. No doubt the increase of leisure presents problems. Affluent societies are full of bored people, jaded with every form of entertainment, unable to find meaning in their work or their leisure time. Protestantism, with an energetic ethic rather remote from Scripture, has not equipped its members for leisure. David Riesman in a famous book has written: "The inner-directed person, if influenced by Protestantism, is . . . unable to waste time." [15] The Protestant churches have been acutely aware that "Satan finds mischief for idle hands to do"; they need to learn also the creative possibilities of leisure. The high culture of most past civilizations has depended largely upon a small leisure

[15] DAVID RIESMAN: *The Lonely Crowd*. New York: Anchor Books, 1953, p. 184.

class; in the affluent society most of mankind can be admitted to that class. As a matter of fact, the traditional class distinctions may be reversed, as laborers enjoy more leisure than professional people.

A final example is health. It may be that some of the gains of the affluent society in this field are illusory, as its wealth barely enables it to treat the illnesses that it produces. But improved diet, research, sanitation and facilities for treating diseases have reduced infant mortality and prolonged life expectancy. A sign of the success is the population explosion, which brings a new set of difficulties. Evidently man is capable of few attainments that do not pose new problems. But improved health is a substantial gain. It not only reduces human misery: it brings an authentic ethical achievement, as it enables society to show a concern for the individual that is hard to realize in societies ravaged by epidemics and starvation.

2. *Against this background of appreciation for the opportunities of the affluent society, the church has the privilege and obligation to call men to responsibility in the midst of their prosperity.*

The church's call will not be a command. In pluralistic, secularized societies, the church cannot demand obedience. But when the church speaks truthfully and lives faithfully, men inside and outside its membership may respond to a prophetic word. An adequate call to responsibility includes several specific notes.

The first and most obvious is the elimination of poverty within the affluent society itself. For centuries the church has quoted— and often misinterpreted—the saying of Jesus: "You have the poor always with you." [16] The church might have compassion on the poor, but poverty was an economic necessity. Today in many societies this is no longer the case. The persistence of extreme poverty is not an inevitable fateful evil but an offense against God and man.

In the most affluent of societies, the United States of America, the relation between wealth and poverty is extremely complex. In some respects the United States has utterly refuted the Marxist expectation that the few rich would increasingly dominate the many

---

[16] Matt. 26 : 11.

poor. The majority of the population share in the benefits of high productivity. The rich and powerful corporations have wide ownership. Many of the great corporations have more stockholders than employees; and the owners include philanthropic foundations, pension funds, labor unions and individuals. But in this affluent society the lowest twenty per cent of the people live in dismal poverty. The Scandinavian countries have shown that affluence does not require neglect of the poor. But the United States stands judged by the words from Isaiah: "What do you mean by crushing my people, by grinding the face of the poor?" says the Lord God of hosts.[17]

Curiously the causes of poverty in this society are not primarily economic. In some regions, economic changes have brought poverty, and increasing automation may bring unemployment and new poverty. But at present most of the poor are not unemployed, and many skills are in great demand. The deepest causes of poverty are cultural rather than economic. The United States is a vast country of diverse peoples. In many cities there is no language that all the residents share. Where there is no common ethnic inheritance, religious belief or cultural tradition, many people live in marginal subcultures. Some of these subcultures barely participate in the main currents of the economy or culture.

The difficulties inherent in the situation are exaggerated by the vicious evil of racial prejudice, although most of the poor, contrary to some opinions, are white; in fact, the biggest impoverished area, Appalachia, includes some of the most racially "pure" Anglo-Saxon stock in the country. But Negroes, Spanish-Americans and Indians have far more than their share of poverty. Hence the answer to poverty will require a major reshaping of society. Limited answers like increased economic activity and better housing programs will help. But the United States will not solve its problem of poverty until it moves a long way toward eliminating racial discrimination, improving education, discovering motivation for frustrated persons and generally relating the various subcultures more effectively to the main culture. The church is called to a difficult and comprehensive ministry in so complex a society—a ministry that it sometimes accepts and sometimes avoids.

[17] Isa. 3 : 15.

A second responsibility concerns the society's decision as to how it will use its wealth. The very abundance of consumer goods may provoke a hunger for more. The advertising which helps maintain high production and employment deliberately stimulates some of the worst motives of pride, greed and envy. Arnold Toynbee has this to say about advertising:

It has made a fine art of taking advantage of human silliness. It rams unwanted material goods down surfeited throats when two-thirds of all human beings now alive are in desperate need of the bare necessities of life. This is an ugly aspect of the affluent society; and, if I am told that advertising is the price of affluence, I reply, without hesitation, that affluence has been bought too dear.[18]

The phrase, "the affluent society," owes its popularity in large part to a book by the economist John Kenneth Galbraith.[19] This book maintains that the United States pampers the private sector of the economy while starving the public sector. Prosperous families consume more and more, at the expense of public services in education, housing, transportation and health.

A large part of the economy of the United States—about ten per cent of the gross national product and about half of the federal budget—sustains its military program. By stimulating research, production and employment, these expenditures promote prosperity. But they also rob other areas of life. The miracle of Japanese economic growth shows what a society may do when it devotes its technology and production to civilian ends. The most public-spirited political leaders in the United States are seeking to cut military expenditures and to shift the effort to other needs. The trouble is that people are usually more willing to pay heavy taxes for military purposes than for schools and housing.

A third responsibility of the affluent society is the redefining of the meaning of useful work. We have noted above how the nature of work is changing. Machines do much of what people have done. This does not mean that people have nothing left to do. But if they are to do worthwhile things, the society must change some of its attitudes.

---

[18] ARNOLD J. TOYNBEE: "Why I Dislike Western Civilization." *New York Times Magazine,* May 10, 1964.
[19] *The Affluent Society.* Boston: Houghton Mifflin Co., 1958.

It is sometimes proposed that when few men are needed to produce the necessities of life, the society will detach pay from work and offer all its members a salary or an income on investments. But a possible alternative is to reconceive work and its compensation. A society usually distributes the fruits of its productivity to its members with some recognition of their social usefulness. Those who make visible, tangible, saleable objects are obviously useful—even if the objects are of dubious value to society. As technology increases productivity, industrialists reap the rewards. So does skilled labor—unless automation makes the labor unnecessary. But the nurse, the teacher and the artists do not increase their productivity proportionately, and the affluent society is likely to deprive them. As industry produces more with fewer workers, society will have to re-evaluate the contributions of its members. It may decide that a nurse is as valuable as an engineer, that a mother at home is as useful as a mother in an office, that a student is as productive a worker as a salesman of unnecessary luxuries.

3. *The church, an international community of faith, is a reminder within each society of the wider world.*

We have been considering responsibility *within* the affluent societies. But this is not enough, because these societies are islands within a world of want. Poverty and need remain gnawing concerns for most of humanity. The church, worshiping the God of all mankind, has the vocation of calling the affluent societies to their responsibility within this needy world.

Christians in many lands may read an essay like this with justified bitterness. It describes a situation so different from their own that it must seem smug and satisfied. Those Christians have an obligation to blast the complacency of churches in more prosperous societies. And the latter have the task of calling their own societies to a world responsibility.

This is not to say that the answers are simple. To talk about rotting food surpluses in one land and starvation in another is easy. To do something about the disparity is harder. The bare logistics of getting the food to hungry people far from seaports is itself hard enough. But this is the simplest part of the task—a part that can be carried out. Thus, on a single day in 1964 the United

States Department of Agriculture set aside $398 million worth of foods to meet famine in one country. The point of this example is not to claim credit for generosity—such acts should be taken for granted among humanitarian people—but to point to beneficent possibility and a limitation of affluence. To offer alms to the hungry is one thing; to strengthen the economy of a hungry land, so that alms are unnecessary, is something else.

Since the Second World War the experience of the more or less affluent societies in helping each other had been remarkable. For example, the Marshall Plan enabled European economies to rehabilitate themselves. But the attempts to strengthen economically poor societies have had no such success. The gap between rich and poor nations has grown greater, despite costly attempts to reduce it. One reason is that many of the efforts have been niggardly, compared with the need. But even the more generous attempts have frequently failed, leaving a sense of disillusion. Apparently the world lacks the skill and imagination for the task.

In this *impasse* there is no reason to expect the church to provide the skill. But it can attack one aspect of the problem. Part of the difficulty is the lack of *rapport* between the affluent world and the impoverished world. People of power look at history differently from those who are on their way to power. The wealthy may have a benign wish to do good, but they do not feel the sting of poverty. Usually they badly misread the dynamics of history. The Christian gospel speaks directly to this blindness, as it tells of the God who loves the poor and powerless:

He has shown strength with his arm, he has scattered the proud in the imagination of their hearts,
he has put down the mighty from their thrones, and exalted those of low degree;
he has filled the hungry with good things, and the rich he has sent empty away.[20]

The United States is often described as a conservative nation in a revolutionary world. That description is not quite accurate. The United States is carrying on its own revolution. It is not conservative in its exploration of space, its automation of industry, its re-

---

[20] Luke 1 : 51–53 (RSV).

shaping of the countryside. But one characteristic of this society—not necessarily inherent in affluent societies—causes specific problems: the United States enjoys its high production partly because of and partly in spite of a devotion to free enterprise. It is out of tune with the majority of mankind in its ritualistic deference to a traditional economic ideology. It wants to make its own experience (which worked in the industrialization of an underpopulated land with rich resources) the model for other societies (which may need to industrialize in quite different ways).

In some respects the fear of socialism in this country is ridiculous. The United States has led the world in socialized education. It has considerable socialized housing, socialized parks, socialized water systems, socialized road nets, socialized dams and power plants. (In the rules that govern public discussion these are not normally called socialism.) When in 1964 a right-wing clique maneuvered its way into control of a major political party, the voters gave its candidate the soundest spanking in any election in this century. But within the United States the traditional dogmatism still inhibits the pragmatic effort to meet problems with a combination of personal freedom and public control. Beyond the water's edge the inhibition is far greater. Far too often this society chooses its friends and enemies by ideological labels rather than by recognition of what they are actually accomplishing.

Surely the church has a special responsibility at this point—to criticize not simply a particular ideology but all the ideologies (leftist and rightist; political, economic, and ecclesiastical) that enslave men. No church can do this job perfectly, because the men in the church are historical men, influenced by the ideologies of their time and place. But the church knows a gospel, which constantly reminds it that the test of any social proposal is not loyalty to treasured traditions but concern for the welfare of persons who are loved by their Creator and Redeemer.

4. *Finally, the church is called to understand and use faithfully its own affluence.*

In prosperous societies, the church may participate in the general wealth. Today the church does not come close to dominating the economy of any major country, as churches in past history have sometimes done. But in several areas an affluent church must ponder the meaning of its Lord's blessing upon the poor and his warning to the rich. The church today can spend large sums on construction of buildings—about a billion dollars a year in the United States. It invests endowments, which it uses largely for educational and missionary purposes. It employs large numbers of people, conducts research, sends representatives on international journeys to ecumenical meetings. In some countries the church still gets support from public funds, raised by taxation. But more often its wealth comes from the contributions of its own members.

It is good for Christians to support the church with their gifts. In this sense, the church, far from apologizing for its resources, has the right to ask for more. But then it must face the critical question: how does a prosperous church live out its vocation of suffering servant, pouring its life out for mankind? At this point the study of church budgets is not encouraging. Most local churches spend a minor part of their income on community service and on work beyond their own boundaries. The major part of the contributions might be designated as voluntary payments to the church for services rendered to the donors.

Of course the issue is not solely a financial one. The affluent church shirks its responsibility, even though it contributes generously to missions and works of mercy, unless it enters into the struggles and sufferings of men. The prosperous church of prosperous members may be rather generous with its gifts, yet still be primarily a pleasant haven for nice people who seek peace in the midst of the world's confusion. It can avoid the issues of the marketplace and the slums, of juvenile delinquency and community discontents, of politics and the clash of ideologies. Such a church —and there are many of them—needs to hear the words of the angel, addressed to the church at Laodicea: "For you say, I am rich, I have prospered, and I need nothing; not knowing that you are wretched, pitiable, blind and naked." [21] The problem is not that the church is too rich, but that the church lets its prosperity betray it into contentment. Its comfort dulls the sharpness of the Word of God. It seeks security in itself rather than in its God.

During the era of Stalinist persecultions, American Christians

---

[21] Rev. 3 : 17.

often expressed concern for churches in communist lands. Reinhold Niebuhr reminded them that they might worry equally about threats closer to home:

> There are signs that Christianity is being subtly corrupted into a glorification of the "American way of life." Sometimes this glorification takes place under social pressure, which our demagogues know how to apply in defiance of our cherished traditions. Sometimes it is merely due to a dissipation of the Christian faith and its corruption by the mood of self-congratulation and complacency to which a rich and powerful nation is tempted, particularly when it is forced to engage in a long conflict with a foe, whose vices seem to prove our virtue. Such a situation breeds self-righteousness, unless there is an actual encounter between man and God, in the pattern of biblical religion; in which encounter even the most righteous men and nations are convicted of their sin. . . .
> Actually the freedom we boast sometimes develops into an idolatrous collective self-esteem. . . . Fatness, ease, and complacency are greater perils for our faith than lean years and the threat of martyrdom.[22]

Some affluent churches are escaping, or at least beginning to escape from this predicament by facing up to an authentic ethical crisis. The racial issue, terrible though it has been for many of God's children, has in one sense been an awakening for some American churches. It has stimulated churches to ask themselves what is their real purpose, to face the meaning of their ministry, to use some of their wealth for a just cause, to identify with the victims of injustice, to accept the hostility of respectable people. The affluent church can emulate the Lord who, though he was rich, became poor for our sakes.[23]

Conclusion

A church that shares the sufferings of the world must also share some of the world's perplexities. Often it must abandon the oracular voice of an authority that knows all the answers and adopt the questioning voice of a people eager both to challenge and to learn. In the face of injustice, greed and the idolatry of systems and privileges, the church may respond with a "Thus saith the Lord."

---

[22] " 'Favorable' Environments," *The Messenger*, Aug. 18, 1953. This essay was published a few months after Stalin's death.
[23] II Cor. 8 : 9.

But when confronted with the need for moral imagination and wise decision, the church must acknowledge its needs.

The intricate problems of ethical responsibility in the modern world are complicated by the fact that the dynamics of an affluent society—like the dynamics of societies in other kinds of revolutions —seem to acquire a momentum of their own that operates almost independently of the human beings within the society. Of course persons keep making decisions. But the big decisions, it may almost be said, are made by the impersonal system. Every act of industrial automation, for example, is the choice of some person or committee, but in each separate case the decision has a kind of inevitability. The system demands it, progress calls for it, the competitors are doing it and this specific corporation obviously has to automate. Nobody has looked at the whole society, assessed the gains and losses involved and decided how to proceed. This fateful quality of the system has been described by one economist: "It is not mere rhetoric to ask if Things are not already in the saddle, riding Man. . . . Man will surely never ride Things unless he is prepared to ask questions which today do not often seem to occur to him." [24]

One calling of the church in the affluent society is to ask those questions. Christian faith has always been concerned with the meeting of the ultimate with the concrete. It can be content neither with visions of eternity nor with purely pragmatic judgments that see decisions only in their immediate contexts. A major part of its calling in our day is to keep questioning society—asking for the purposes, the values, the effect upon persons of the processes the society takes for granted.

This task may be less satisfying, humanly speaking, than providing answers. Yet Jesus himself often met a situation with a searching question. His church may readily grant that it cannot always tell the society the right thing to do. The technical knowledge needed to make wise decisions in the social process comes from many sources. Helpful guidance often comes from stubbornly secular men, who have no interest in the church or its

---

[24] ROBERT L. HEILBRONER: "The Impact of Technology: The Historic Debate," in *Automation and Technological Change,* John T. Dunlop, ed. Englewood Cliffs, N.J.: Prentice-Hall, Inc., 1962, pp. 7, 25.

message. Such men too can serve God. The church has the vocation of declaring its faith, exercising its ministry of reconciliation and ceaselessly confronting society with the questions and challenges that rise out of that faith and ministry. Surely there is no refuge from the task in a nostalgia for the good old days when life was simpler.

One of the great texts of the New Testament reads: "I have learned the secret of facing plenty and hunger, abundance and want. I can do all things in him who strengthens me." [25] People usually turn to that text when they are in want, for life is obviously hard then, and they need support. But the text is equally important when people live in abundance. It tells us that there is a secret of living in plenty, that a person can live faithfully in prosperity.

So it is with Christ's church. Probably wealth is more dangerous to the church and its members than poverty. But an affluent church can use its resources, as a poor church can use its poverty, in obedience to God.

---

[25] Phil. 4 : 12–13.

4

CONVERSION AND SOCIAL TRANSFORMATION

by EMILIO CASTRO (Uruguay)

As pastor of a congregation in the heart of a large city in Latin America I preach a gospel of salvation calling to repentance, a change of life, an experience of "conversion." When someone is converted, I feel intense joy like that reflected in Luke 15 and rejoice when statistics show the Evangelical Church's impressively rapid growth. But a cruel doubt gnaws at me: To what extent will the fruits of these statistics be seen in real life in Latin America— in what is taking place in the countryside, in politics, in the factories? To what extent are the structural changes which our Latin America needs, if it is to emerge from its present semifeudal state, helped and encouraged or upset and retarded by this growth of the Evangelical Church? We see character change in individuals. But how shall we explain the social conservatism of many Christian leaders? How shall we understand the relation of conversion to social quietism?

Some will say that conversion and social change are two totally independent realities, the study of the one belonging to theology and the other to sociology. Or, if you prefer, the one to psychology, the other to history. This attitude cannot be quickly set aside. Has not the reality of conversion been presented independently of any social system, in the Roman Empire, in feudal times, in liberal democracy and in socialist regimes, in Eskimo tribes and in modern industrial society? The gospel works in freedom and requires no particular social system through which to reach man. Evangelists can claim that "man is the same all over the world" and that therefore "the message should be the same," irrespective of its social setting.

The same argument applies to the other end of our equation: society has been transformed independently of the religious experience of its members. Desirable social changes have been brought about by men who had no conversion-experience and who rejected even the possibility of it for themselves and denied its reality in others. We might even say that social change has been effected in the face of firm opposition from "converts," and that consequently our topic should be treated from a negative angle: the obstruction to social change resulting from conversion.

But this duality or separation of our terms is not acceptable. For very different reasons we are obliged to focus our attention on the relation between conversion and social change.

The Link Between Conversion and Social Change

We often hear the assertion: Change man's heart, and society will change. The fallacy of the argument is immediately evident. No such thing as "man's heart" exists apart from man's relations. I am I and my circumstances, Ortega y Gasset would say. Martin Buber would say that I exist as a person only in the reality of my relation with a "thou." In plain language, I exist in a whole collection of relations that make up my being. To change my heart means in some measure also to change those relations.

Furthermore, there is a paradox in the original assertion. On the one hand, to escape from social responsibility, from the discipline of studying the techniques and relativities of society is to revert to a religious primitivism. The magic wand of the fairy godmother, "conversion," will turn us into model citizens. Thus we know nothing about the complexities of the social structures. We do not pose the problem that Reinhold Niebuhr defined so clearly in the title of his book *Moral Man and Immoral Society*. But, on the other hand, the assertion "new men, a new nation," reveals our conviction that as an integral part of its existence conversion carries with it a consequence, a social militancy. At the very moment when we simplify and superficialize the social problem, we are declaring the indissoluble relation between conversion and social structure.

We are also obliged to examine the views of sociologists (whether they call themselves Marxists or Christians) concerning the indissoluble relation between the religious phenomenon —including conversion—and the given patterns of society. For example, Karl Marx could argue that criticism of religion was unnecessary because it is merely the consequence of the order of production-relations in a capitalist society. In such a society the laborer needs religion as a comfort—it functions as an opiate— and the oppressing classes need it to justify their exploitation. Once the conditions of production are changed and exploitation is eliminated, the need for religion has gone and conversion as such will be impossible. It will have disappeared by virtue of the social revolution which eliminates classes and puts the means of production into the hands of the proletariat. Though there is general agreement today that Marx fails to do justice to the interdependence between the economic structure of society and the factors that make up what he called the superstructure—conscience, culture, religion and so on—we must ask what is the true relation between faith, culture and society, and how far the patterns of a given society condition the possibility of conversion and the forms that it will take.

Even Christian sociologists working in modern industrial areas confirm the futility of the churches' traditional methods: the church is completely ignored by the working classes, who are "sociologically predestined not to believe." In 1960, when the Roman Catholic Church carried out its great mission in Buenos Aires, mobilizing thousands of priests from all parts of the world in an unprecedented effort to rechristianize a city, it was virtually a failure. It was unable to project itself beyond the circles of those who in some form or another were already connected with the life of the parish. The social pattern that is given shapes a mental pattern that is impervious to the Christian message. The exceptional case of a conversion here or there simply proves the rule. We must ask ourselves where the problem resides—in the structure of society or in the forms and content of the church's message. And we shall have to look carefully to see how much wisdom was shown by the biblical writer when he prayed: "Give me not riches lest I forget thee, nor poverty lest I deny thee."

Our problem is present also in the current debate concerning the mission of the church. Traditionally we thought we had understood it: to spread, to gain through the conversion of the greatest possible number of individuals who thus came to be saved. Today the growth of the world population, the fact of a church that is not growing numerically as fast as the increase in population, the secularism of technical society, "the adult world" of Bonhoeffer, all cause us to look again to the problem of mission and evangelism. Does God will that all men should be converted? Scripture tells us clearly that God wills that all should be saved. This is plain. But Scripture speaks to us of a divine plan for salvation that includes the representation of all humanity on the one hand. The story of salvation is the story of the people of Israel, the messiah, the church, chosen to act on behalf of all humanity to be the witnessing people who proclaim and live in the light of revelation. Consequently, we must ask: What should be the church's immediate concern—its numerical growth, or the serving presence of Jesus Christ in the world? To seek the conversion of individuals or to seek the transformation of society, so that man can live a truly human life? Is this a real alternative?

In the New Testament integration into the group of disciples—whether those of John the Baptist or of Jesus himself—has clear consequences for social activity. John the Baptist, in replying to different questions about the way in which to manifest repentance, offers plain directions respecting relations with one's neighbor: for example, the man with two shirts must share with him who has none. Jesus shows that his new commandment is "Love one another." His call to service is clear. There is no greater measure of greatness than the capacity to serve. To draw near to Christ is to be placed in a position of service to your neighbor. It is to have a changed attitude toward society. To enter into discipleship means to follow him who identified himself with the needy.

Technical society adds urgency to our subject. The society that in the New Testament was concerned with personal relations, and in which love could be expressed directly, has been transformed today into an impersonal society in which love has to be expressed in social patterns. However much I may love my neighbor, I do not contribute effectively to helping him if I do not see to it that modern society has the social elements and mechanisms that serve to protect him. Or, if you will: The good Samaritan could look after the wounded man, treat him with oil and wine, lift him onto his donkey and take him to the inn. Any one who did that today would be indicted for "illegal practice of medicine. . . ."

The same charitable spirit toward the wounded must be expressed in the complexities of urban life, in the thousand and one social relations that determine the kind of help that the needy person is to receive. To know how the converted man expresses himself, can express himself or should do so, in this technical society, is most important for Christian testimony. To know how far a society of impersonal relations conditions, determines, hinders or aids "conversion" is important for the church's strategy. To know God's purpose as it is manifested in the patterns of society and to know the particular calling to which God summons the convert is demanded by our obedience to the lord of history who is the lord of our life.

The Biblical Understanding of Conversion

Conversion is the word that has been applied in the church's history to different biblical episodes. In the Old Testament it is synonymous with repentance, a complete change in the whole life, taking God's word seriously. It was expected that conversion would occur in response to the prophetic word, which was admonition and proclamation of judgment and hope. In the face of God's word, a change of direction was produced in the people or in an individual. Hence conversion.

The New Testament puts the accent on the objective quality of what occurs. Jesus speaks to Nicodemus of rebirth, of a new beginning of life. But this is the work of "the Spirit that breathe where it wills." An objective condition is necessary if this rebirth is to be produced: the Son of Man must be lifted up. The metaphor of the healing of the people of Israel in the desert by their contemplating the serpent suggests that it is the contemplation of the crucified one that produces salvation and initiates the action of the Holy Spirit, toward rebirth.

In the synoptic gospels we recognize as calls to conversion the call that Jesus made to his disciples—"Follow me and I will make you fishers of men"—or to the rich young man—"Go, sell all you have, give to the poor and come, follow me." In every conversation with anyone who wishes to be his follower, Jesus insists on radical rethinking—to follow in his steps. He chooses his friends and expects them to decide to follow him conscientiously. It is hard to speak of the reality of conversion in the gospels because the events of the cross, the resurrection and Pentecost had not yet come. Nevertheless, experiences like that of Zacchaeus show us how that change (which later was to be called conversion) implied a relation to the person of Jesus that was a new orientation for relations with one's neighbor.

Paul uses the expression "a new creature." "If any man is in Christ he is a new creature." Here the objective character of conversion is safeguarded to the utmost. A new birth is not produced in an individual, making of him a being different from the others. The new creation has taken place in Jesus Christ. Being in him, bound to him, we are joined to the new creation and we become a new creature. The apostle constantly describes this union with Christ, and its sense is not mystic, but real and objective. Dead and raised up with Christ, our true life is hidden with Christ in God. In this union with Christ, our neighbor is present: we are placed in a position of service to him. In the Pauline ethic we are called to be what we already are, to let the inner reality of our relation with Christ manifest itself in our conduct.

The Acts of the Apostles stress the receiving of the Holy Spirit as the way in which the congregation in Jerusalem was established and the converts' adherence to the true faith ensured. The Spirit came down through the apostles' laying-on of hands. Objectively the church, through the apostles, extended recognition to the new brethren. But very intimately there remained in the convert the consciousness of the action of God's Spirit. This interplay of objective and subjective facts suggests to us a complementary dialectic: God's objective and subjective action, the cross and the Holy Spirit, man's subjective and objective action, our attention focused on the crucified one and the confirming testimony of the Christian community.

The relation of the Christians to the wider society was one of tolerant suffering: obedience, within certain limits. No claim was made to destroy the religious institution: the Christians worshiped in the temple. Civil authority was not disowned. When the apostles were arrested, there was no protest, no denial of the state's authority. But obedience was conditioned! "Judge for yourselves whether it is right to obey men rather than God." This attitude, expressed here in the purely religious sphere, comes to permeate the whole Christian outlook toward social patterns—respect and esteem so long as they do not threaten the Christian conscience, which is bound by obedience to God. What was still not seen very clearly was that obedience to God should be shown in all orders of life, and not only when the state directly attacked the church. There was still no clear conception of what it meant "to be the voice of those who have no voice in society." But it was already understood that those who for the world were worthless—slaves, thieves, prostitutes—were precisely those who were called by the gospel to make up the church. This world soon passed. Meanwhile, its poor received attention within the church.

From this rapid analysis of the New Testament we deduce that conversion means that we become aware of a relationship with Jesus Christ, and this means, in time, relationship with our neighbor. It means becoming part of the discipleship of those who serve. These two elements—relation with Jesus Christ and relation with my neighbor—can be distinguished, but they cannot be separated. No relationship with Jesus Christ exists that is not a relationship with our neighbor. "He who says he loves God, whom he has not seen, and loves not his brother whom he has seen, is a liar." The lack of a correct relationship with one's neighbor is authentic proof of the absence of a correct relation with God. Conversion understood as a personal advantage does not exist. It is always understood as a call to form part of the movement of God's mission of love to the world.

We are not dealing with an event that takes place in two moves —first, conversion to Christ and then, a "second conversion" from Christ to the world, to which we would hasten as servants. The preaching of two moves in this way has caused damage in the church, in that it has permitted people to remain at the first stage with a self-centered religiosity, in a self-complacent church that makes its own welfare a norm for judging the world. Readiness to serve my neighbor forms part of the essence of conversion. But conversion is always in reference to Jesus Christ. It is not a state. It is a relationship. It lives by its object. It is not a personality that is somehow different from the others. The difference is in its perspective. It wishes to see nothing isolated from the person of Jesus Christ. The convert is not a superman in either the moral or the intellectual sense. He is a man who lives in relationship with Jesus Christ, in the twofold sense of the expression: in relation with the historic Christ and in relation with the Christ who finds him as he ministers to his needy neighbor. And that twofold encounter is effected by the mediation of the Holy Spirit, who actualizes yesterday and leads in the world of today.

This is not to be interpreted only in terms of direct interpersonal relations: assistance to one's neighbor, the concrete individual, and unrelated to changes in social institutions, in forms of production, in power-relations between social groups. The call to follow Christ is not the traditional religious call of withdrawal from the world. On the contrary, it was a call that sent man back to the society from which he came. Becoming a Christian did not mean abandoning the duties that belonged to life in a pagan society.

The pagans or Jews converted to Christianity faced the structures of the empire with the same limitation of view as any pagan of that time possessed. Moreover, their eschatalogical vision could foresee the disappearance of the system, and so its sanctified and absolute character was removed. But that disappearance of existing social forms was not to be the result of man's action in history, but rather the result of the breaking in of the *Parousia*. We could also say that the Christians were laying new bases for human relations that would inevitably destroy the fromework of the society. (Slavery was not attacked, but there was a call to love the "brother slave"; Roman militarism was not condemned, but a vocational pacifism was taught.) Nevertheless we must recognize that such consequences were a subconscious fruit of the activity of the Christians and were not the result of a clear comprehension on their

part. Later we shall discuss this problem in detail. It is sufficien
here to affirm that the New Testament conceives neither of a
Christian separated from the world, nor of a Christian life that does
not express itself in interpersonal relations.

The Social Factor in Conversion

But to what extent does the social situation condition conversion
in the Bible? An initial answer, though a partial one, indicates that
the prophets and the apostles utilized social facts for their call to
conversion. The prophets did not hesitate to interpret what hap
pened to the people, both internally and externally, as vehicles for
God's call to repentance. The apostles used the Jewish dispersion
the *oikos* of the Roman houses, Paul his Roman citizenship. We
should not interpret the expression "fullness of time" in a sociologi
cal sense, but we cannot overlook the fact that a series of social
economic and political conditions was present in the Roman
Empire that favored the spread of the Christian message. We can
not know how much weight those circumstances bore in condition
ing the kind of decision that the isolated individual who embraced
Christianity through a "conversion" took. But at least the historical
possibility that the call to conversion can reach its object is given
or negated by the total situation.

We can also understand that although in New Testament time
Christianity spoke to man, approaching the situation from the out
side, without any involvement with the existing society, today it ap
pears involved in the situation, since it is the result of twenty cen
turies of Christian history. It is logical to suppose that the social
conditions today play a much more important role, favoring o
hindering the proclamation or the reception of Christianity, in
short, affecting the reality of conversion. Even if God is powerfu
in the midst of any circumstance to bring about the change in th
individual's life, it does not mean that he does not work with du
consideration for all the circumstances of human existence, no
that the church (which claims to be the vehicle of God's call
remains blind to these factors.

When Moses struggled with Pharaoh, God's demand was plain
"Let my people go, so that they may serve me." Liberty was a basi

requisite for worship. Could God work among slaves? Undoubtedly he could, but slavery is not what he willed for his children. Liberty makes genuine worship possible. The fact is completed when, in the book of Joshua, after the conquest of Canaan, the people are faced with this choice: "Choose you this day whom you will serve." Liberty makes conversion possible. Or at least in the biblical revelation, the decision (taken in freedom) is what God seeks. And the struggle for freedom—with all its biblical components, which far exceed political liberty—is a task that belongs to the church's being, since it constitutes the human possibility of responsible decision before God.

We must focus attention now on the other term of our equation: social change.

By the transformation of society we understand those changes in its structure—its forms of production, property, class and the like—that affect the life of whole groups of people. In ecumenical circles the expression "rapid social change" has been coined to indicate areas of the world where people are rapidly abandoning the traditional society and are entering the modern industrial world. These changes can be the blind outcome of historical events, or they can be changes that are sought and guided. Without a doubt, to a greater or lesser degree, they are everywhere the result of objective factors and conscious planning. In the political struggle people speak of "revolution," where there is a radical change of those who hold power in a given society.

In traditional societies, the idea of social transformation plays virtually no role: Things are as they are, and that is the way they ought to be. The common man takes no part in decisions. He endures invasions or goes to war because of a factor outside himself. Where slavery exists, it is a given fact of his experience, as unchangeable as the natural laws that govern his whole life. Here or there an exceptional man may cross the barrier of social conformism. But it is precisely the exceptional person whose life is given an aura of legend who confirms the common man in his acceptance of the status quo. At times he is an unconscious agent of change. He joins masses that are filled with anger about an unbearable situation. But the historical possibility of a different kind of society never crosses his mind. To him the form of society is as fixed as the cycles of nature. An invasion, a war may mean a change of master but not a change of the forms of society. It is only in the past two centuries that we have begun to experience the era of the common man and to recognize that it is not only possible but necessary for the citizens to participate in the formation of social structures.

The Christian, as a citizen of stabilized societies, shared the same social quietism. In the first centuries his quietism was even greater, because of the Christians' awareness of their insignificant numbers and their expectation of an early end of the world. We can claim that the Hebrew-Christian tradition has contributed to the formation of the western conscience, with its idea of a future open to man's action, history to be fulfilled, a goal toward which to press. But it is also true that upon the establishment of the *corpus christianum* in Europe, the historical goal was regarded as having been reached, and there only remained the projection of the individual toward eternity and the geographical missionary expansion that would spread the hierarchical Christian society throughout the world.

Conversion in itself did not alter this outlook. It involved man with his neighbor. It placed him in a responsible situation toward society. But it did not exempt him from submitting to the disciplines of the study of society and of its problems.

If we understand this fact, we shall be freed from many fallacies. We shall not be optimistic as to whether the conversion of a greater number of citizens in a country solves its structural problems. We shall not ask, as is so often done: after twenty centuries of Christianity, what is wrong with the world that it is still unable to overcome such problems as war? We shall understand that conversion is not the irruption of the religio-magic solution into the problem of society. There is a relative autonomy in politics that is not affected by religious conversion. We say "relative," because logically any change in a person's spiritual orientation has some social consequence that will (at least slightly) affect social forms. But anyone who wants to take part actively in the struggles by which social changes are effected must do so without illusions, submitting to the technical disciplines of his specific field: economics, politics, culture, or whatever.

This understanding of conversion in a given social context enables us to grasp the senselessness of so many Christian centuries during which the "converts" failed to attack slavery as a social institution. It can help us to comprehend even certain segregationist attitudes of our day. We can find in this situation a horrifying mixture of personal compassion and social insensitivity.

Often, too, we have to deny that there has been a real conversion. There can be a psychological experience of "warmth," or a kind of "decision" that fits the traditional rules of conduct and experience that the church calls conversion, without that incorporation into Christ that is characterized by a regard for all life, in the light of our relation with his person and teaching, having taken place. We can be in the presence of psychic phenomena without spiritual reality or of ecclesiastical events without serving power. In either event, the word conversion will be used, but it does not correspond to the reality that the Bible calls rebirth. "By their fruits you shall know them." Insofar as there is an openness toward Christ's judgment and a responsible involvement with one's neighbor, we can judge—with all the human relativities of judgment—that a conversion has taken place. The definite judgment in this connection is left to the divine wisdom. But though we are willing to understand that social myopia is possible in persons whose Christian character and genuine conversion to Christ we cannot doubt, we ought not to recognize any spiritual kinship with those who (consciously or unconsciously) make use of the gospel to cover up their personal prejudices and conveniences.

The Problem of Christian Conservatism

It is a historic fact that the church's tendency in social matters has been conservative. And it has been so, basically, because of ignorance of the autonomy of political life to which we have referred, and because of its desire to preserve a status quo situation within which the phenomenon of conversion occurred. The fact that conversion had been experienced within a certain social framework served to sanctify that framework as "the" framework within which conversions were possible. At the same time, to the extent that the "converts" and the church established forms of social service that expressed their responsibility for their neighbor, they moved with more confidence in familiar primary social patterns, which did not demand any great technical preparation. Hence the social fruits of pietism. Hence also the "social gospel." All were intent on being loyal to the conversion experience within the structural framework of known society. They lacked a comprehension of the responsibility to view society as a whole and to see the dynamic of love of one's neighbor expressed in action in the interest of justice in social structures. Our century offers the possibility of the common man sharing in this task of change. We still have to see whether the conversion experience, permanently the same, will today include an intelligent view of the forms of change in modern society.

The biblical idea that applies best to the concept of the convert is that of holiness. "Called to be saints—holy ones" is the title that the apostle applies to Christians. Holiness is separation for God's use. In many Christian circles, the emphasis has been on what was called "holiness of life," with insistence on the personal virtues that should make the convert. But it is necessary to go deeper into the concept of holiness to understand that those moral gifts of character are not ends in themselves, but marks of a life that has been placed at God's disposal. The saint ("holy one") is a person who is available. He awaits orders.

Such holiness includes a responsible attitude to one's neighbor: bearing one another's burdens, loving one another. Just as holiness can degenerate into an obsessive concern for the "beauty of our soul," so also the call to love our neighbor can degenerate into a sterile, sentimental idealism. But there is no reason why it should. The marks of a Christian character and the consciousness of being always bound to one's neighbor must find forms of expression, of placing oneself at God's disposal, in any social pattern. Moreover, they must find ways to make themselves effective in order to be genuine instruments, available for God's use in working for social change.

Our problem today is to discover what role the traditional virtues recognized in "converts" can play, in technical society, with its complex patterns. Then we shall ask: To what extent does conversion equip people to go ahead with social change, or is it in itself socially conservative? Lastly we shall inquire whether the struggle for social change is part of the church's mission.

1.   As society becomes more complex, it becomes more impersonal. The bureaucrats' decision affects real flesh-and-blood people. Planning-measures that promise marvels for the many sacrifice the interests of the few. Bureaucratic machinery itself is becoming depersonalized. Officials at different levels of administration cannot see all the consequences of their actions. The sense of responsibility is becoming diluted. Personal interest is disappearing. Here indeed is precisely the situation in which the "convert" could best apply the traditional virtues of honesty, responsibility and interest in the individual. A complex society needs outstandingly the person who is dedicated to higher values to carry out routine tasks with a sense of fidelity to the very end. Revolutionary regimes seek to implant all kinds of moral stimuli to attain that grade of responsibility that is indispensable if the social machinery is to yield its fruits. The Christian must be concerned for justice in the patterns of society, and must learn the technical disciplines that can equip him to serve in society, but he must not lose sight of the importance of the basic moral virtues in every social situation.

2.   But the technical world offers a field for more than the exercise of the traditional virtues. The simple fact of conversion, which includes a personal decision, places us like a brake on the tendency to mass men together—which is a by-product of technical society. In the measure in which we speak of genuine conversion to Jesus Christ, and of a person who has taken a decision that gives perspective to his whole life, we are speaking of an individual who maintains an island of humanity in the midst of dehumanizing tendencies. It is not that the convert remains unaffected by the collective influences of the systems of work, communication and so forth; but in the midst of a society that is molded by all those systems, he has taken a responsible decision of an ultimate character. He has resisted affection by all the "massifying" influences, and therefore he makes decisions, conditions the things in which he takes part and has an authority to which to refer—all of which surprises the multitude. He remembers that there is a sphere of personal responsibility and privacy that is part of man's nature; and simply by living on the consequences of his experience

of encounter with Christ, he becomes a personalizing influence in society.

3. Responsibility and decision are the personal values that the convert brings to society. To what extent does he participate in the revolutionary dynamic? To what extent does he understand that his conversion demands it?

We must begin by recognizing his conservative tendency. It is no use deceiving ourselves by pretending to be revolutionaries. A person who has experienced conversion to Jesus Christ goes through an initial period of revolutionary inhibition. Social changes frighten him. There is no reason why the period should last very long, but it is unavoidable until one goes deeper into the nature of conversion and into the intelligent forms of expression of the Christian life in the areas of society. An old militant communist of Dresden once said to me: "You Christians will never conduct a revolution, because you do not dare to accept the consequences of one." There is much truth in this statement. As a man relates his life to Christ, he can but hesitate when he faces what he must do in the fields of political and military action. With every concrete decision we are treading holy ground.

This sense of responsibility brings a temptation to avoid public dilemmas, thus taking refuge in an area of private irresponsibility: any participation in the political arena means dirtying our hands, so we withdraw from such areas, in order to maintain our personal purity. As though by doing so we were not just as guilty! There is no way of escape, by action or by omission.

This same sense of responsibility, this vacillation, can bring us to a practical expression that is both timorous and confident, reverent and daring. It places us in the position of pardoned sinners who fulfill their duty trusting in the forgiveness of sins. Converts' political activity should be characterized by deep humility, since it is carried on without illusions as to its purity. There is a risk that this realism may restrain such activity, but it should not, and so long as our conversion binds us to our neighbor and prevents us from forgetting the concrete injustices that must be combatted, it will not do so.

But the convert also tends to be conservative out of ignorance. We have already spoken of the failure to recognize the autonomy of political life. Here the teaching work of the church is basic. But more basic still is the fact that the convert should learn something from the events in his own country. We have said that this is the century of the common man. At least it is the century of the masses. In the measure that the Christian shares in the concerns for change that are manifest in his own country, he will find himself infected with them and obliged to ponder the relevance of his faith to the social conditions of his country.

If conversion places us in the midst of our brothers and identifies us with them, we shall thereby learn the importance of structural factors in our society. We shall understand how traditional kindness has definite limits. We shall understand how love demands knowledge in order that it may be poured out in service to society. But we must not deceive ourselves. The convert *per se* has no reason to possess a greater knowledge of the laws that govern the life and death of human societies. Conversion does not make us wise in any particular field. There is no substitute for serious and responsible study and an open mind toward society.

Conservatism, whether caused by fear of losing personal purity or by ignorance, has in it the basic ingredient of its correction in the very experience of conversion, which places a person face to face with his neighbor. Returning a number of times to my specific neighbor enables me to overcome inner hesitation and prevents my being satisfied with the tradition of "benevolent action." This is what is happening in the countries that used to be called "mission lands." The church brought them the message that called to conversion, but it also unavoidably increased their myopia toward social change. The missionary, being a foreigner, or through his tacit or explicit connection with the occupying power, or because he had difficulty in adapting himself to a completely new situation, added to the convert's legitimate hesitation illegitimate factors that tended to distract him from concern for social structures. Christian schools and institutions had, it is true, their influence on society; but it is only in our generation that throughout the world the need to draw the social consequences of the conversion-experience that brings us to see Christ in every neighbor is being forcefully brought home. The cup of cold water that we give in his name should be given through public health measures or economic planning. Inevitably the gospel has to bring us to take part in these decisive aspects of community life. As our knowledge of the laws that govern human societies increases, our discovery of specific ways of exercising our Christian responsibility will also increase. But the starting point will always be the concrete neighbor: "Thou shalt love thy neighbor."

The Spiritual Power for Social Action

Anyone who struggles to serve in the political and economic forms of society knows how often he is tempted to become discouraged. Lack of understanding, hatreds, power factors—all combine to dissuade him. There are moments of bitter defeat, others of Pyrrhic victory, still others in which we do not know whether we are betraying the very thing we want to support. In all these circumstances a true conversion-experience is a source of power and of support. It gives a Christian a fixed point of reference for his life and work, and a dynamic in God's love for mankind whom he is seeking to serve.

Conversion, relating our life to Jesus Christ, ought to make us more open than anyone to the changes that are taking place in society. Our trust cannot rest definitely in any particular social or economic system; we cannot sanctify either private property or collective ownership. If God is behind the motivation of our public activity, we know that he is the lord of tomorrow and that he will also be present in other social forms. If God is the only lord of our life, we cannot judge changes in society according to how they affect our patrimony or personal interest; we shall look at them rather, with an unselfish interest to judge all things in terms of the highest justice which God wills for us. In short, we shall be able to measure the reality of our conversion by the extent of our involvement in the struggle for social justice and the detachment with which we move in the midst of the prevailing social systems.

God has placed the church in the world out of love for that world of which it forms a part. Jesus Christ is lord of the world and those who recognize his lordship ought to show it by the serving spirit that characterizes such a lord. It is for the church to discern God's activity in the secular world, to cooperate with that activity and to point to Christ's presence in it. To proclaim his lordship, to point

out, to discern his presence, to be an instrument of his lordship—
all these are tasks of the church that bring it within the framework
of social change. God himself is at work in them. God himself is
concerned with them. His church cannot be indifferent without betraying the very lord which it claims to announce.

But if we wanted to limit our understanding of the church's
task to thinking of it as a simple quest for individual conversions,
we should at once discover that this is impossible. Conversion requires a neighbor, and I find my neighbor today in society. No
man is independent of his relationships. In loving God in my neighbor, I love him in the setting of patterns that—for better or for
worse—condition his life. And that search for my neighbor cannot be motivated by eagerness to proselytize. It is a search that
blossoms from love toward God. And that love is directed upon
my neighbor regardless of how many of them become aware of it.
If there is no love, there has been no conversion. If there is love,
we are neither able nor willing to avoid those areas that determine
and condition man's life on earth.

From the other extreme of the equation, we are equally led to
incorporate into the church's mission a genuine concern for the
transformation of society. The gospel requires certain historical
conditions if it is to reach people: freedom of conscience, peace,
communications. If we are to assure the conditions of orderly
life that make the proclamation of the gospel possible, we must
enter into the social struggle.

We would go further on this point: every true struggle to create
humane living conditions in which man may express freedom and
responsibility seeks to establish a situation in which the call to
conversion finds a man free to respond. The transformation of society—in itself a good thing if it involves the changing of injustices
into forms of justice—is also a positive fact from the point of view
of the preaching of the gospel, since it liberates man for the great
decision of his life: his answer to God's call in Christ.

We must safeguard ourselves here against misunderstanding. We
are not saying that conversions do not take place within every social pattern, or that you must first change society and then preach,
or that we are interested in social change so that men will accept
the gospel that is offered them. But we are saying that the procla-

mation of the gospel is not something isolated from given social situations, and that as far as human factors are concerned, social change affects the possibility of conversion. We must always respect the miracle of grace, the mystery of God. In other words, what we do for the whole man in society bears a relation to his salvation. By our responsible attitude in the transformation of society, we help to set the stage in which God's Word can speak freely to man. The rest belongs to the mystery of God, and to human liberty. "Let my people go, so that they may serve me. . . ." "Choose you this day whom you will serve."

5

AWAKENED PEOPLES, DEVELOPING NATIONS AND THE DYNAMICS OF WORLD POLITICS

by M. M. THOMAS (India)

THE Papal Encyclical *Pacem in Terris* describes three revolutions of our age that have made a tremendous impact on world politics: the awakening of the working class to a new sense of dignity, the emancipation of women and their increasing role in public life and the awakening of subject nations and races to their rights to independence and equality of status. When we set these revolts of suppressed groups within the framework of a world that technology is transforming into a neighborhood, we are confronted with the new dimensions of the problem of building a world community. This essay will concentrate on the third revolution—the emergence of nonwhite peoples into world politics.

The Struggle of Awakened Peoples and Races for Their Human Rights

The struggle of the peoples of Africa and Asia against colonialism and foreign political domination and of nonwhite races everywhere against racial paternalism, discrimination and segregation, are two aspects of the same revolution. Pope John XXIII saw them together as the expressions of the same aspiration of men for freedom from the subjection of "political powers located outside . . . [their] own country or ethnic group," and for "the rank of citizens in independent nations." [1]

Daisuke Kitagawa, in *Race Relations and the Christian Mission*,[2] also sees this relationship, pointing out that behind Afro-Asian solidarity lies the dynamics of racism:

Today in Africa and throughout the world, members of coloured races are being united. It is wishful to think that they are not necessarily united against the white race, for quite frankly they are. The element of counter-racism is very strong. . . . To be sure . . . [the] conferences of Afro-Asian nations have not openly declared "racial war" against the West. However, racial feeling is one of the strongest factors that keeps the otherwise precarious solidarity among Afro-Asian nations from breaking down completely.

The struggle against racial segregation in the United States has been inspired by the political emancipation of African people, and its leaders have acknowledged their debt to Mahatma Gandhi, who used the techniques of nonviolent resistance on a large scale in India's struggle for national freedom. James Baldwin says, in *The Fire Next Time*,[3] that the decision of the American Supreme Court ten years ago against segregation in schools cannot be understood apart from "the fact that Africa was clearly liberating herself, and therefore had, for political reasons, to be wooed by the descendants of her former masters." [4] This view is generally

---

[1] "Men all over the world have today—or will soon have—the rank of citizens in independent nations; no-one wants to feel subject to political powers located outside his own country or ethnic group. Thus in many human beings the inferiority complex which endured for hundreds and thousands of years is disappearing, while in others there is an attenuation and gradual fading of the corresponding superiority complex which had its roots in social-economic privileges, sex or political standing.

"On the contrary, the conviction that all men are equal by reason of their natural dignity has been generally accepted. Hence racial discrimination can no longer be justified, at least doctrinally or in theory. And this is of fundamental importance and significance for the formation of human society according to these principles which we have outlined above. For, if a man becomes conscious of his rights, he must become equally aware of his duties. Thus he who possesses certain rights has likewise the duty to claim those rights as marks of his dignity, while all others have the obligation to acknowledge those rights and respect them." (*Pacem in Terris*, Part I).

[2] New York: Friendship Press, 1964, pp. 26-27.

[3] London: Michael Joseph, 1963.

[4] Dr. Paul Sigmund, of the Department of Politics of Princeton University, makes the following comment: "I personally would doubt that the

accepted by American Negroes, and it is a fact, as Kitagawa charges, that the sense of common struggle has brought "the people of Negro racial background in Africa and the United States closer together" in a new way, which it has not been possible for "the missionary movement of the last century and the first part of this century" to do.

The movement in the world toward full political rights for all citizens within independent nations is the direction in which world politics is moving and makes men conscious of the remaining vestiges of old western colonialism, which keeps one people subject to another, and of neocolonialism, which keeps peoples from the right to determine their own political and economic life.

No doubt, the peoples who still remain under an old type of colonialism are few. But the fear of neocolonialism will continue among the new nations; it will be enhanced by the frustrations of nation-building and reduced by its achievements.

The practice of some nations of giving only second-class citizenship to certain racial or ethnic groups because of their color is becoming therefore more and more intolerable and something that the people, thus deprived of their human dignity, are prepared to fight. There are indications that the struggle for racial equality will be a prolonged one and that it is likely to become a dominant factor in world politics in the years to come.[5]

---

decision of the Supreme Court in 1954 was much influenced by the emergence of Africa; at that point, the African independence movement was not sufficiently important to act as a major influence on the thinking of the Justices. Much more important was a long train of judicial decisions widening the implications of the constitutional guarantee of equality embodied in the Fourteenth Amendment to the American Constitution."

And Dr. Leroy S. Ronner, professor at the United Theological College (Bangalore, India), writes: "I think your assertion that American Negroes have felt a closer affinity with Africans as a result of the Civil Rights movement is generally wrong. It is certainly true for the Negro extremists of the Black Muslim variety, who regard the NAACP, CORE, SNICK and all other organizations which have a large white constituency as traitors to the Negro cause. But there is evidence that the majority of the Negroes—James Baldwin is chief among them—are protesting, not on the basis of the rights of the black race, but on the basis of their citizenship as Americans."

[5] Dr. Rupert Emerson, of the Department of Government, Harvard University, comments: "It is perhaps no more than wishful thinking, but I hope that the statement that race conflict is likely to become a more dominant factor in world politics in the years to come will prove to be wrong. If the

In the United States, the rights of the Negro "to go to school, to get a job, to vote and to pursue his life unhampered by the barriers of racial segregation" have the protection of the federal law. Yet, those rights may have to be secured by bitter struggles against state laws, organized white racists like the John Birch Society and the Ku Klux Klan, vested social interests and the legitimate fears of demoralization that inevitably follow in the wake of the disintegration of a traditionally segregated society. The combination of conservative extremism with religious pietism and individualist morality that found expression in the campaign of Goldwater, although he was massively defeated in the Presidential election, remains a potent force in American politics and may keep alive white racist groups in other parts of the world.

The growth of extremism on both sides of the race conflict is evidence of the failure of liberalism to achieve its ideals of equality and fraternity through moral persuasion, education and agitation, within the framework of the Constitution. The use of extraconstitutional means of exercising power is more or less taken for granted by most, if not all, of the groups fighting for racial equality. The only question is whether these means should be nonviolent (the "extremism of love," as Martin Luther King, Jr., calls it) or should involve the use of arms.

In general, Negro leadership has advocated a combination of constitutional process and the Gandhian technique of nonviolent group resistance as reinterpreted in the light of the Christian faith. In his book *Stride Toward Freedom*, Martin Luther King warns the American Negro against following the path of violence and says that, where violence is used, "future generations will be the recipients of a desolate night of bitterness, and our chief legacy to them will be an endless reign of meaningless chaos." He offers nonviolence as the path whereby the Negro can bring justice "for both himself and the white man." In his speech accepting the

United States can manage really to get over the hump of dealing with its own racial problem, I should think that a tremendous advance would have been made, since the great bulk of the colonial problem is already disposed of. South Africa certainly remains a danger spot of very real consequence, but I hope that it will become possible to deal with it not in terms of racial division in the rest of the world but on some more general ground."

Nobel Prize, he reiterates his faith in nonviolent means not only for the situation in the United States but for that in Southern Africa as well.

In certain parts of Africa, the situation is in fact more fraught with violence than in the United States. South Africa, with *apartheid* and its militant defiance of international opinion; Rhodesia, where the whites are determined to continue minority rule and recently declared their independence as a white nation-state; and Angola and other Portuguese territories are dangerous spots, where the struggle for racial equality and human rights may take a violent turn, especially as the newly independent African nations find the situation increasingly intolerable. (The United Nations seems helpless in the face of the needs of subjected African peoples. The big western powers do not take seriously the economic boycott of South Africa.) It is in this context that the words of the Kenya Home Minister must be read: "The remaining colonial territories in Africa will not be liberated until the independent African states jointly are prepared to wage war against South Africa." Sixteen independent African states are committed to liberate black Africa, and have already met twice, in Addis Ababa and Cairo, to organize their forces. The African members of the Commonwealth have been successful in pressing on Britain its responsibility for establishing in Southern Rhodesia an independent nation with majority rule. The policy of some African states, of withdrawing from international conferences because of the participation of South Africa or Portugal, is self-defeating. But at least it shows the frustration caused by the racial situation in Africa.

Many erstwhile followers of the nonviolent Chief Luthuli and his African National Congress, like Nelson Mandela (tried, convicted and sentenced to life imprisonment), have been converted through long years of frustration to the inevitability of armed uprising inside and armed intervention from without. They have organized the Spear of the Nation movement, whose aim is sabotage and armed overthrow of the South African government. This kind of conversion from nonviolence to violence is taking place every day. The consultation on Race Relations in Southern Africa, held under the auspices of the World Council of Churches and the South

African Institute of Race Relations, in Mindolo (Zambia) in 1964, declared:

> The urgency of the situation in South Africa is further increased by the conviction of leading Africans that, as all peaceful measures tried by African political organizations over a period of many years to bring about an ordered change have proved abortive, only one avenue remains open—that of violence. On the other hand, it is precisely this conviction and possible resultant action which consolidates the white electorate, hardens its general attitude and leads to ever-increasing measures which eventually precipitate the danger they wish to avoid. For many Christians involved in the struggle for a just solution, the question of possible violence as the only remaining alternative has become an urgent and ever-pressing one. Reports indicate that many are convinced that war has already begun.

This picture may be too pessimistic, and I have not, perhaps, given due recognition to the achievements of liberal humanism. But, unfortunately, liberalism is breaking down through fear of the dynamism in the revolutionary upsurge of suppressed groups; it cannot face the fact that such hate and violence can exist in decent men! Liberal Christians are so conscious of their own guilt that they feel unable openly to condemn the extreme fascism expressed in *apartheid*. Those theologians who say, "Let the sinless among us condemn South African whites," tend to paralyze even those Christian groups that want to act. They are profoundly wrong in thinking that, because all men are equally sinful before God, they should not distinguish between the greater and the lesser evil in any situation, and then take the necessary action justified not by their own works, but by faith. There still seem to be some theologians who have not learned the necessity of dealing with the relativities of politics and society. There is no evidence that the forces of liberal humanism, Christian humanism, or even nonviolent militancy have fully understood the working of the political, economic and social powers that are seeking to consolidate white extremist elements, especially in Africa. Men are thus left struggling for their rights, with the path of violence their only choice.

The Relationship Between Developed and Developing Nations

In an article entitled "Brazil: An Underdeveloped Giant Wakes Up," [6] Caio de Taledo gives a few lines of a revolutionary song of Brazil, "Song of the Underdeveloped."

> But one day the giant awoke,
> He ceased being a sleeping giant,
> And lo! a dwarf arose;
> He was an underdeveloped country!

The description fits all the peoples of Africa, Asia and Latin America. They have all become conscious in a new way of their rich spiritual and cultural heritage, and feel themselves to be giants; but they know also that, given the modern criteria of economic and technological power, they remain dwarfs. And it hurts. The struggle of the poor nations today to develop themselves and to raise their people's standard of living not only determines in large measure the direction of politics within them but also shapes the character of international relations, especially those between the developed and developing countries of the world.

There has always been poverty and famine in the countries of Africa and Asia, accompanied by a spirit of resignation, often reinforced by religion. Today, this spiritual situation has changed. The struggle for national independence, the emergence of independent nation-states and the process of nation-building have disturbed "the pathetic contentment of the masses," who now realize that poverty is not their inevitable fate, but can be overcome through organized effort. Therefore, "the revolution of rising expectations" is part of the self-awakening of Africa and Asia and of the search of Afro-Asian peoples for their self-identity.

When hungry men begin to discern that a higher living standard is a fundamental human right, any obstacle to its realization, either within the nation or in other nations, seems like injustice. While this sense of injustice feeds on memories of colonial exploitation, by which the nations of the West developed their own economies,

---

[6] *motive,* Nov., 1963; *Student World,* No. 1, 1964.

it is not primarily a product of the past but a new awakening of men to their own human selfhood. Therefore, any slackening in the world's effort to promote the economic welfare of all peoples becomes intolerable. The new sense of economic injustice will have no less revolutionary results than did the old feeling of direct exploitation.

The nations of Africa, Asia and Latin America realize that their economic development is primarily their own responsibility. They seek to remove the causes of economic stagnation in their culture and society and to mobilize the financial and technical resources by increased agricultural and industrial productivity and social welfare. But they know only too well that they cannot succeed without international economic cooperation.

A large volume of opinion in the developed nations today is urging increased aid to the developing nations in their economic struggle. Such opinion has found expression not only in such voluntary movements as the Freedom from Hunger campaign but also in putting pressure on governments and business to evolve systems of financial aid and technical assistance to underdeveloped countries that show a sensitive awareness of their political and social goals. The United Nations is committed by its Charter "to promote social progress and better standards of life and larger freedom" and "to employ international machinery for the promotion of the economic and social advancement of all peoples" (Preamble). Bilateral and multilateral international machinery has been developed to support national development plans. However, they all remain inadequate, and then are sometimes subordinate to political and ideological interests, unrelated to the problem of economic development. Further, public opinion in this field is so closely circumscribed that the richer nations have not yet taken the more costly step of making the interests of developing nations a criterion, if not *the* criterion, of policy in international trade, common markets and world economic development. Even in international economic relations, charity and justice must be closely related. International charity must express itself in impersonal institutional structures and the obligations of international justice if it is to have the character of true charity. It is in this connection that the recent Geneva Conference on World Trade and Development and the

Final Act of the Conference deserve attention.[7] But the general reaction to it in the developed nations confirms that they have not adequately recognized the deeper implications of the ever-widening gap between the rich nations and the poor on world politics and on the issues of war and peace.

The gulf between the rich and the poor countries can be gauged by the fact that "the joint income of the developing countries, with two-thirds of the world's population, is not much more than one-tenth of that of the industrialized countries." As world economy swiftly expands, the result of vast scientific and technical progress widens the gulf still further. The value of world exports has been more than doubled since 1950. But the developing countries' share in them has been declining steadily "from nearly one-third in 1950 to only slightly more than one fifth in 1962" and at a time, we should note, when development in the poorer countries requires imports of capital goods and technical skills from developed nations. The growing gap between their import and export earnings has put the severest strain on development plans.

Many factors in underdeveloped economies no doubt contribute to this situation. But even when "their plans, policies and institutions are designed to achieve the transformation of their economic and social structures and to provide for maximum saving, investment and output to a pre-determined order of priorities for a targeted rate of growth," their realization has been hindered "by the instability of international markets for primary products and by conditions restricting the access of primary commodities and semi-manufactures and manufactures to the markets of the developed countries."

The Geneva Conference spelled out some of the "specific policies" of wealthy nations that hinder the plans of developing nations and affirmed that, "In order to facilitate the industrial exports of developing countries, their products should have freer access, particularly to the markets of the developed countries"; and it is recognized that "substantial imports of manufactures and semi-manufactures may involve some readjustment in the industrial structures of the developed countries."

---

[7] *United Nations Conference on Trade and Development: Final Act.* Duplicated report.

It is not yet clear, however, that the richer societies are prepared for this necessary "readjustment." The main resolutions at the conference were, in fact, generally carried by the votes of the majority of the economically underdeveloped nations, and it is therefore too early to assess their value. The hostile reaction in developed nations of the West, moreover, seems indicative of their irritation at the sight of the poorer nations forming themselves into a bloc and demanding sacrifices from the richer—almost as a matter of fundamental right. The Economist [8] commented on the conference that "the underprivileged nations at Geneva have been winning votes by losing heads." But, whether by exercising heads or votes, or by losing them through more explosive measures, the poor nations are determined to battle with the rich to realize the economic means of the fuller life. The Economist rightly said, "There are limits to the extent to which you can bully someone into giving you money for nothing, when you leave no bargaining power but a hubbub of voices." But this bullying spirit on the part of the powerless is an important factor in determining new trends in world politics. There is little doubt that the poor nations are determined to use their numerical majority in the continuing international machinery that has been set up. As they state in a joint declaration, "the developing countries attach cardinal importance to democratic procedures which afford no position of privilege in the economic and financial, no less than in the political sphere." And they do envisage that "the progressive strengthening of the machinery that is now contemplated" will lead to an international cooperation that will "serve as a decisive instrument for ending the division of the world into areas of affluence and intolerable poverty. This task is the outstanding challenge of our time."

By common consent, the forging at Geneva of the United Front of the Developing Nations was "the outstanding feature of the entire conference and an event of historic significance." The "seventy-five developing countries" have pledged themselves to strengthen it as "an indispensable instrument for securing the adoption of new attitudes and new approaches in the international economic field." And many rightly believe that this new bloc is the most dominant emerging force in world politics.

---

[8] London: June 6, 1964.

Ideological and political blocs along other lines continue to have validity. But it is also clear that, with the unity of the poor and the division between rich and poor becoming more dominant, they will cut across other divisions and make them less important. We find, for instance, that Japan, though a nation of nonwhite people, voted against, or abstained from voting on, many of the crucial resolutions at Geneva, because it is a developed nation. Free World alliances simply broke down in the conference, dividing themselves into rich and poor. Russia had its embarrassing silences, as it could not identify itself fully with the poor nations. Here the ideological rift between the Chinese and the Russian Communists has a certain relevance. As Edward Rogers writes in *Living Standards:* [9]

If the gap between rich and poor continues to widen, and if the world does polarize into opposing camps, the almost certain outcome will be war. From that point the estimation of probabilities moves into the realm of science fiction—where it had better stay. The advanced nations could win a nuclear war, ending, if they were lucky, with a world crippled, decimated in population and pock-marked with lethal radio-activity. The poorer nations could by force of numbers win a conventional war, dragging down the West to the level of their own poverty, and in the terrible enterprise destroying for generations their own prospect of escape from its thrall. Either prospect is grim. A serious, urgent campaign against poverty is the alternative to war.

Search for a New Political Morality

In the industrialized West, the debate in the field of political and economic morality has for long been primarily between individualism and collectivism—in politics between a multiparty system of democracy, with its emphasis on individual freedom safeguarded by the Rule of Law, and a one-party structure of communist government, with its emphasis on the state and law as the instruments of the party that represents the people's collective interest and purpose; and in economics between *laissez-faire* capitalism and socialist planning. In the world today, capitalism and socialism have ceased in practice to be watertight systems, with capitalism accepting a good deal of state initiative and socialism accepting the stimulation of private enterprise and the price mechanism; and the

[9] London: SCM Press, 1964, p. 82.

ideological issues, though very much alive in some quarters on both sides, have not much moral significance. It is a different matter with the debate on political morality and the discussion of the nature and function of the state as conceived and practiced by the democratic and communist regimes. The ideological power blocs led by America and Russia continue to determine the character of the world political discussion.

Three new facts, however, are beginning to influence the debate on political morality. First, the awareness that nuclear technology, by increasing the utter destructiveness of a nuclear war, has eliminated it as a political weapon. Second, the logic of technological development and the move toward affluence, which, coupled with natural human urges, have led Russia to liberate itself from Stalinism and to ease its internal controls and tensions. This has altered its position in relation to other countries of the Russian bloc and has caused the breach with China; it has diminished the communist threat and made America readier to look toward peaceful coexistence with communist societies. Third, the struggle of Africa, Asia and Latin America to build up viable and dynamic political structures that are effective in consolidating self-conscious religious, linguistic and ethnic communities as national communities, in order to satisfy their expectation of higher standards of living and to meet the demands of the masses for fuller freedom and opportunities to participate in state and society at the level where power is exercised, has challenged static definitions of constitutionalism and the Rule of Law and has brought about a new consciousness of the dialectical relation between freedom and justice in a dynamic political situation. As a result, new forces and new perspectives have been introduced into the debate on political ethics.

When nuclear war can only annihilate both the victor and the vanquished, it certainly cannot be a continuation of politics through other means; and the idea of a "just war" loses its meaning. Can any political decision be more immoral than the decision to unleash a nuclear war, which would exterminate the major part of mankind and leave the rest hopelessly diseased?

The elimination of nuclear war from among the political weapons does not mean eliminating possession of nuclear bombs. Such possession does impress as a symbol of a nation's economic and military strength, and its prestige effect has tremendous political power. That is why nations are eager to enter the nuclear bomb club. But, at the same time, the peoples of the world strongly resist the entry of more nations into the nuclear arms race.

As a result of the nuclear impasse, several things have happened. First, world peace has acquired a new priority in world politics, which has led to the breakdown of the rigid ideological military blocs led by America and Russia and to a general acceptance of coexistence and cooperation between different social and political systems and ideologies. Second, it has deepened the awareness of all people of the interdependence of nations, the interconnection between the struggles for world peace and social justice everywhere, and the virtual elimination of the distinction between foreign and domestic affairs within the nations. The bargaining power of the non-nuclear nations has strengthened and increased their freedom to be rid of traditional structures of international law and to look for more dynamic relations in national and international life. Non-alignment in international affairs has a new respectability, and the new nations have scope to experiment with new political structures and ideologies and to build up their own political ethics.

The new nations need to develop new political ethics applicable to their own particular situations. They cannot, it is true, throw away the insights of political morality that have emerged in the debate between the advocates of liberal democracy, socialist democracy and communism. But the dynamics of their situations are in many ways very different from those of the West.

These differences arise in several ways. First, the revolutionary changes that came to the West one after another over a long period are coming to the new nations simultaneously and within a much shorter time. Demands for increasing agricultural and industrial productivity, for the participation of all the people in government, for more equal distribution of the wealth of the country and for public responsibility for health, education, social welfare and security, all pressing together, make strong state initiative and state-imposed discipline in large areas of public life essential, not primarily on ideological, but on sheer pragmatic grounds. It is significant that the United Nations Conference on World Development and Trade in Geneva assumed that state sectors would be required along with private sectors in the economic life of the developing nations. Second, industrialism, socialism and community development in relation to the traditional religious and cultural background pose many problems. If they are to attain stability, these new techniques and ideas must have indigenous cultural roots and a certain continuity with indigenous humanism through reform of traditional religions and cultures. In this process, it is necessary and legitimate to reinterpret as far as possible the techniques and ideas themselves in indigenous forms. But, inevitably, the spirit of traditional collectivism and authoritarianism will also seek to absorb the imported techniques and institutions, yet leaving aside the spirit of western humanism that lies behind them.

We face new situations where the relation between order, freedom and justice has to be worked out in new dynamic patterns without being too meticulous about using only well-tried political molds imported from the West. There has been a series of experiments in building political structures that represent attempts to adopt the insights of the West to new situations. Nehru's democratic socialism, Nasser's Arab socialism, Nkrumah's African socialism, Sukarno's guided democracy, Castro's communism and Mao's communism cannot be classified in the traditional categories of the West. Even India's parliamentary democracy has had to be adapted to the needs of a developing situation, by recognizing techniques of the states' planning of economic life; and Chinese communism has developed its own distinct patterns in seeking to revolutionize the agrarian pattern of a traditional Confucian society.

I do not claim that all these patterns should be accepted indiscriminately as equally legitimate and moral; or that morality should be dispensed with; and that stability and/or an alliance with either the communist or the anticommunist power bloc alone should become the criterion. But the moral evaluation of the emerging systems must be based on a new set of criteria that are creatively relevant to the context, and not merely on formal western categories. The new criteria will include the essence of democracy, but without identifying it with its traditional western forms. They will include, that is to say, the demand that the structure of any political order should, at some point, express concern for persons and their destiny beyond the state; that people should have the opportunity to participate in political power and to oppose power; and that power should be made responsible by minimizing the arbitrary exercise of it. But such criteria must also recognize that freedom and responsibility cannot be worked out except in the specific context of the search for the dignity and identity of new groups that lies behind the dynamic of awakened peoples, developing nations and reviving cultures. It is therefore a complete mistake to impose an ideal on the situation, pitting the individual against the awakening class, nation or race, or debating the moral priority between freedom and justice; the main concern should be to relate the forces and ideals that are already in operation in the actual complex situation.

No doubt, the idea of a responsible society that emerged from the discussions at the Amsterdam Assembly of the World Council of Churches can be developed into a criterion of the kind we seek. But, at Amsterdam, the main debate was between democracy and communism and therefore, as it emerged, the idea of responsible society did not reckon with the situations of the new nations. As a result, it is too comprehensive and balanced and too much lacking in the sense of the tragic tension existing between the urgently necessary and the ultimately significant to be relevant to the moral complexities of our situations. It is perhaps not impossible to work toward a new criterion of political ethics, expressed in a new understanding of responsible society, and relevant to the moral dynamics of the new situations.

What I have in mind is best expressed in a statement of the East Asia Christian Conference on "Responsibilities of the World Community for Asia's Political and Economic Development":

Abstract judgments of these different systems serve no useful purpose. Each has grown out of political forces and social needs of a particular situation. Moreover, they all have one common aim: to create an independent nation-state serving the urgent social and economic needs of their peoples. While each nation should be free to develop the patterns of political life which suit its genius best and correspond to its stage of political maturity, this freedom cannot be absolute. It should be exercised with understanding of certain basic political and moral requirements of community, both national and international. Christians concerned with the spiritual and ethical foundations of society have a duty to work within the limitations of the different situations for the basic principles of a responsible state even though they may be expressed in different forms of state and can be realized only partially in any.[10]

The statement goes on to speak of three values of responsible political life that should be the concern of the newly independent nations: 1. "The State must be based in some measure on the consent of the people." 2. "The State must express in its own structure its recognition that man has ends and loyalties beyond the State." 3. "The power of the State should never be absolute and must be limited by political means, legal processes or custom." But the statement recognizes that no political order can realize these values in its structure unless, in the first place, it is able to convince the people of its effectiveness in promoting national solidarity, economic development and social justice.

In fact, the real debate among people and parties accepting the responsible state as the goal of politics is not about moral priorities but about the chronological ordering of things. The question is whether radical structural changes and rapid development in society can and ought to be achieved with the minimum possible curtailment of individual freedom, with built-in safeguards for their restoration; or whether there are many situations that make it legitimate for responsible people to conclude that a government has to be at least pragmatically authoritarian to effect the necessary social transformation and that the urges of human freedom have a better chance of asserting themselves when the forces of development have achieved strength and when the larger inequalities between classes, castes, races and other groups in a society have been overcome. It is important that this debate continue within the framework of a responsible search of the nations for a new political morality. This is not said to minimize the threat of totalitarian ideology and politics, either of the left or of the right, but to distinguish a type of authoritarianism of the left that may be a necessary means toward an eventual strengthening of responsible state and society in some of the developing countries.

---

[10] *Christian Community Within the Human Community,* Minutes of the EACC Assembly, 1964. Part II.

Chinese Communism Today and the New Polarization of World Politics

The struggle against colonialism and racial discrimination, the united front of the poor nations to secure a fair deal from the rich in matters of aid and trade and the efforts to build state structures that can effect modernization of traditional societies—all these have their distinctive characteristics, cutting across one another. Nevertheless, they are closely related and, broadly speaking, strengthen one another and work together to form some sort of new international proletariat, fighting for their liberation against the West. In this context, Chinese communism, with its concept of world polarization and its program of pushing this division of the world between the rich and the proletariat to extreme limits, poses a serious threat. It does so precisely because it speaks relevantly to the militant mood of the nonwhite peoples and the poor nations in their search for effective fighting power, and because it appeals to the human urges behind that mood. In the present situation, China seems to have great power to convince the leaders of the several liberation movements in Africa, Asia and Latin America that totalitarian communism and war are the only effective means of successful liberation. China's testing of the nuclear bomb has enhanced its prestige and its image as a rapidly growing military and industrial power and impressed the Afro-Asian nations with its capacity for militant leadership. In contrast, India and some other countries have represented a more liberal view of state structure and a more nonviolent form of political struggle; and they are committed to using nuclear science only for peaceful purposes. Will such nations retain an influential role, and will their ideas have some chance of success among the awakened peoples and developing nations of the world? Will Chinese communism move in the direction of the liberalization these countries represent, or will the extremist spirit overcome them, too? It is anybody's guess. The answer depends on many factors and forces within these nations. But much also depends on whether the white races and the developed nations, be they capitalist or socialist, will recognize the human urges behind the revolutionary awakening of peoples throughout the world and make the readjustments and sacrifices necessary in their own lives, enabling their countries to participate, in an imaginative and costly way, in the struggle of all peoples for a new society.

Perhaps, in the new decade that we enter, the churches' main task will be to prove that Christian and human solidarity can render unnecessary (or at least less destructive) wars and violences that seem inevitable today.

Postcript: Comment by Professor S. Rouner of the United Theological College, Bangalore, on the middle section of the preceding paper. He writes to Mr. Thomas as follows:

"There is an interesting shift in your argument from the concept of *rights* to the concept of *responsibility*. My feeling is that the basic issue is also one of responsibility rather than rights. You raise —by implication—the complicated philosophical question as to whether an individual or a nation has a 'right' to wealth. Your argument is that the affluent societies have it, and the poorer nations have a right to demand sacrifice by the rich. You go so far as to argue that the economic policy of the affluent cannot be regarded as moral in the fullest sense until they accept the national goals of the poor as their sole consideration in economic policy, rather than the present mixture of self-interest and interest in the future of the other fellow.

"Basic to the argument about rights is the democratic credo that 'All men are created equal.' This is not an empirical statement, but a legal principle essentially, which has now been applied to some social areas, and tentatively to economics in the principle that all men have a *right* to equal opportunity, or a 'fighting chance.' If they lack the ability or the situation which gives them a genuine 'fighting chance,' the welfare state declares, rightly, that society has a responsibility to see that none of its members suffers great hardship economically. This is not far from the communist goal of 'to each according to his need.' And I take it that what you mean to say here is that the rich ought to recognize the needs of the poor, and are responsible for meeting them—and I couldn't agree more.

"I am uneasy about the use of *rights,* however, because—while it highlights the sins of the rich, it tends to cast a cloak of piety over the sins of the poor. It has the revolutionary advantage of pitting rich against poor and clarifying the problem, but it tends to authorize any demand made by the poor on the rich. Psychologically speaking, it is an expression of the resentment of former colonies against the colonialists who often bled them. Because the colonialists feel guilty for their sins, the charge of 'economic colonialism' becomes an effective weapon of the poor in urging their demands. It also tends to further the false economic assumption that the major problems of the poor can be met by large increases in aid of one sort or another from the rich.

"Economic rights are tied almost solely to nationalism. The poor are concerned only with their rights as a poor nation. They are not concerned, for example, with the internal problem of poverty in the 'rich' nations, or with the complex difficulties which the 'rich' have in maintaining economic stability. Their demand is based entirely on self-interest, but they do not recognize self-interest as valid for the rich. The rich, because they are 'rich,' have no right to self-interest.

"From the perspective of the poor, the ethics of the situation is clear to the point of being maddening, further adding to their resentment. But economically there is a certain lack of realism involved, because the poor know that their economic problems are so much greater than those of the rich that they find it hard to understand that a rich nation has many genuine economic problems. Price supports for grains in America is probably a good example. Unless the poor are prepared to admit the right of the Americans to deal with this as a real economic problem, the real difficulty of sharing America's incredible agricultural overproduction isn't going to make much headway.

"I would say, rather, that the question of rights is rooted in the deeper question of responsibility. The real problem of relationship between rich and poor is a problem of mutual responsibilities, both to one's own people and to each other. Each nation's primary responsibility is to its own people, economically, politically, culturally, etc. This is what makes it a nation. This much 'self-interest' is valid for everyone. What we are all gradually learning is that our national identity takes place under a more inclusive and increasingly felt identity of mankind. We are our brother's keeper. We must reach out politically and economically, and we must do it responsibly. America must solve the surplus agricultural problem not only for its own sake, but for India's (etc.) sake as well. India must be prepared to recognize that this is an American problem and not impose an Indian solution on it, in the same way that America must recognize that India's planned economy affairs are appropriate for her and not insist that India's internal affairs be ordered along an American pattern. India has a right to urge on America a solution of the problem, because it is a mutual problem; in the same way, American AID [Agency for International Development] people urge particular solutions on the Indian economy because they are involved in it.

"I agree entirely that the whole question of mutual economic responsibility takes place within the context of the moral requirement of the rich to aid the poor. Let there be no question about that. But any economy, rich or poor, is a dynamic thing, subject to its own particular operations, and liable to collapse if dealt with insensitively. The poor always envy and resent the rich for being rich when they are poor, and this resentment is a crucially necessary ingredient in any movement for economic justice, for the rich seldom share unless they have to. In this context, perhaps the emphasis on rights is both inevitable and necessary. But there is at least some evidence in the modern world that the rich are also 'awakening' to their responsibilities. And as this awakening increases, the poor will begin to realize that their own needs are part of the larger problem of a new economic pattern based not on the divisive cry of *meum* and *tuum* but the problems of the entire international community."

6

THE POLITICAL DYNAMICS OF LATIN AMERICAN SOCIETY TODAY

by MAURICIO LOPEZ (Argentina)

THE world has received two contradictory pictures of Latin America. The traditional image, drawn largely from the eighteenth century, is that of lands "flowing with milk and honey," rich in natural resources and precious metals. The Tower of Gold, on the banks of the Guadalquivir River in Seville, where the coveted metal made its first stop before getting into the hands of European kings, nobles and merchants, bore mute but eloquent testimony to that abundance. Two more ingredients completed the picture: the fact that here were educated peoples who had an unlimited capacity to assimilate European culture but who were unable to produce a stable political order for themselves, a rather surprising combination of a delicate cultivation of the spirit with a kind of civic irresponsibility that has been so well illustrated in an almost interminable series of comic-opera revolutions.

This traditional picture was not false; it was simply incomplete. Hidden behind the scenes was a continent impoverished by the continuing existence of structures and patterns of life that have kept two thirds of the population of more than 200 million in harrowing conditions of misery, injustice and cultural backwardness. What makes this situation different is the fact that the people have become aware of their condition. They are now conscious of being an irresistible political force, and, spurred on to action by politicians and intellectuals, they are ready to use any and all means to attain a fuller and more worthwhile life. The revolutionary ferment that has taken hold of this continent is nothing but the reflection of this impatience of the masses to put an end to an old social order, which has continued almost intact since the colonial period, and to share in the development of a more brotherly and just human society.

The Slow Decline of the Colonial World

1. Those who undertook to subdue and rule the Americas from the end of the fifteenth century onward came upon sizable native populations which had in some instances—such as those of the Incas and Aztecs—a well-advanced social and political organization and which had succeeded in building up vast empires. Wielding the yardstick of European anthropology, the conquistadors regarded the Indians as "barbarians," to be liquidated, driven away or used, whichever was most convenient. In general, the Spaniards decided to make use of them as farm laborers, miners and artisans. To dispel any doubts that they were human beings, one of the popes decreed that they had souls and could therefore be evangelized. The Roman Catholic Church, in concerning itself with this task, did much to elevate the Indian's condition and to lighten the yoke imposed by the secular arm.

The conquistador brought with him the institutions, culture and forms of community life of a Spain that refused to move into the modern world and preferred to shut itself up in its medieval dream. This heritage was to make itself felt heavily all over the American continent. The colonial Administration created the *encomienda* system, turning over to the conquistador a large expanse of land—*latifundium*—and a certain number of Indians who would cultivate it in exchange for clothing, food, shelter and spiritual care. Obviously, there was thus established a feudal system of property and economy. The products of the land and the mines were sent off to the big city, and the fabulous profits that were obtained by their exploitation were not reinvested but were wasted away in a life of luxury or in erecting ostentatious churches. When the colonies broke off their political ties with Spain, economic practices were n no way changed. The economic liberalism that was brought in was to benefit the industrial nations of Europe and the tiny Latin American *bourgeoisie*. The feudal regime of agrarian property survived, as did the one-crop or one-product system, yielding coffee, bananas, sugar, cotton, copper and silver that were exported to Europe. Latin American economy continued to be complementary to that of Europe. To the latter went the products extracted from the ground and from under the ground; to the former went the manufactured products. When the economic interests of Britain or France were considered to be threatened, there was recourse to armed intervention or some other show of strength.

This tributary character of the Latin American economy was not altered when the United States assumed an imperialist role. During the colonial period, the two parts of the American continent lived in ignorance of each other; when independence arrived for both, the southern "Americans" felt inspired by the ideals of liberty of their northern brothers. The latter helped the South American patriots to break loose from their Spanish tutelage; and when the struggle against the colonial forces took shape, the enunciation of the Monroe Doctrine strengthened still further the solidarity between the two Americas. Together they were to work for the prosperity of the American peoples, for relations of common interest and for defense against any new European attempt to assume control. At that time, there were no points of friction in economic matters. The two had paralled systems, and both were providers of raw materials for Europe. It was a brief idyl, which began to fade as the United States emerged as a great world power. Having finished its march to the West, the United States established its borders by buying Florida from Spain and Louisiana from France and seizing half the territory of Mexico. It managed to disencumber itself from nearby competitors by snatching Puerto Rico from Spain and occupying Cuba. Continental solidarity was a vehicle no longer of friendship but of imperialist purposes. Especially since the First World War, United States commerce and capital has established the third colonization of Latin America in the name of democracy and free enterprise. They did so with the tacit consent of the Latin American oligarchies, whose herodian mentality caused them to live with their backs turned on their own country, unmindful of the privations of its people.

2. The crisis had a social dimension. Latin American society is far from homogeneous. Indians, whites, mestizos and Negroes make up, to a greater or smaller degree, the racial ingredients of society in the different parts of Latin America. The pure Indian has remained on the fringe of national life, neither participating in community affairs nor sharing in political decisions. There have been, it is true, a number of serious attempts to integrate him into society—some of them showing visible signs of progress, for instance in Bolivia. The Negro was brought as a slave from Africa, especially to the Caribbean regions and Brazil. Unlike the Indian the Negro assimilated the habits, food and dress of the white man. In Brazil, he was recognized as a full-fledged citizen; and, although some social and economic discrimination exists, it has no legal sanction, nor is it supported by any idea that he is naturally inferior. The mestizo had very insecure beginnings. He steered between two worlds, with his father's Spanish culture and his mother's Indian mentality. Hence his first unsure steps; hence the ambiguity that harassed him; hence the lack of historical background to which he could attach himself. But, unlike the Indian, he was ambitious and he steadily gained ground and social stature. Today, especially in Mexico, he constitutes a true lever for social and cultural advancement and is a decisive factor in political leadership.

Latin America's diverse racial origin forms in itself an invaluable contribution to the cultural and human wealth of the continent. The disquieting factor, therefore, is not the diversity, but the marked dualism to be seen in the social sectors. True, we can speak of an increasing rise of the middle classes, but these are not sufficiently large to counterbalance the extremes. This dualism has economic bases. A very small number of families monopolize most of the wealth, while the great mass of the population exists at a standard of living that borders on misery. At first sight the statistics that indicate an average annual income of $370 per inhabitant would seem to indicate a substantial rise in the living standard of the whole population. Nothing is further from the facts. The inequality of income, national and individual, contradicts any expression of optimism. Actually, more than half the population—that is, more than 100 million people—have an average income of $120 a year. While there are countries, like Venezuela, that reach some $500 per inhabitant, others, like Haiti, do not exceed $55. A mere 5 per cent of the families has from 30 to 45 per cent of the national income. In every country, the oligarchies, which have become wealthy, chiefly in agriculture and cattle-raising or in foreign trade, have not reinvested their capital but have transferred it to bank accounts abroad. It is estimated that over $15 billion belonging to the Latin American capitalists have been sent to Europe and the United States. It is not surprising that the foreign companies should do the same, exporting their gains much more substantially than reinvesting them.

The most noteworthy demographic feature today is the phenomenal population increase. Human beings are multiplying in Latin America at a higher rate than in any other part of the world, and the demographists calculate that the population will be tripled by the end of this century. Two characteristics mark this rising human tide: its youth and its mobility. Children under fourteen years of age make up 40 per cent of the population. This is a great blessing for a developing continent, which needs the contribution of young blood fired with hope, but for the present it forms an onerous burden that weighs heavily upon the active population. Moreover, the poor conditions of farm life are causing a sizable internal migration from the country to the city. It is a phenomenon that is repeated everywhere—Buenos Aires, Mexico City, São Paulo, Santiago, Lima, Caracas, Bogotá; yet that generator of dreams, the city, becomes a place of disillusionment for new arrivals. They are kept on the outskirts and allowed to enter only to perform their daily work. When they return to their shacks at night, the meal is scanty, the single room a confused symbiosis of human beings and animals crowded together, and each morning brings the anxiety of uncertain employment. It is moving to see, only a few yards from the elegant beach of Copacabana in Rio de Janeiro, those pigsties of dwellings that hang like clusters of leaves on the hillsides. From the mountain top, the Christ of Corcovado looks down not only upon the city but upon thousands of poor, upturned faces, animated by feelings of rebellion against a rich society that forgets its obligations in respect to social justice. These belts of misery in our metropolises constitute an excellent broth-culture for social revolution.

3. The crisis has also a political aspect. In contrast to Africa and Asia, which began to free themselves from political colonialism at the time of the Second World War, the countries of Latin America obtained independence from Spain in the first quarter of the nineteenth century. The wars for independence, fought out locally at an impressive cost in lives and property, broke up the unity of the empire and subdivided national units to the point of exaggeration. Brazil was an exception. While other countries poured out their blood in internal struggles that retarded the establishment of order, Brazil was ruled by an enlightened and progressive monarch. Even the introduction of the republic did not cost a single drop of blood, for Pedro II, a liberal who abolished slavery at the cost of support from the oligarchy, finally packed his bags and abandoned Brazil for good.

When the Latin American countries severed their ties with the mother country, they looked to the Anglo-Saxon democracies for a constitutional model. Liberal democracy was introduced and "imposed" by the ruling classes, who thought that they had thereby found a political instrument with which to weld together their country's national unity and social life. Liberal politicians were so dazzled by the Anglo-Saxon democracies—indisputable examples of "political and social order," the importation of which would eliminate all problems of national organization—that they were blinded to the real needs of their countries. Democratic institutions could hardly function in countries where there was almost no middle class in which to establish them and where enormous sectors of the population could neither read nor write and were not even socially integrated into the nation's life. Accustomed to the authoritarian government of the Spanish crown, the masses tended toward the *caudillo* type of ruler, who governed with a strong arm and a paternalistic spirit. In such circumstances, democracy was more a name than a reality—a formal apparatus benefiting the privileged classes and utterly devoid of social content. This does not mean that there has been no opportunity to practice a genuinely democratic form of government. In the balance of accounts, the examples of Uruguay, Chile, Costa Rica and Mexico belong on the credit side, but it is also true that as long as the crude social dichotomy persists, democracy will be more of a slogan than a vital reality.

4. Ignorance and illiteracy are other evils that corrode society. Much has been done to promote education and to develop popular culture. Argentina, Uruguay and Cuba have literacy rates that compare well with those of many European countries; Mexico spends more on education than on arms. Nevertheless, that task remains gigantic. Generally, the illiteracy rate is alarming—as much as 90 per cent of the population in certain countries. Among people over fifteen years of age there are more than seventy million illiterates. It is easy to imagine the disadvantages that confront this enormous mass. Their participation in society and their chances of influencing it are reduced to a minimum. Incapable of giving thought beyond their own daily concerns, they are unable to assume by themselves any significant political role.

Furthermore, the bilateral relations of economic and political dependence with the United States constitute another symptom of their delayed development. Democracy and free enterprise, imposed utopias from abroad, have proved incapable of raising the living standard of the population and of laying the foundations for a constructive national political life. United States diplomacy —and sometimes the Marines—have always operated to protect economic interests and to blow away the spirit of revolt, thereby paralyzing popular recovery. To these ends, use was made of pseudodemocratic regimes as well as of dictatorships. The Organization of American States (OAS) appeared, with suspicious unanimity—the honorable exception being Mexico—to be dedicated to no other task than to serve those interests.

As the colonial world collapsed, it left a continent unsettled and adrift in its inner being. There was, on the one hand, a minority that possessed all the wealth, lived and thought *à la Europea,* was educated, cultured and democratic. On the other, there was the great mass of the urban and rural population—underfed, illiterate and ill-housed, which began to be aware of its condition and to be awakened to a revolutionary frame of mind that no one could check. This precarious economic, political, social and cultural development is today the source of one of the most explosive revolutionary situations in the world.

The Awakening of Social Conscience

1. The attempts to end this colonial heritage can be fairly well identified from 1920 onward. About that time, a vast social and political process began that was directed toward achieving a more equitable and economically free society. There was a real mobilization of ideological forces and tendencies, an urgent desire to give the continent a modern face-lifting. The European model of community life appeared worn out and decadent; it no longer served as a guide for new paths and aspirations. The urban middle classes felt that their hour of history had come, and, undergirded by new political parties, they took over power. The small industrial *bourgeoisie* displaced the landholding oligarchy in determining the course of economic life. The working class began to organize, listening to the far-off echo of the Soviet Revolution and to the campaign cries of European socialism nearer at hand. Some of the Latin American countries have shown themselves able—albeit precariously—to practice democratic ways, but in general the political life has seesawed between constitutional governments and dictatorial regimes. Art and culture have sought for inspiration that is rooted in the soil and have tried out new ways of expressing the national ethos. The university "reform" movement has championed the democratization of academic life through the admission of students from all social strata; and in the ideological plane, "Aprism" has summoned the peoples of Latin America to fight for social justice, reintegrate the Indian population in national life and uproot economic imperialism.

The balance sheet of the four decades that have passed is far from satisfactory. Progress has been recorded here and there, but there has been no over-all development to set in motion all the forces of a country. Moreover, the resistance of the ruling classes, in connivance with foreign economic powers, has blocked the most promising undertakings. The land problem has received the attention of governments, and, in some places, plans for agrarian reform have been put into effect that would enable the peasant to work his own land. Farm work has been mechanized and steps have been taken to diversify the crops. But these have been partial attempts that have not noticeably modified the physiognomy of the country-side. Thus we have, side by side in the same country, zones of vast production with adequate agricultural technology and other zones with the most primitive farming methods, which barely serve to keep their inhabitants from starving. Josue de Castro expressed it in a moving way when he wrote of northeastern Brazil as the land of desolation and death. Buenos Aires, São Paulo and Mexico City are powerful industrial complexes, developed under a policy to protect the national capital. Labor unionism is awake and has managed to get its rights protected through measures of social legislation that in some cases, as in Uruguay, are truly progressive. But the rhythm of industrial expansion has slowed down, the with-drawal of capital resources hinders the creation of new enterprises and the policy of low salaries is inflicting a severe malaise upon the working class, which finds itself helpless and frustrated in the face of the violation of its rights and the constant threat of unemployment.

The middle class is today more numerous and more prosperous than it has been in the past. It has unquestionably succeeded in strengthening its position, but it is not very much open to initiative that would draw it closer to the working class. Jealous of the ad-vances it has won, it fears that social effervescence may signify a temporary reversal in its living standard and it prefers to entrench itself behind the façade of an irresponsible liberalism. This amounts to a dangerous polarization of society that fails to find a way to combine interests and aspirations for the good of the national development.

2. All this shows how difficult it is to know whether Latin America should be included in the sphere of western countries or would fit better among the countries of the so-called "third world." Development is not wholly absent, but more in evidence in an un-derdevelopment that gnaws away at the continent's deepest entrails. The twenty countries of which Latin America is composed derive from a common conquest and colonization; they are related in Latin languages and cultures; they have maintained their distinc-tive ethos; and they have always spoken in favor of continental

solidarity. But this historical and cultural community begins to break up when we look at it from the ethnic, geographic, economic and political points of view. The limited value of generalizations is perceived when one has to deal with rich or poor countries, lands with high or low literacy rates, those with temperate or tropical climates and countries populated in varying proportions by American Indians, Caucasians and Negroes. But this Latin American ambivalence does not succeed in hiding the difficult conditions of population growth. Thus the central problem of Latin America is the radical transformation of its social patterns and institutions and of its way of life. A real political and social upgrading of the masses must be effected, for they are tired of living a marginal existence; they know, or at least instinctively feel, that technical advances have been attained that would give them access to material welfare and cultural life, and they are driven by a harsh revolutionary determination to achieve these ends. No one has described the situation better than did the Argentine economist, Raul Prebisch, when he said in his farewell speech upon leaving the Secretariat of the Economic Commission for Latin America in July 1963:

In Latin America, the systems of production and life must undergo deep changes, and something new must be built up. And if we do not succeed in doing it now with our own hands, if a resolute, firm, clearsighted response is not made to this present imperious demand, the new generations with bold, fearless and perhaps irreverent hands will wipe the slate clean of the world that we have not known how to transform and will erect another that may not be what we would have desired for ourselves and for them.

3. That challenge had already been taken up several years earlier by those 'bold, fearless and perhaps irreverent hands" of which he spoke. The Cuban Revolution of 1959 constitutes, in the wide scope of its aims, the most important social and political event in Latin America in this century. A true mirror of a continent in ferment, it reflects all the problems, tendencies, aspirations and temptations of our time; it is a miniature world of destiny's threats and promises to a whole people in tension. Its rhythm is felt in every sphere of Cuban life, and its influence—though apparently becoming less resounding—extends everywhere. The first

fruits of a new society in formation, it offers itself as the most radical pattern on which to lead Latin Americans to break their remaining ties with their colonial past and to plunge into the still-confused and ambiguous domains of a society that is more brotherly, more progressive, more just.

The objectives of Castro's Revolution had been fixed in 1953 in the Moncada Program, which included agrarian reform, nationalization measures, urban reform and educational reform. The revolutionaries considered it impossible to carry out a revolution of the classical or bourgeois type that would be limited to the re-establishment of the formal freedoms of democracy without touching the capitalist structures of the national economy. If they had done so, they would not really have changed anything, and they would have sacrificed vigorous and decisive popular support to assure their position and gain their ends. The goals of the revolution, apart from any ideological definition, would inevitably go counter to the United States' interests. It is not surprising that, after a certain initial enchantment that the "romantic" aspect of Castro's action helped to encourage, the United States government showed an attitude of caution and hostility, followed by threats of economic sanctions. Faced with the danger of seeing his movement shipwrecked, Castro sought and obtained economic and military assistance from Soviet Russia and decided to give his revolution the ideological dress of Marxist Leninism. It is the task of impatient biographers to recount Fidel Castro's ideological history and to establish his supposed or actual Marxist affiliation before he started his movement. For better or worse, Castro introduced the first Latin American experiment with an economic, social and political regime in open rupture with liberal capitalism. Here is an economic revolution of a socialist kind, in which the benefits of agriculture and industry are put at the disposal of the centralized planning state; it is also a revolution against the economic colonialism exercised by the United States. Deep reforms in the system of land control and production, changes in urban property ownership, a decentralization (still at the planning stage) of the industrial centers and a vast plan of reforms in the realm of education (in the main already carried out) have all helped to raise the material and cultural living standard of the working masses and have done away with endemic unemployment of a structural kind. Gross errors committed in different sectors of the economy are being recognized and corrected. The Marxist dogmatism of the early days is giving way to an attitude that is more flexible and more mindful of Cuba's historical and social reality. The absence of rigid official instructions contributes to a more spontaneous and variegated cultural life. The state continues, as before, to be secular and neutral in religious matters, and there is no reason to suppose that the present government—which, incidentally, maintains diplomatic relations with the Vatican—will assimilate the militant atheism of some of the people's democracies of eastern Europe. There are also some shadows that could jeopardize the revolution itself. The lack of technical teams to advise and direct the social and economic development is still felt; an enlarged and barely competent bureaucracy constitutes a real short circuit between the government and the people, and there is an inevitable but costly distraction of energies and resources to assure the internal and external security of a country that still feels threatened by invasion. However, the effectiveness with which it has attacked the real problems of underdevelopment, and the way in which it has been able to stimulate and fill with hope the masses who have been raised to the status of essential components of the new society, should be counted to its credit.

As might be expected, a revolution of such a nature has had ample repercussions throughout Latin America, though "Castroism" does not express itself everywhere in the same form. There are groups inspired by the Cuban Revolution who have embarked on the course of guerrilla warfare, with the support of the peasant masses, in order to overthrow legal constitutional order. Other groups, made up of leftist intellectuals, some of them Christians, express their sympathy with the Cuban regime, criticize the policy of the United States and defend the principle of nonintervention in the affairs of other countries, but believe that the revolutionary struggle should be launched constitutionally.

The OAS has decreed the ostracism of Cuba; all the countries that form part of the OAS, and even Bolivia, which does not, have severed diplomatic relations with Cuba. Only Mexico has refused to take part in this "quarantine" or in any other joint action against the Castroist Revolution.

Nevertheless, the revolution has had its immediate catalytic effects. In the first place, it laid bare the widening gulf between Anglo-Saxon America and Latin America. Already, in 1958, the then President of Brazil, Juscelino Kubitschek, in what he called "Operation Panamericana," proposed a plan in which North and South Americans would commit themselves to the struggle against underdevelopment and its habitual train of evils. This scheme was left in the limbo of neglected dreams until action was needed to block the way to Cuban influence. President Kennedy, in the presence of the Latin American diplomatic corps, announced at the White House on March 13, 1961, his Alliance for Progress program to "end the dictatorship of misery in Latin America." This was a genuine economic and social charter for decisively embarking on the road of development within the framework of the liberal institutions of the West. The plan calls for grants totaling some $20 billion from public and private capital, for the most part by the United States, for a period of ten years.

In the four years since it was started, the Alliance has proved to be inadequate and ineffectual. The financial aid has not been used for the promised reforms—as was to be expected—in view of the fact that most of those governments are made up of representatives of the oligarchies and that private companies are the source of such investments. To initiate a structural reform would therefore mean acting against their own interests. Moreover, the Alliance as planned is insufficient. To foster a minimum required annual rise of 2.5 per cent per person, it would be necessary to double the proposed investments. Hitherto, it has been effective chiefly in the political sphere: It has checked the spread of Castroism and has shut the door to leftists, with the threat of economic sanctions on any government that shows any degree of sensitivity to the demands of the masses. It is handcuffed by a basic contradiction, namely, that of trying to bring about a social revolution with the cooperation of reactionary forces.

Relations between the United States and Latin America are today placed in the widest context of the division between rich and poor countries by the definition of a problem which is more exactly economic and ideological, but which also has its moral effects. The problem is to discover how world commercial relations can be changed in order to overcome the economic dictatorship of the wealthy countries—to which Russia "objectively" belongs—over the underprivileged countries and thus enable the latter to enter upon the road to development and progress. In this connection, the Conference on Trade and Development organized by the United Nations (Geneva, March-June, 1964) is a beginning that promises hope. It is a great opportunity for the "civilization of the privileged" to find here a way of involvement in a humanism that is less materialistic and more closely associated with a common cause.

Ideological Choices, Political Spectrum and Christian Responsibility

1. The ideological dimension of the revolutionary ferment in Latin America covers a wide gamut of choices. It is evident here that we are no longer dealing with the abstract and universalist ideologies of the nineteenth century but with a collection of ideas and values which respond to a specific historical circumstance and which become more concrete upon being related to the economic and social development of the continent. Among those most commonly in practice are liberalism, authoritarianism with popular support, reformism and revolutionary socialism.

Liberalism is the ideology of a kind of industrial and commercial *bourgeoisie* which recognizes the need to modernize social patterns but which, in the face of social mobilization, is more closely concerned with preserving order than with assuring justice. Nothing, therefore, distinguishes it from conservatism, with which it comes to terms in matters of private property, free enterprise and liberal democracy. At present it lacks intellectual vigor, but it maintains its political and economic power almost intact, and its aggressive counter-revolutionary activities are evident everywhere.

Popular authoritarianism is the ideological pattern that seeks to give expression to the feelings and desires of the urban and rural laboring masses. It is colored with a strong nationalistic spirit, and its political authority assumes the form of a protective state. The nation is above any private interest and constitutes an organic whole in which the workers play a front-rank political role. It trusts to the people's struggle to obtain new social forms and to create a more just community. The people's movements in Latin America have been fostered especially by political leaders who have established charismatic relations with the masses. Among the most important are those that belong to "Varguism" in Brazil and "Peronism" in Argentina, two experiments in authoritarian democratization that have left deep impressions in the political sands of those countries. Popular authoritarianism is kept alive in our days by certain groups of young Army officers who gather round so-called socialist "Nasserism." They hold that the Army should enter the political struggle openly and become the vanguard of the nationalist people's revolution. They consider that the democracy so far practiced has been an exclusive privilege of the oligarchies and that the parties that have popular roots have been powerless to change the situation. They fight against capitalism because it is incurably linked to imperialism and against communism because it does not succeed in combining social justice with religious belief.

Reformism is the ideology that gives greater attention to the economic and social slant of development than to its political dimension. It favors a government in which technocrats hold key positions and which will make possible the launching of a full and harmonious development of the nation's economic resources, the application of more technology to agriculture, the fixing of a more rational position for the industrial forces and the promotion of education, especially for the training of professional workers and technicians. The reformists prefer to think in continental terms; they focus upon Latin America as a whole and advocate measures to coordinate the structural development of every nation with that of the others. Its chief exponents have been feeding their theories to public opinion through the Economic Commission for Latin America, a regional organism of the United Nations. They not only condemn economic imperialism, but dedicate themselves to creating the appropriate structural conditions that will enable each nation to emerge from its situation of dependence. In this, capital and foreign companies can play an important role as long as they identify themselves with the highest interests of the country.

Revolutionary socialism gathers together the tendencies toward the left and postulates a strong central government and a radical and complete change of the present patterns. It constitutes an important focus of attraction for the masses of workers and peasants and is a fertile laboratory of ideas for students and intellectuals. It shows a strong Marxist influence, which, along with other characteristics, distinguishes it clearly from the bourgeois-influenced democratic socialism—and the working people become the motive power and the nervous system of the revolution. There are those who choose the revolutionary war because within the present democratic system they see no prospect of a total renewal of Latin American life. Only the force of arms can knock down pillars of traditional society. Other leftist groups believe that peaceful life is still viable and think—at least in some countries—that within the present constitutional system bread and justice for all can be achieved.

2.   The political prism of what has come to be called the "revolution of development and social justice" reflects this ideological panorama. There is a manifest loss of support for the traditional political organizations which developed out of the middle classes and which are instruments of the oligarchy. They have wasted themselves away by their use of power, and they have no new and imaginative program to offer. They stay in power by means of shady electoral machinations, or by regulations that hinder the illiterate masses in getting to the ballot boxes or by skillful divisive maneuvers in the area to the left.

People's parties have grown in importance, as would be expected, in the countries where trade unionism has developed the furthest, such as Chile, Argentina and Brazil. Peronism has achieved great electoral successes in Argentina, where it can claim more than half the voters. Its weak flank is its ideological vagueness. The Popular Action Front in Chile binds together Marxist leftists and has shown itself to be a disciplined force able to make itself significantly felt as an opposition party. Castroism, by its very nature, is forced to carry on underground and, in countries like Venezuela, Guatemala and Colombia, still watches for its opportunity. The armed forces are being trained in guerrilla warfare and have managed to limit the field of action of these revolutionary movements. In Brazil, Popular Action, a combination of Christian and Marxist elements, has achieved outstanding results in awakening the political conscience of the masses through a persistent campaign of education and promotion of popular culture.

The most important political event after the Cuban Revolution has been the vertiginous entrance on the scene of the Christian Democratic party. In some countries it remained a rather embryonic force, with a scanty, fluctuating number of voters. It has belatedly come to pick up the postwar triumphs of the European parties of the same name, after the maturing of a political point of view based on serious reflection about Latin America in a state of revolution. Credit should go here to the contribution of the *Centro Bellarmino* in Santiago, Chile, which provides the Christian Democratic party with the ideological platform that enabled it to define the lines of its political, social, economic and cultural activity. Depending on the color of the glasses through which one looks, it can appear as either rightist or leftist. To Latin America, it looks like a modern, dynamic, progressive party with a pinkish tinge if compared with traditional political bodies. Furthermore, it enjoys the sympathy of the Roman Catholic Church, which is unquestionably a formidable asset, giving it a badge of respectability and prestige that makes it palatable—although with a slightly bitter taste—to the conservative classes. Its anticommunist views—enlightened and not hysterical—make it trustworthy in the eyes of the great power to the north. In power today, in Chile and Peru, with vigorous activity in Venezuela and other countries, its goal for the future is to fulfill a desire to accomplish the "revolution in freedom."

According to its leaders, this revolution carried out by the Christian Democrats in Chile has a double meaning: on the one hand, to loosen the power of the privileged classes in the economic and political realms and, on the other, to restrict considerably the freedom of foreign capital to maneuver and to make it play a decisive role in the development of the country. The aim is therefore to do away with this double dependence—external and internal—which was suffocating the life of the masses. The government has drawn up a program of land reform and is striving for a decisive say in the exploitation of the copper mines, which are the main resources of the country and are, at the moment, in the hands of foreign enterprises. On the social level, the Christian Democrats are busily trying to carry out a thorough promotion of the rural and urban masses, avoiding any kind of class struggle. On the political level, the government will call, when necessary, a referendum to give the people an opportunity to express democratically their views on the crucial problems of nation-building. The private sector of the economy will not lose its initiative if and when it accepts the rules of the game of a policy of development.

This Christian Democrat Revolution is much more interested in political action and efficiency than in a carefully defined ideology. For this reason, it is eagerly seeking the support of a people renowned for its generosity, openmindedness and tested endurance. This is solid ground to start with, but it must be said that time is against any delayed and soft action. The Chilean masses still live in great poverty, and a greater material austerity than that to which they have so far been subjected cannot be imposed. The question is how to obtain a progressive and rapid improvement of their standard of living and how best to integrate them into a more just and dynamic community. If the government succeeds in doing this, it will then be the first significant achievement of a political movement that, throughout Latin America, is endeavoring to make compatible, from the very outset, economic development and political freedom.

3. The Christian Church in Latin America faces a challenging and difficult new period. Political and social change oblige it— whether it wants to or not—to revise its theology, its structure and the form of its presence. This is true for the Roman Catholic Church, which has been in the continent for more than four centuries, and for the Protestant Church, which has been there for about a hundred years.[1] The Roman Catholic Church is deeply rooted in the colonial world; it was the instrument of mass evangelization of the Indian—a task that never really reached his soul; it established the standards of thought and conduct of millions of people; and it remained closely bound up with the ruling classes. It approached the masses in a paternalistic manner and generally

---

[1] See GONZALO CASTILLO CÁRDENAS: "The Challenge of the Latin American Revolution," *Christian Social Ethics in a Changing World.* (Vol. I in this series.)

preached submission and respect toward those in high places. The winds of revolution are not blowing over it for the first time; it suffered a buffeting in the Mexican tempest of 1910, which stripped if of a great part of its material possessions, leaving intact its way of life and thought. Relations with the state were noticeably changed; the church remained confined to the "spiritual" sphere, and the secular state took care of politics, tolerating no interference. With time, this *modus vivendi* came to be firmly fixed, and it has not hindered the church from proceeding to recover its lost influence. The Bolivian Revolution of 1952 did not enter the religious sphere, and, although the socialist tinge of its social concerns annoyed the hierarchy, this did not seriously affect its influence on the Bolivian scene. It should be underlined that the Protestant Church experienced a notable upswing after the revolution.

The Cuban Revolution (1959), with its clear Marxist-Leninist accent, has raised the question of the relation between the church and the world in the most radical terms. This event brings to life, with almost brutal evidence, a new form of society, with all its promises and threats—a society that undertakes to revise aims and values, leaves behind all ideological or spiritual homogeneity and takes possession of technical resources for a better mastery of nature and city life, with a population in explosion, restless and, for the most part, secularized.

It is thus a critically difficult situation for the church. A new stage in human history is opening up, and Christians, who are involved along with other men in the world revolution, are summoned by God to pay attention to the signs of the times. What is occurring in Latin America is part of a revolution of worldwide dimensions. It is the elevation of humanity to the technological age, the passage of mankind from a dependent status to a kind of maturity that leads it to sever its ties with metaphysical or religious guardianships. It is a time in which man is discovering the realities of history as essential to his being, and technical skill as a fit instrument with which to construct a more just and brotherly community life.

The church has had to learn about this circumstance through a crucial experience: the Cuban Revolution. Cuba's abrupt mutation into the socialist world took the church by surprise; it felt excluded from this new world and concluded that it had nothing to do with it. The church fell into the trap of defining its relations with society more by its attitude toward communism than according to the profound significance of the changes. From there to its present eclipse was only a single step; all the efforts that the church is now making to come out again into the light show how long and hard the process of recovery will be. The same can be said of the Protestant Church in that country. Church attendance is increasing and religious practice is deeper, and yet the general atmosphere seems to make of the church a place of quiet refuge for disenchantment.

The social change has sharpened the conflict between the generations in the church. The older wing remains closely bound to the old order, pronounces anathemas against the dangers of communism and minimizes the need for changing patterns and forms of life. The younger wing looks at the revolution and, without being in unanimous agreement, encourages Christians to take part in it as the most responsible way to witness today. Someone has spoken of the "ghetto church," which erects a wall around itself and rests on its splendid past, and the "dialogue church," open and communicative, present in the struggle that man may be more humane and may live in a more responsible community.

Pastors, theologians and laymen feel summoned today to a task of reflection that will lead the church to a renewal of the form and fashion of its presence. On the basis of biblical revelation, they see the Lordship of Christ not only in the community of believers, but in society and in history. They feel that the signs of the times move God's people as such—and not only its members as individuals—to live in a new Diaspora, a dispersion whose environment is the post-Christian world. On the frontier of the dispersion, the *koinonia*—unification in Word, Sacrament and the bond of life —lives in the midst of men, shares in their problems and hopes and with them weaves the fabric of history. It does so in the steps of Christ—in a life of service among men—and not in order to implant a program dropped from heaven. And, in the midst of men, the witness of Christ also includes keeping the whole human enterprise on a plane of relativity; on that level of the penultimate where Christians participate in the struggle for economic development and social justice as a preparation for the coming of Grace.

The ecumenical movement (involving Roman Catholicism more and more) is of great significance for the renewal of Christ's Church in Latin America. Theological faculties, study centers, "church and society" organizations, student and youth movements and laymen's institutes are enabling the church to appear in a new light and are making of the Christian faith not an article from the past but a living and efficacious reality for our times. These are signs of hope in the midst of perplexities and confusions.

In the mind and feelings of the people, the Latin American social revolution is like a second War of Independence that will lead to the creation of basic conditions for a true and concrete democracy. A growing drive to do away with old structures of exploitation, to create new patterns of life for the benefit of everybody, is under way. This is not an easy task; multiple obstacles and suffering still lie ahead, but the hope that a more just and human society can be established is stronger than ever. The Latin American man seems to have his future and that of his fellow worker in his own hands; he sees himself as the decisive force for bringing about a new order and a new purpose in life. For him, the only alternative is injustice, submission and nonbeing. If the constitutional means to achieve this aim are blocked for him, the revolution will have to resort to violence and civil war.

Along with that, there is a general dissatisfaction with the traditional ties between the great power to the north. Pan-Americanism intended as relations between unequal partners does not make any sense today when the republics from the south are coming of age and are determined to have their own voice in the international arena. This does not mean a breaking of relations between the two Americas but the recognition that a new system of communication should be worked out whereby, through mutual respect, both the United States and Latin America might develop the kind of society more akin to their peculiar ethos and values.

It has been said that Latin America is on the threshold of a new way of life by the assimilation of technical progress and social planning and the natural vocation of its people to human freedom. Here is a continent with a wealth of humanity and opportunities. The earth's treasures are provided in quantitative balance—neither too little nor too much—just enough, as Dr. Arnold Toynbee would say, to shut out easy answers and sharpen the intelligence. The Christian Church is called to provide men of heart and thought to join in this challenging but promising enterprise, because it is a struggle of people to free themselves from beliefs that cripple the human spirit, and a struggle where men dare to oppose unjust laws and crippling social barriers.

7

AFRICAN NATIONALISM:
THE AFTERMATH OF
COLONIALISM

by JOHN KAREFA-SMART (Sierra Leone)

WHEN Sir Winston Churchill made his "famous last words" re-
mark that he had not been appointed His Majesty's first minister
in order that he should preside over the dissolution of the British
Empire, little did he guess that in actual fact he would live to see
all of the territories under British colonial rule—except the small-
est dependencies in the Pacific—attain self-governing status, if not
complete independence.

The process of decolonization, which began at the end of the
Second World War with the granting of independence to India and
Pakistan, gained momentum in Asia, Africa and the Caribbean,
with the result that one new country after another was added to
the list of free, sovereign and independent states, thus qualifying
for membership in the United Nations. It was no longer possible
to hold back the forces of liberation, or to prevent the revolutionary
effects of what another British Prime Minister, Harold Macmillan,
so aptly described as "this wind of change."

The liberation struggle was nearly everywhere directed first toward the achievement of national political independence, yet political change was only one aspect of a three-sided revolution,
which had as its other aspects technological and social changes.

Dr. Kwame Nkrumah had this interrelated nature of the political, technical and social struggle in mind when he was tempted

to give the injunction to his followers—with apologies to the New Testament—"to seek first the political kingdom and all these things will be added." Since it was the necessity for economic exploitation of natural resources and raw materials which led to political domination by foreign powers, and which also resulted in deliberate retardation of social development, any change in each of these areas must have direct effects in the other areas as well.

The relationship between political independence and economic development must be emphasized. Although, in moments of crisis during the struggle for independence, a nationalist leader might proclaim that "it is better to be independent in poverty than to enjoy economic wealth under political subjugation," yet the underlying motive for wanting independence in most cases is to obtain the freedom of making decisions about the use of the resources of the nation for the benefit of its citizens instead of being forced to share these benefits according to the ideas of the foreign masters.

The mass of the people, in most cases, become involved in the struggle for political independence only because of the promise of rapid and tangible improvements in their private material circumstances. Existing conditions of poverty, illness and a generally low standard of living are blamed on the fact that the people are not free to organize their own national life and to exploit the resources of their country. At the same time, the much higher standard of living in the metropolitan country is explained by the economic exploitation of the colonial territories.

Independence thus becomes not a final goal but in effect only the beginning of a revolution aiming at transforming the whole previously colonial society. The leaders of the newly independent nations find themselves immediately confronted with the equally important need for revolutionary activity to achieve both technological progress and social development.

The objectives in the political sphere, following the birth of the new independent nation, may be listed as follows: to maintain the newly won independence; to frame a Constitution that would safeguard the highest goals for which the anticolonial struggle was carried on; to maintain democratic rights for all individuals and groups in the nation; to provide the machinery and the processes of good government; and to enable the free choice of the people to be expressed through an unrestricted exercise of their franchise under universal suffrage.

The danger of what has been loosely termed "neocolonialism" is very real. This embraces every attempt, overt or otherwise, to bring the new nation under some form or other of political attachment to the previous colonial rulers.

In addition to its political application, the concept of "neocolonialism" also includes all forms of economic relationship that place the newly independent nation in a position of dependence for the continued exploitation of its resources and for general economic development. Such neocolonialist economic power may arise through financial loans or through subsidiary industrial or commercial corporations, which, although they may be registered in the new nation and under its laws, are nevertheless owned and directed by a parent company in the previously metropolitan country.

Another important neocolonialist phenomenon is the creation of associations whose aim is to control the external market for the raw materials and natural and mineral resources of the former colony, which, at the same time, continues to be a ready-made market for the manufactured goods from the metropolitan country. Although some benefit will accrue to the newly independent state, the major financial and economic advantages lie with the controlling groups abroad.

It is only fair to note, however, that in some cases the neocolonialist slogan serves another purpose: namely, to divert attention from inefficient attempts by the leaders of the new nation to plan and to execute programs for the economic development of their country. It is convenient to find a scapegoat, and the old colonial masters are blamed for continuing economic ills and for internal political instability.

Most of the new nations have agreed that their first line of defense against neocolonialism is to adopt a policy of nonalignment with respect to the major power groupings of the former imperial countries and of neutrality in the struggle between the contending blocs.

The objectives of the technological revolution, although equally clear, are not so readily achieved on the basis of independence. The aim of this phase of the revolution is to bring all available knowledge and technics to bear on the problems of health, education and the profitable use of the natural environment, including both natural and human resources. There is almost always an overwhelming lack of the physical facilities through which knowledge and technics become available. High illiteracy rates among both adults and children are characteristic of colonial dependency.

The provision of educational facilities therefore tends to receive almost undisputed priority in the new nations. To give effect to this priority, however, is quite another matter. Not only do schools have to be built but enough teachers have to be found. As only those who have themselves been to school can teach, it soon becomes a serious problem to decide just where the major emphasis should be placed and the maximum of funds expended—on schools or on teacher-training.

The problem is further complicated in that the national technological objectives also depend for their achievement on the degree to which the available knowledge can be passed on to the whole population. The control and prevention of disease, the technics through which the land could be used to produce more and better food and the primary products required by industries and the economic use of local materials for providing such important physical necessities as good and healthy housing all require the communication of knowledge—usually through the written word.

Furthermore, none of these goals can be met without the expenditure of money. There is usually very little spare money available as savings in societies that have almost literally lived from hand to mouth during the colonial regimes. The only sources of capital for technological and social development are external. Often the very nations that have only recently relinquished political domination now become the only immediate source of assistance for further development.

Quite apart from the provision of capital for economic and technological development, the former imperial nations are also often the only source from which trained personnel can be made available for the planning and for the execution of development schemes and projects.

This double dependence on the nations, which, it is legitimately feared, might evolve a suspected neocolonialist relationship with the newly independent states, is one of the most important factors leading to instability in the post-colonial era. The new states are faced with the problem of how to achieve the goals to which they are dedicated in the post-colonial revolution and, at the same time, to safeguard their independence. The solution would be made considerably easier if the new nations could obtain the assistance they need, without mortgaging their nonalignment and their neutrality at the same time.

The problem is, however, only a part of the larger and more universal problem of the relationship between rich and poor nations, although it must be noted immediately that not all newly independent countries fall under the classification of poor nations, and that poverty may be, as in the case of Portugal, a reason for refusal to sever the colonial and imperialistic bond.

As long as some nations remain poor while others continue to increase in wealth, the tensions that threaten world peace will remain unrelaxed. The truism that a nation cannot long survive half slave and half free can be revised and applied in a world-wide context. Universal peace and security cannot be maintained as long as the world is half rich and half poor.

At the same time, however, efforts to put some of the accumulated wealth of the rich nations at the disposal of the poor nations will only lead to failure if they are not rid of the element of charity and if they appear to threaten the human dignity of the recipients of aid in the poor countries.

It is in this connection that the existence of the United Nations is regarded by all the new and developing nations as an absolute necessity. The dangers inherent in bilateral agreements for technical assistance (both for personnel and capital) can be minimized where these agreements are entered into on a multilateral basis, preferably through the United Nations.

Through several of the specialized agencies of the United Nations, considerable results have already been achieved, notably in the fields of the control of disease (World Health Organization), the improvement of agriculture (Food and Agricultural Organization), the development of programs of education at all levels (United Nations Educational, Scientific and Cultural Organization) and the betterment of the conditions of human labor (International Labor Organization).

The results of the past can be matched in the future if the United Nations succeeds in coping with the problems the new nations face in their efforts to transform their economics from being principally those of primary-material production to those of industrial production; from an entire dependence on the industrial nations and the prices they pay for primary products to mutual agreements that would take the interests of the developing countries into full consideration.

The continuing technological revolution in the developing countries, together with the struggle for power and for spheres of influence among the powerful, developed nations, will result in strains and tensions, which constantly threaten to produce physical conflict.

Is it not, therefore, in the best interests not only of the new nations but also of the developed nations that maximum efforts be made to bridge the economic gap as quickly as possible between the developing and the developed nations?

In the light of this urgent challenge, responsible Christian citizenship must urge a serious re-evaluation of the priorities that are currently given to such other uses of national resources as space projects and the development of nuclear weapons as well as conventional defense programs.

The wind of change that swept away colonialism could turn into a refreshing breeze bringing health to all the nations; or it might be fanned into a tempest if all human efforts are not directed urgently toward making the post-colonial era a period of reconciliation, of interdependence and sharing of resources and the enhancement of human dignity for all men.

8

ECONOMIC DEPENDENCE AND INDEPENDENCE — AS SEEN FROM SOUTHEAST ASIA

by A. C. Espiritu (Philippines)

In this second half of the twentieth century man can no longer depend for survival or progress on the traditional structure of nation-states. Not only is the small nation-state politically helpless without the protection of great power; but as an isolated unit it is no longer economically viable and must look to an economic union or regional grouping if it is to develop its economy and make its influence felt in world affairs. And man's needs and desires can no longer be fully satisfied within national boundaries. The fantastic world array of consumer products is fast producing a common mass taste and a universal mass demand. The advances in the technical and scientific fields have further emphasized the interdependence of the modern world.

However, the idea of international union or integrated economy is still far from realization. We still lack the necessary political and social skills. There does not yet exist, in the international context, that sense of solidarity which induces individuals and social groups to accept rules and regulations, some of which are not to their own immediate advantage. Greater internal integration is also needed before any political unit can participate fully in the building of one world.

Economic Dependence: Historical Roots

Because of the wealth of commodities within the region of Southeast Asia trade has always had a large influence in its historical development. Its links with the two big neighbors, India and China, were established over two thousand years ago. Until the end of the first century India traded mostly westward until the pattern shifted and Bengal ships began to make their way through the Malacca Straits to Sumatra and Borneo, and along the Malay Coast across the Siam Gulf to the southern coast of China. Moreover, India's midway position in the Indian Ocean gave her a strategic maritime advantage which was complemented by the spread of the Hindu and Buddhist religions, with their pervasive influence on the culture of the region.

After a slower start, China had developed, by the latter part of the second century, regular trading contacts with the Indianized city-states on the Gulf of Siam, which, before the Christian era, were already its vassals. Commercial exchanges were made at southern Chinese ports of entry, and successive tributary missions completed their leisurely journey to and from various Chinese courts. When the Imperial era was over and the Yang-tze lowlands had been assimilated, China's direct influence extended to the lands bordering the South China Sea; and in the meantime, commercial intercourse increased with all Southeast Asia, with India and Ceylon and with the Near East.

Though the influence of these two giants was to some extent checked by the arrival of Muslim merchants in the seventh century and by the religious impact of Islam, especially in Sumatra and Java and some parts of the Philippines, many of the greatest achievements in Southeast Asia, whether in the realm of art or of statecraft, were basically of Indian or Chinese inspiration.

The capture of the city of Malacca, at the peak of its commercial prosperity in the early sixteenth century, by a daring band of Portuguese explorers bent on seizing control of the fabulously profitable spice trade to Europe—followed by the Spanish entry into the Philippines and the Dutch control of Java as the hub of a vast trading operation from Persia to Japan—led to the region's sub-

jection to remorseless European rivalry. Trading supremacy fluc-
tuated; and, as that of the Dutch declined, British and French
hegemony was established in the Indo-Pacific Peninsula. The continued control of Vietnam, Cambodia and Laos by the French
constituted the only serious challenge to the commercial supremacy
established by the British at the end of the eighteenth century.

Thus, the countries of Southeast Asia became parts of different
imperial groupings under a western dominance, which, though relatively short-lived, brought deep changes to the region, transforming its political and economic life and forging new and powerful
ties with the major industrial centers of Europe and the United
States.

The achievement of independence after the Second World War
has not completely changed the colonial structure of the economies, since, within the former imperial spheres, "special economic
ties" have been forged and the lopsided pattern of these countries'
foreign trade has been largely maintained. Politically the trans-
formations in international power structures have made of independence little more than a system of alliances and collective
defense arrangements; and the sun-and-planet relationship, between
the United States and Britain on the one hand and the states of
Southeast Asia on the other, has become still further entrenched
since China fell to the Communists in 1949.

Political and Economic Instability

The current situation in Southeast Asia is one of political instability and economic stagnation, and the Asian peoples recognize that a long and difficult road lies ahead. During the struggle
for independence, the goal was clear-cut and identifiable. Today,
the problems are far more complex. Nationalist leaders who were
effective as instruments of protest against the colonial regimes
have proved less effective as instruments of progressive reform.

In the face of the chronic instability of much of the region, the
former imperial powers who now lead the free world feel almost
compelled to interfere in the internal affairs of some of these
countries. Thus, the desire to keep Vietnam safe from communist
invasion, Laos, Cambodia, Burma, Thailand and even the Philip-

pines from the threat of communist infiltration provides the continuing and natural justification for the system of alliances that
has grown up in the region. In spite of some grounds for hope
the present pattern of social and political development by no means
guarantees the eventual acceptance of democratic institutions. The
search for an appropriate political system is a perplexity that, in
varying degrees of urgency, confronts each nation. Liberal democracy, as practiced in the West, has not always been acceptable
Though some countries pay lip service to liberal political aspirations, their crucial need is for stability, however this may be
achieved politically.

There is little prospect that in their present situations, the coun
tries of Southeast Asia will achieve the modernization of their
economies to which they aspire. Their problem is aggravated by
the unbalanced structure of their economies, dependent as they
are on the western powers for an international market for their
exports, which are almost wholly agricultural. Economic aid has
only reinforced this dependence.

Foreign Aid and Economic Dependence

It is interesting to note that as a dispenser of foreign aid, the
United States has changed the character of its aid from emergenc
relief to long-term development. Strengthening the economies o
the underdeveloped countries has become, with defense build-up
a major purpose of American aid, because of the conviction tha
economic stability is the best defense against subversion.

But military aid, though it is imperative in emergency situation
such as Vietnam, is never really effective in building the founda
tions of a stable, viable economy. Pouring billions of dollars int
the Southeast Asian countries has not liberated them from the age
old problems of poverty and illiteracy. It is, moreover, almost im
possible for foreign aid planners to penetrate far enough into
country to make careful and adequate assessments of the socia
environment and of the apparatus of power. Consequently, muc
aid has fallen into the wrong hands and has not been widely share
by the masses of people or significantly used.

The magnitude of United States aid to East Asia ($3,500 mi

lion in 1964, a substantial portion of which went in military aid to Laos, South Vietnam and South Korea) is indeed impressive. But the tendency to evaluate aid in terms of magnitude, rather than in terms of its positive effects on economic growth, has made the benefits which accrue grossly incommensurate with the amount of funds expended. Foreign aid, whether direct or indirect, has done little to broaden the base of exports in the primary-export economies of Southeast Asia and has, in many instances, perpetuated the old structure of international trade. It has precluded the exporting countries from spreading their imports and exports equally over a large number of countries. Foreign aid is predicated, again, on the lack of external resources, especially capital, technicians and specialists. In fact, in assuming that capital is the missing element, foreign aid programs are doing precisely what colonialism did. Out of his experience as American ambassador to India, Kenneth Galbraith [1] affirms that economic aid cannot be effective unless instituted simultaneously with four other, noneconomic measures: an increase in the literacy rate and the improvement of a higher system of education; the adoption of social justice measures; the creation of an effective system of public administration; and the infusion of a clear and purposeful view of what development involves.

Since it is hardly possible for any country to give aid without increasing its influence over the recipient country, aid programs should be developed on lines that would preclude a further relationship of dependence and influence. There should be increasing provision for fellowships, scholarships and training grants to the nationals of the recipient countries. Some way, moreover, should be found to channel a larger share of foreign aid through the United Nations or its agencies, as has already been done, for example, through the Expanded Program for Technical Assistance (EPTA), the U. N. specialized agencies, the U. N. Special Fund, the World Fund Program and the U. N. Children's Fund (UNICEF). Such agencies as FAO, UNESCO, ILO, WHO, ICAO, ITU, IBRD, IMF, and IFC should all be utilized to minimize interference with national sovereignties.

---

[1] "A Positive Approach to Economic Aid," *Foreign Affairs*, April, 1961.

Increasing Regional Trade

Any increase in the regional trade of Southeast Asia (and of East Asia in general) would lessen dependence on the former colonial rulers. Fortunately, such trade is increasing. As a result of postwar American policy, Japan has re-emerged as a major competitor for the Southeast Asian markets. Its geographical location makes it a natural trading partner for the agricultural countries of the region. The hoped-for expansion of Indian trade with the region has not materialized, but Australia is increasingly active in Southeast Asia as a potential market for its manufactured goods. The economy of the Philippines is still closely tied to that of America; but, as these old trading links weaken and the Filipinos begin to solve their own problems, the accidents of history will take second place to the facts of geography. In fact, one might say that the recent attempts at regional economic groupings—the Association of Southeast Asia (ASA), constituted by the Philippines, Malaysia and Thailand, and the Maphilindo (Malaysia, Philippines, Indonesia)—are, in spite of congenital weakness, symbolic of future trends.

Foreign Trade as an Instrument of Power

In the final analysis, the most significant factor in the economic relations of states is to be found in the power structures that are established. As a result of economic inequalities and the differences in stages of development between countries, and also because of the differences in the extent to which they need each other's products, foreign trade becomes an instrument of national power. Take, for instance, relations between the Philippines and the United States. The Philippine Trade Act of 1946, as amended by the Laurel-Langley Agreement, provided for a transition period of twenty-eight years before the final termination of the special trade relations between the two countries, on the assumption that Philippine traditional exports—copra, sugar, abaca, minerals, tobacco— would require such a period to prepare for the eventual loss of a protected position in the American market and at the same time the Philippines could establish a viable, independent economy.

But the United States imposed a condition which required the Philippines to confer equal rights on American citizens to exploit the natural resources of the Philippines and to operate public utilities in the country—privileges reserved under the Philippine Constitution to its nationals. In addition, through the Philippine Rehabilitation Act of 1946, the United States Congress made Philippine acceptance of the parity condition for Americans, and the corresponding amendment of the Constitution to that effect, a condition of payment of war damage claims.

The Philippine Trade Act of 1946 did not, however, fulfill the expectations of independent economy, and in fact it made it difficult for the Philippine economy to wean itself from dependence on the American market. There is increasing pressure in the Philippines for parity to be scrapped from the constitutional and treaty commitments of the Philippines, and for the treaty to be allowed to lapse after 1967.

Philippine-American economic relations also illustrate the problems of trade adjustment, when trade relations are not equal. The effect of American economic policy toward the Philippines having been to encourage Philippine overspecialization in a few agricultural exports, among them sugar, the Philippine economy would be seriously dislocated if it suddenly found its sugar exports cut off from the American market. The American economy, on the other hand, could cut off its preferential treatment for Philippine sugar without any disadvantageous effect on itself.

Marshall, the great English economist, was fully aware of this aspect of trade. The rich country, he said, can with little effort supply a poor country with implements for agriculture which she could not make for herself; and the rich country could, without much trouble, produce for herself most of the things that she purchased from the poor nation, or, at all events, could get fairly good substitutes for them. A stoppage of the trade would therefore generally cause much more real loss to the poor than to the rich nation. Moreover, in the classical pattern of colonial relations, "influence" derives from the fact that the trade conducted is critically essential to the underdeveloped country, which therefore grants the former colonial power certain advantages—military, political, economic.

The Struggle for Self-Sustaining Growth

Underdevelopment is the key reality in Southeast Asia. Though, for the moment, in countries like Indonesia and Vietnam basic political issues take precedence, in the long run the vital need is to infuse the economies of the whole region with such a dynamic upward thrust that they will be enabled to take off to self-sustaining economic growth, free from violent swings in foreign exchange and from fluctuations in international markets. Underdeveloped societies have not experienced growth as a built-in, self-sustaining economic process over long periods. Sporadic outbursts of growth and the occasional achievement of great peaks of productivity have been countered by long stationary periods.

Except in Malaysia and to some extent the Philippines, both the momentum of economic growth and the enthusiasm of political leaders for its acceleration have waned. Whereas elsewhere great strides have been made in the 1960's toward doubling national incomes, Southeast Asia shows, by and large, unimpressive rates of economic growth, which have, in any event, been cancelled out by growth in population.

Apart from the need to avoid dependence on former colonial rulers, it is important to achieve economic development on all fronts. Such development demands social, psychological and political changes that are preconditions for the process of economic modernization and also its consequences.

It has been discovered that economic growth is directly related to the existence of an elite entrepreneurial class. The achievement of higher rates of growth seems to depend on the successful activity of some group in society which is prepared to accept innovations. Thus, we are faced with the psychological problem of generating in enough people the motivations, creativity and purposeful sense of innovation required for growth, and at the same time with the economic problems of investing sufficient resources in human capital and of training enough people in public administration and in the managerial and technical skills to operate a modern economy.

It is generally accepted that in most of Southeast Asia, the governments must take the initiative in economic development But then comes the problem of creating adequate machinery for government-controlled development, since the managerial skills and the sense of efficient and dedicated public service demanded are precisely the qualities that are lacking in public administration in Southeast Asia.

It is fortunate for the underdeveloped countries that they can bypass the trial-and-error period: the clear lessons of waste and error in the economic history of Britain and other countries of western Europe are there for the learning. Moreover, recent experience seems to suggest that modernization is proceeding more by a process of adapting resources, techniques and institutions from the industrialized societies than by innovation. But the overall problem is that of accomplishing in one generation the social, psychological and economic changes that took many decades and even centuries in the western world and of generating, both in the political leadership of Southeast Asia and in the general population, the genuine determination and purpose that are all too often lacking.

The undue concern of Southeast Asia, leaders and people alike, for politics, when the basic issue is beyond all doubt the economic one of liberating people from poverty, is a decisive problem in itself. How are the people to be provided against hunger when they are themselves unwilling to tread with single-minded direction the path to progress? Nor does the problem end there. We can make no progress unless the people learn the most fundamental lesson of all: to sacrifice short-term gains for long-term goals; to create a disciplined society in which everyone, whether in the public service or in private life, is willing to refrain from scrambling for his own advantage, disregarding the welfare of the nation as a whole. The tragedy in the Philippines, which finds a parellel in other countries in the region, especially in Vietnam, is the fragmentation of society into cliques and factions and groups, each seeking to cut the other to pieces and to identify its own narrow motives with the national interest.

Foreign Capital and Economic Independence

W. W. Rostow points out [2] that both Britain and Japan achieved economic maturity without the assistance of foreign capital and that actually, the loanable funds required to finance a country's take-off to self-sustaining growth have generally come from two domestic sources: the shifts in the control of income-flows, including income-distribution; and the ploughing back of profits in rapidly expanding sectors, including that of exports. But foreign loans and investments can help to make good the lack of necessary capital and foreign exchange.[3]

However, attitudes to foreign investment vary as people become aware that their economy is not entirely under the control of nationals. At one extreme, Malaysia is hospitable to foreign capital and has in fact advocated for the countries of Southeast Asia an international charter to regulate the treatment of foreign private investments to be drawn up with the help of the United Nations and in consultation with the U. N.[4] But Malaysia's attitude is explained by the remarkable production and prosperity achieved during the short period of British occupancy of the peninsula. Though the modernization of the economy has been accomplished at the price of British control of a very high proportion of the total tin and rubber production, Malaysia has by far the highest income per capita of any nation in Southeast Asia after Japan.

Though the Philippines, on the other hand, imbibed great political and liberal ideas under the American occupation, it did not get the benefit of an enlightened economic policy. Nor did it achieve the increase in per capita national income achieved by Malaysia, and its foreign trade, communications, banking system, mining industry have all been mainly in the hands of foreigners.

The awakening has, however, come, and Philippine policy on foreign investments now revolves around two mutually antagonistic objectives: a faster rate of economic growth and greater Filipino

---

[2] *Stages of Economic Growth.* Cambridge University Press, 1960.

[3] See, e.g., United Nations, VII, *Economic Bulletin for Asia and the Far East* (No. 1), 1957.

[4] See ECAFE, Annual Report to the Economic Social Council, 1957–58, United Nations Economic Social Council, Official Records: 26th Session, Supplement No. 2.

control of critical areas of the economy. The simultaneous pursuit of both goals often results in tensions that slow down the process of growth. In the Philippines, moreover, there is a tension between the legitimate desire to attract foreign investments and the valid fear that they may dislodge Philippine investments on their own home ground. There is a persistent pressure for industrial development to be promoted only under conditions which give Filipinos the main control and the country the primary benefits of its own economic progress. The policy is therefore to discourage foreign investments in the form of branches of wholly foreign-owned subsidiaries and to expect substantial participation by Philippine nationals, particularly in those ventures concerned with basic industries and the exploitation of natural resources.

The nationalistic impulse involving hostility toward foreign investments has been most clearly manifest in Indonesia and Burma. In Indonesia the Economic Declaration of March 30, 1963, declares that

... the basic strategy of Indonesia cannot be separated from the general strategy of the Indonesian Revolution. According to its basic economic strategy Indonesia, during the first stage, is to build a national and democratic economy, free from the remainders of imperialism and feudalism. The first stage is a preparation which ushers in the second stage, namely, an Indonesian Socialist economy, an economy without the exploitation of man by man.

But the Indonesian economy is only now completing the first stage. "Our duty in the economic field at this first stage," the Declaration states, "is to wipe out the remainders of imperialism and feudalism in the economic field; activate all national potentials as an effort to lay the foundation of a national economy and stimulate its growth, which will be free from imperialism and feudalism and which will become the basis for the creation of an Indonesian Socialist community."

In Indonesia, though foreign investment is officially equated with colonialism, many businessmen and professionals are hungering for increased foreign trade, foreign investments and joint ventures; and there is a growing feeling, privately shared even by many government leaders and, ironically enough, encouraged by overly rigid governmental restrictions, that foreign investments are not entirely identical with colonialism and that a planned and well-directed introduction of capital is urgently required. But the trend is toward greater government restriction on foreign investments, and crises over such questions as the government's share in the profits of the three oil subsidiaries, Caltex, Stanvac and Shell, continuously arise. Moreover, Indonesia's withdrawal from the United Nations may even more significantly affect her attitude toward foreign investments.

How much further nationalism and political ends should be pursued at the expense of economic development is the crux of the Indonesia problem. The economy is in a condition of static equilibrium, and it does not look like moving ahead significantly in the foreseeable future. By any standard nothing seems more pressing in the lifetime of this generation than to lay the foundations for initiating a self-sustaining growth. And yet Indonesian leaders are compelled to erase every vestige of western dominance and to create a sense of national purpose.

Nationalism can be turned in different directions. In the main, however, it has taken two definite forms in Southeast Asia: (1) a fierce pride in asserting national sovereignty, accompanied in some instances by an extreme reaction against vestiges of western influence and a loosening of economic ties with the West; and (2) a desire to transfer to indigenous hands the productive assets of the country, which were formerly largely held by aliens, including affluent Chinese and Indian immigrants.

Nationalism and the Idea of Complete Independence

Nationalist feeling is essential both for the development of a sense of national community in young and rising nations and for their drive toward economic maturity. It can be turned outward to remove past injustices suffered under colonialism or to exploit opportunities for national aggrandizement, once the industrializing economy develops sufficient momentum. It is nationalism that provides the social force to unleash individual initiative, creativity and organizational skill for the task of economic, social and political modernization which the old feudal structure had obstructed, in some instances in collusion with the former colonial powers.

In a sense, nationalism is simply a matter of self-assertion and self-affirmation. In this sense it is both natural and necessary. But it is always in danger of distortion and of being made the supreme goal of every activity. The moment nationalism thus becomes an end in itself instead of a means to achieve greater opportunities for development, it leads to destruction.

The dilemma of many Christians in these countries is acute and not easily resolved. Many of them feel that the reawakened national feelings are part of God's plan and that it is only just, in this century of enlightened perspectives, that the people of every nation should shape their own ideals, draw up their own political structures and symbols, manage their own foreign policy and assume primary responsibility for the modernization of their economy. But there is also an obvious need to moderate the more destructive aspects of the change-over, not the least of which is the growth of intolerance, prejudice and hostility.

Nationalism is a reality, and the clamor for a more effective exercise of nationhood has become insistent and compelling. But can there be complete freedom in the context of new developments in power structures and of the reality of Chinese expansionism? Countries that are too small to be militarily self-reliant or economically viable cannot assume that complete freedom comes as a result of liberation from western domination. Indeed, the dominant scene in Southeast Asia is that of countries living under the shadow of China, the colossus of the North, whose influence over the area is now turning full circle and may, in the long run, prove to be more significant and lasting than that of the West.

Structure of World Trade

Southeast Asia's economic dependence has been to some extent perpetuated by the steadily increasing inequalities between developed and underdeveloped countries, a pattern that can be changed only by a structure of trade that reverses the economic trends and insures the poorer countries a share of the world market. They depend almost entirely on a narrow base of primary exports for which the demand is often inelastic and where excessive price fluctuations upset producer expectations. There is also the danger that the decline in commodity prices is becoming a permanent trend. Tied as they are, economically, to their international trade, the underdeveloped countries must boost their trade if they are to achieve higher rates of growth.

One solution might be to fix minimum commodity prices in the world market at approximately the present level, though even this may not be enough. There is much significance in the new concept of aid tied to trade that was propounded by the underdeveloped countries at the U. N. Conference on Trade and Development (UNCTAD) in 1964 (to guarantee the purchasing power of the exports of primary commodities).

It is also encouraging that UNCTAD was able to set up a new organization for the promotion of international trade (The Trade and Development Board, established as an organ of the United Nations General Assembly)—even if only with the grudging consent of the developed countries and in the face of a lack of genuine concern on the part of the industrial powers, including Japan. Paul Prebisch, secretary-general of UNCTAD, put the case succinctly:

Many developing countries bear the deep imprint of thousands of years of civilization. They could do much to ensure that, in our efforts to control economic forces, we do not subordinate man to the demands of technology or purely economic process, but enable him to free himself from economic need, from poverty, and from his inherent ills, so that he may improve his life and achieve that full existence which, in the developing countries, has until now been traditionally enjoyed only by a few.

Conclusion

In spite of the inevitability—and indeed the growing reality —of interdependence of peoples and nations, our world is still plagued by the fact of so much plenty in some areas and so much want in others. The strong and rich nations do not easily comprehend their responsibility and they are constantly tempted to use power without discipline, as we can see in the perpetuation of conditions of dependence in the economic field and of unfair trade relations. Foreign aid to underdeveloped countries is too often regarded as a painful necessity, given in order to keep these countries out of the communist camp!

Notwithstanding the obvious difficulties involved in reconciling outside assistance with the understandable pride of newly independent states, it should not be impossible to provide them with a measure of strength in their struggle for economic progress without depriving them of the effective exercise of their nationhood. Southeast Asia needs, above all else, a reasonable space of time within which to work out its own solutions to the vexing problems of increasing the living standards of its people.

The Southeast Asian peoples are striving to modernize their societies in the full exercise of nationhood, freed as much as possible from the constraints and limitations of dependent relations with the former colonial powers. Western responsibility must see them not as objects of exploitation but as a people for whom the strong bear some burdens not only because every man's suffering is a concern from which there is no escape, but because these people have already suffered for centuries from the injustices of colonial relations.

No task can be more exciting in the interdependent world in which we live than that of closing the gap between rich and poor. But nothing can be more difficult. And yet this is our ultimate responsibility.

9

THE ROMAN CATHOLIC CHURCH AND ECONOMIC PLANNING—AT THE NATIONAL AND INTERNATIONAL LEVEL

by ABBÉ FRANÇOIS HOUTART
AND A. DELOBELLE (Belgium)

The Question of Economic Planning in the Roman Catholic Church

QUESTIONS concerning planning and underdevelopment have only recently been included in the social teaching of the Roman Catholic Church (not at all until the last years of Pius XII, and not substantially until the great encyclicals of John XXIII). Earlier similar concerns were formulated in quite different terms, more closely related to the politico-social structures that existed before 1960.

Within the general setting of the papal doctrine of social justice, we find the first indications of a planned national economic policy in the analyses of the principle of "the fair wage" and of the type of economic order that it requires, in the analyses of an international economic policy, and also in the documents concerning the obligations of the colonizing countries toward the colonized. Admittedly the problems of planning and of mutual aid at the international level still seem to be of secondary importance. But these documents do contain a complete doctrine of economic relationships in national or international life. The problems of the national economy are already examined in the light of technical considerations, whereas the sphere of international economic relations is dealt with only at the level of first principles.

This situation is the sociological outcome of the strong ties that still existed at that time between the Roman Catholic Church and the western world, especially Europe. The economic and social questions dealt with by the Popes were essentially questions which arose out of the industrial societies of the West, with their own particular social pathology and their own characteristics. The economic and social problems in the rest of the world were usually dealt with from the viewpoint of western experience, and the ethical principles applied to them were extensions of the principles applied in the West. Consequently, Roman Catholic social doctrine was primarily derived from the Christian analysis of the position of the wage earners in Europe, and touched only indirectly, when political reports were drawn up by the European colonists, upon what is today called the problem of underdevelopment in other continents. The attention of the Popes seems to have been drawn to this question in the first place in connection with the problem of the indigenous clergy. The question came up again after the Second World War when the former colonial countries in Asia became independent because the ecclesiastical structures had to be separated from the political and economic structures imposed by the colonizing countries.[1]

It was on the occasion of the encyclical *Evangelii praecones,* published on June 2, 1950, by Pope Pius XII, that concern for the underdeveloped countries was clearly expressed for the first time. But it was in his encyclical *Fidei donum* of April 21, 1957, that Pius XII definitely and explicitly introduced this question into his teaching. He reverted to it several times in his public addresses.[2] It was Pope John XXIII, however, who brought a new

---

[1] Older papal documents could be quoted, however, concerning the slave trade and the liberation of slaves.

[2] See J. Y. CALVEZ and J. PERRIN: *Eglise et société économique. L'enseignement social des Papes de Léon XIII à Pie XII* (1878–1958). Paris: Aubier, 2nd edition revised and corrected, 1961, pp. 139–140.

light to bear on the problem in his encyclicals *Mater et Magistra*
and *Pacem in Terris,* though the space specifically devoted to underdevelopment is still relatively small and the principles are set
forth largely from a western point of view. It is mainly due to the
spirit that inspires these two encyclicals that the social doctrine
about underdevelopment has been, as it were, renewed and given
a fresh start within the Roman Catholic Church. Since then an
increasing number of the pastoral letters written by the different
conferences of bishops in the underdeveloped countries have taken
up the problem and examined it in relation to their various national
settings.[3]

Although the theme of underdevelopment has thus been included
in the social teaching of the Popes its importance has been greatly
strengthened by the changes that are now taking place within the
Roman Catholic Church as a general consequence of the spirit of
the Second Vatican Council, and especially of the presence at it
of many bishops from underdeveloped countries. Consequently the
approach of our church to the world can no longer be solely from
the West, but will be far more universal in outlook. A social
process is going on within the Roman Catholic Church parallel
with the process of decolonization in the political world. It expresses at the summit a movement which has been taking place
for a long time at the local level, through the creation of indigenous
bishops and clergy in the young churches.

On the one hand, therefore, we have a clearly defined doctrine
concerning the economic relationships and the social life within the
countries based on the pattern of the industrialized countries of the
West. On the other hand, we have the first judgments and the expression of certain principles concerning international economic
relations and the specific social problems of the underdeveloped
countries themselves. In order to be understood, the attitude of the
Roman Catholic Church to problems of national or international
economic planning must be seen from this sociological, dynamic
and historical point of view. This means that, where possible, many
problems should be treated by analogy with the situations described

---

[3] See Father HOUTART and A. DELOBELLE: "Doctrine sociale de l'Eglise
catholique romaine et les problèmes du sous-développement" in *Background
Information,* WCC, Geneva, June/July, 1964.

in the existing papal documents. But this social doctrine also benefits from the current thinking in the church; many of the documents written by bishops contain preliminary answers, which await the papal sanction. In addition to the teaching of the bishops, the Vatican Council and the Pope, the analytical work undertaken by Roman Catholic experts—clergy or laymen——must be taken into account. Although their conclusions do not enjoy the same authority as pronouncements by the hierarchy, they constitute a basic element of the church's social doctrine, as a part of the dynamic whole in which the authority of the church, the clergy and the laity all have their place.

The Doctrinal Point of View and Planning

In order to simplify the statement of principles, we shall distinguish between the two fields to which they are applied: the national and the international. Although the points of approach remain the same as far as principles are concerned, the ways in which they are discussed and presented are different.

A. *The State and National Economic Planning.* National economic planning is joint action, undertaken at different levels and under different names, drawn up by the public authorities and carried out under their supervision, general or direct, with a view to improving the economic and social development of an area or of a whole country. The church has not hitherto directly stated its position with regard to planning and methods of planning; but through the Popes it has stipulated certain conditions and ethical rules that should be observed by the public authorities of all states when carrying out their tasks. These rules, which are inspired by a basic personalism, were laid down in a general way as they applied to states with a liberal or democratic structure, but they also apply to states whose structure is more authoritarian. And whatever the political structure of the country, they remain fundamentally valid for all types of economic planning, from the most rigid systems to the most flexible. The Roman Catholic Church has formulated the rule of subsidiarity (of which we shall speak later) as a fundamental principle which applies to them all.

1. *Conditions for action by the public authorities*

a. *Respect for the common good:* The acts prescribed by the authorities must be

formally perfect, the content ... must be morally good, or at least capable of being directed towards good. Indeed, since the whole reason for the existence of civil authorities is the realization of the common good, it is clearly necessary that, in pursuing this objective, they should respect its essential elements, and at the same time conform their laws to the needs of a given historical situation.[4]

This general rule also applies both to the public authorities and to all the physical or juridical persons of which society is composed, who are engaged in political, economic or any other form of action. "All individual citizens and intermediate groups are under an obligation to make their specific contributions to the common welfare." [5]

It is also made clear that the common good, which is the common goal of the action of the individual, the social organization and the state, "embraces the sum total of those conditions of social living whereby men are enabled to achieve their own integral perfection more fully and more easily." [6] The social encyclicals of the previous Popes from Leo XII to Pius XII had frequently defined these conditions of social living, and how they should be envisaged from the economic point of view.[7]

b. *Principle of subsidiarity:* In actual fact these general principles draw attention to certain stipulations according to whether one is in a developed or an underdeveloped country. Obviously, in the latter the public authorities have a primary role to play in implanting a modern type of economy, especially in the initial phases. In some of the least favored countries, there is nothing between a few political, social or economic leaders on the one hand and the illiterate masses still living in an independent economy on the

---

[4] Encyclical Letter *Pacem in Terris of* POPE JOHN XXIII. Vatican: Polyglot Press, 1963, p. 17.

[5] *Ibid.,* p. 17.

[6] Encyclical Letter *Mater et Magistra* of POPE JOHN XXIII, quoted in *Pacem in Terris,* p. 18.

[7] See J. Y. CALVEZ and J. PERRIN: *op. cit.*

other. Between these two levels hardly any social groups exist at all. Owing to this absence of specialized intermediary organizations, and to the rudimentary organization of the leaders and the *elite*, all the problems, whether social or economic, assume a political hue. In most of the underdeveloped countries, therefore, even when the internal structures are more developed, the state exercises an indispensable function in regard to initiative and organization.

None of the papal documents has hitherto dealt directly with the problem, although some of the episcopal letters refer specifically to the necessity for the public authorities to take the initiative in certain spheres, especially with regard to agrarian reforms.[8] However, in the teaching of the Popes a general rule is found for these matters in which the initiative of the state is dominant; this is the principle of *subsidiarity*. It was affirmed by Pius XI in *Quadragesimo Anno* (1931) and was stressed again by John XXIII in *Mater et Magistra*.

Although the public authorities have at their disposal methods and instruments that are being increasingly perfected to reduce the economic discrepancies between the different areas of a country, or between different sectors of economic or social life, they are still subject to the rights of the individual.

But the principle must always be reaffirmed that the presence of the State in the economic field, no mater how widespread and penetrating, must not be exercised so as to reduce evermore the sphere of freedom of the personal initiative of individual citizens, but rather so as to guarantee in that sphere the greatest possible scope by the effective protection for each and all, of the essential personal rights; among which is to be numbered the right that individual persons possess of being always primarily responsible for their own upkeep and that of their own family.[9]

In this the Pope fully recognizes the right of the public authorities to take the initiative in the economic field, and to move on to planned development. The important point, in these matters, is not to confuse the end with the means.

---

[8] See, for instance, for Latin America, the documents published by the Bishops in Venezuela, Sept. 16, 1960; in Chile, Sept. 18, 1962; in Paraguay, April 28, 1963, and in Brazil, April 30, 1963.

[9] *Mater et Magistra*, p. 14.

c. *The phenomenon of socialization:* The Popes have been dealing with this phenomenon for a long time, but it was John XXIII who drew attention to it by giving it a special name. By "socialization" he means: "A progressive multiplication of relations in society with different forms of life and activity, and juridical institutionalization." [10] This is a specific feature of socioeconomic development, and the Pope points out that the public authorities side by side with private initiative play an important role in extending it. He recognizes the many social and economic advantages of this assumption by the growing number of organizations in public life. But at the same time the Pope asks that the individual should not be crushed beneath their weight, and that these "intermediary bodies" should enjoy "effective autonomy" in face of the public authorities, so that they can "pursue their own specific interests in loyal collaboration between themselves, subordinate, however, to the demands of the common good." [11]

Such principles are clearly important in evaluating forms of planning in the underdeveloped countries. However, they describe the situation in countries which already enjoy a certain level of development, and in which private initiative is beginning to operate.

2. *Functions of the public authorities*

In his social encyclicals John XXIII also draws attention to the aims of action by the public authorities. The first of these aims corresponds to the primary function of protecting the individual, which is still valid today, but which formerly constituted the essential task of the state. The second aim, the promotion of the person, corresponds to the modern concepts of the state's economic and social role. It is important to affirm this dual function, in order to evaluate the forms of economic planning.

a. *Reconciliation and protection of rights and duties of individuals:*

One of the fundamental duties of civil authorities, therefore, is to coordinate social relations in such fashion that the exercise of one man's rights does not threaten others in the exercise of their own rights

---

[10] *Ibid.,* p. 14.
[11] *Ibid.,* p. 16.

nor hinder them in the fulfilment of their duties. Finally, the rights of all should be effectively safeguarded and, if they have been violated, completely restored.[12]

b. *Duty of promoting the rights of individuals:*

It is also demanded by the common good that civil authorities should make earnest efforts to bring about a situation in which individual citizens can easily exercise their rights and fulfil their duties as well. For experience has taught us that, unless these authorities take suitable action with regard to economic, political and cultural matters, inequalities between the citizens tend to become more and more widespread ... and as a result human rights are rendered totally ineffective, and the fulfilment of duties is compromised.[13]

In this connection the Pope emphasizes that the public authorities have an obligation to concern themselves with the social and economic conditions in their sphere. On this point he mentions the substructure (roads and communications, drinking-water, housing, hospitals, schools, churches, leisure), the insurance systems, all the services which deal with employment (recruitment of workers, fair wages, coresponsibility in enterprises, associations of all kinds connected with work) and cultural services.

3. *Conclusions at the national level*

Although the basic principles for the general evaluation of systems of economic planning can be found in the social teaching of the Popes, we lack certain details required for their application to the developing countries.

We have already shown the extent to which this social doctrine is still largely dominated by the example of the countries in the industrial West. But even so, many of these statements have a certain relevance to the underdeveloped countries, because of their preference for crafts or home industries rather than for gigantic enterprises. However, the papal documents do not always recognize the difference in economic utility between the two, nor the possibility of forming human groupings within such great combines

---

12 *Pacem in Terris,* p. 18.
13 *Ibid.,* p. 19.

—a development that tends to restore to these latter their human dimension. But on this point, if a certain confusion still exists, there are a large number of papal documents which express support for co-management and the transformation of the enterprises and social organizations into associations of responsible collaborators.

There remain, however, certain problems that have been directly tackled by the leaders in the underdeveloped countries, and that have not yet been officially or adequately dealt with by the doctrinal authority of the Roman Catholic Church. Among these are the questions of the concentration of landed property, of the population explosion and of the control of capital and its utilization for the benefit of the country.

B. *The State and International Economic Relations*. The mutual obligation of states to respect one another constitutes an ancient principle in the political doctrine of the Roman Catholic Church, because all men are linked by their common origin, nature and destiny. Moreover, just as a "common good" exists at the national level, so it also exists at the international level. It is a basic principle of social doctrine that the good things of this world are intended for everyone. This approach opens the way to international planning.

One of the consequences of this last principle is precisely that individual economic advantages are subordinated to the common good of the political communities.

These two principles (the community of nations and the fact that the wealth of this world is intended for all men) give rise to two rights: first, the right for people and goods to circulate freely (in the past this has been used to justify certain forms of colonization, on the pretext that political protection and security must be ensured for people and goods); and, second, the duty of the developed countries to aid those which are still underdeveloped. Thus, the universal utilization of wealth which indirectly justified the colonization of certain countries (still incapable of exploiting their own natural wealth) forces the rich countries in a much stricter and more general way to help the poor ones.

This doctrine (that the wealth created by God for all men must be equitably available to all, in accordance with the principles of justice and charity), while recognizing that everyone has the right of access to the wealth of the earth, also establishes an equally natural right in international relations—the right to social justice which makes it incumbent upon the more fortunate peoples to help the less fortunate countries. Consequently adequate study of the relations between population-density and means of subsistence must be developed on a world-wide scale, and the problem which it involves can only be solved on the same plane, in the solidarity which operates between all peoples. So that when the artificial barriers which divide them are removed, a more systematic movement of peoples, capital and material wealth may be organized.[14]

Thus, although in the past, when no high international authority existed, the church accepted certain rights of interference by particular states in developing the wealth of underdeveloped countries (without actually going so far as to affirm the right to colonization) its main concern was to formulate the duties of the colonizers toward the colonized countries. These duties included respect for the indigenous culture, since the fact that all men are linked by a common origin, nature and destiny does not mean that anyone has the right to impose cultural uniformity. There is also an obligation to pay fair salaries, by adapting to local conditions the legislation passed in the western countries. Lastly, there is the right of the underdeveloped countries to aspire to independence and the duty of the colonizing states to prepare them for it, in accordance with the general welfare, at the international level.

This social doctrine, inspired by the political supremacy of the West (especially of western Europe) over the rest of the world, remains valid in its basic principles, even after the process of decolonization and the radical transformation of the political scene since the Second World War.

Something far more important than a change of vocabulary is involved. Behind the basic principles, which remain the same, a vast development is taking place in the social doctrine of the church in relation to the specific problem of underdevelopment. The Vatican Council's schema on the relations between the church and the world have a special section on this question.

---

14 MGR MONTINI, at the social week in Palermo. Quoted in G. BLARDONE, P. CATRICE, J. FOLLIET, G. MATAGRIN, R. PADIRAC, R. VOOG: *Initiation aux problèmes d'outre-mer. Colonisation, décolonisation, sous-développement.* Lyons: Editions de la Chronique sociale de France, p. 259.

Indeed, although the process of political decolonization is almost complete, the economic decolonization of the ex-colonial areas, and especially the radical readjustment of international commerce (in which the influence of western domination is still very strong), are still far from realization. And it is within this context that one can envisage the social thinking of the church taking shape in connection with international economic aid. Just as the church refused to leave the fixing of wages to the free play of supply and demand on the market, so today the church cannot agree to fix the remuneration of the poor peoples in the world simply through the mechanism of an anonymous market. Some of the Popes' previous statements have already been largely on these lines. In *Quadragesimo Anno* Pius XI wrote: "The free play of competition cannot be expected to bring about a well-organized economic régime." [15] Just as the employer has a moral responsibility to fix a fair wage that covers the social needs of the workers, the states that control international commerce have strict moral obligations toward the poorer countries, including the duty to remunerate them adequately so as to ensure their social development.

The doctrinal statements which have already been made by the church, especially by John XXIII, relate essentially to the conditions for, and certain aims of, external aid.

1. Conditions for external aid

The encyclicals draw attention to four conditions which should be borne in mind by the more-developed countries, when helping the less-developed:

a. *Concern for full development:* Here John XXIII was especially anxious that certain errors committed in the past be avoided, since they had been fraught with serious consequences that influenced the social development of the more developed countries for a very long time. The states must be concerned both about economic and about social development, since the one cannot exist without the other. The process of development must be both harmonious and gradual—a fact that must be borne in mind in the process of development. It will simultaneously affect every sector

---

[15] Quoted by J. Y. CALVEZ and J. PERRIN: *op. cit.,* p. 385.

of economic life: primary, secondary or tertiary. It must produce an equitable distribution of wealth.[16]

b. *Disinterested work:* The bigger temptation with which the economically developed communities have to struggle is that of profiting from their technical and financial cooperation so as to influence the political situation of the less developed countries with a view to bringing about plans of world domination. It is, therefore, indispensable and corresponds to the need of justice that the above mentioned technical and financial aid be given in sincere political disinterestedness.[17]

Otherwise this would be tantamount to neocolonialism and would strike an irreparable blow to the formation of a world community "in which each member, whilst conscious of its own individual right and duties, will work in a relationship of equality towards the attainment of the universal common good." [18] John XXIII attached so much importance to this point of view, and to the need to avoid forms of aid which would be counter to it, that he reverted to it over and over again: "It is vitally important, therefore, that the wealthier States, in providing varied forms of assistance to the poorer, should ... avoid any intention of political domination." [19] The peoples must be "conscious of their own duties and rights, working on a basis of equality for the bringing about of the universal common good." [20] This is a clear reminder, at the international level, of the principle of subsidiarity already stressed at the national level.

c. *Respect for the characteristics of the individual communities:* Respect for others must be observed in international relations, as much as in relations between individuals. That is an old principle which has already been affirmed many times, especially in connection with the relations between colonizers and colonized peoples. The new vocabulary is transposed in view of the new context: "The political communities on the way toward economic development generally present their own unmistakable individuality, due either to their resources and the specific character of their own

[16] *Mater et Magistra,* p. 38.
[17] *Ibid.,* p. 39.
[18] *Pacem in Terris,* p. 31.
[19] *Ibid.*
[20] *Mater et Magistra,* p. 39.

natural environment, or due to their traditions frequently abounding in human values, or due to the typical quality of their own members." [21] Every people is called upon to make its own special contribution to the world society that is coming to birth. Its own special values must therefore be respected and not destroyed by borrowing from other peoples (whether under compulsion or not).

d. *Respect for the hierarchy of values:* In the process and policies of raising the standard of living by means of economic development or scientific and technical progress, it must be remembered that "scientific and technical progress . . . are not . . . the supreme values . . . but are essentially instrumental in character." [22]

On this point the Pope condemns the neglect, or negation, of spiritual values in the most developed countries, and the way in which these values are sacrificed to scientific, technical and economic factors or to material wealth: "This constitutes an insidious poison, and one of the most dangerous, in the help which the economically developed peoples can give to those on the way to development: people in whom ancient tradition has quite often preserved a living and operating consciousness of some of the most important human values." [23] John XXIII has no hesitation in saying, "to undermine this consciousness is essentially immoral." [24]

2. *Functions of external aid*

On this point the Pope draws a distinction between long-term and short-term objectives and problems.

a. *Short-term aid:* This refers essentially to needs that require urgent assistance, and John XXIII is thinking primarily of the chronic famines in the underdeveloped countries. He contrasts them with the surplus of consumer goods (especially agricultural products) in the more developed countries. However, though fully realizing that a surplus in production (especially in agriculture) may "cause economic harm to a certain portion of the population" in a state, the Pope makes it clear that "this is not a motive for exonerating oneself (in the developed countries) from the obligation of extending emergency aid to the indigent and hungry." [25]

21 *Ibid.*
22 *Ibid.*
23 *Ibid.*
24 *Mater et Magistra,* p. 40.
25 *Ibid.,* p. 37.

The principle that the wealth of the world is intended for all men suffices to explain the moral obligation incumbent upon countries that have a surplus to share it. On the other hand, the principle of subsidiarity could be invoked, to prevent this surplus being distributed in such a way as to destroy the national or local efforts of the poor country to provide for its own needs.

b. *Long-term aid:* This emergency aid is not sufficient "to eliminate, or even to reduce, the causes which ... bring about a permanent state of want, misery and hunger" [26] in many countries. Other methods must therefore be sought, and the Pope is thinking in the first place of cooperatives.

These cooperatives could give those inhabitants who have the necessary qualifications the technical and scientific advice that they need, and the capital required to initiate and to speed up their economic development. But in addition to these forms of basic community development, the Pope also refers to many initiatives (both public and private) begun by the more developed countries for the purpose of helping the less developed. Among these the Pope mentions the granting of study-scholarships to young people from those countries, so that they can come for training to the specialized schools and universities of the more-developed countries. He also mentions the granting of capital by the World Bank, by the wealthy countries or by individuals, and investments effected in the developing countries.

3. *Conclusions concerning international aid*

However, the various forms of external aid (some of which are mentioned in the papal documents) are far from adequate, either in the scope that they have hitherto attained or in their present aims or even in their form. It is not the Pope's task to define what form such aid should take. He can only indicate certain basic moral principles. However, he aptly points out "that the scientific, technical and economic cooperation between the economically developed political communities and those just beginning or on the way to development needs to be increased beyond the present level." [27] And he concludes: "It is our hope that such a develop-

---

[26] *Ibid.*
[27] *Mater et Magistra,* p. 38.

ment will characterize their dealings during the next decades." [28]
This reflection and this conclusion leave the way open for the
church's social doctrine to develop significantly in regard to the
different problems of underdevelopment and the obligations of the
industrialized countries. The insights of Pope John XXIII are like
the opening of an entirely new chapter.[29]

However, this chapter can take the form only of a dialogue with
the actual evolution of international economic relations. And during the next few years these relations are bound to be influenced
by the demands of the underdeveloped countries for a fairer system
of international trade, in which the industrialized countries will no
longer exercise almost supreme authority, and in which the conditions for exchange will not be fixed in such a way as to enrich the
developed countries and to drain the poorer countries of their
resources.[30]

It is becoming clearer every day that the development of the
underdeveloped countries cannot be adequately assured through bilateral financial aid or through international bodies (with or without interest, reimbursable or nonreimbursable). And in addition to
financial or technical aid, the mere stabilization of the price of materials is not sufficient, because the resulting returns would themselves be inadequate (in addition to the fact that many of these
products can in future be produced synthetically by the industrialized countries themselves). Thus, the policy which must be envisaged is the opening-up of the markets in the industrialized
countries to the manufactured products of the developing countries. Having accepted the reform of the political structures, the
countries of the West will have to accept the reform of the international economic structures. And this reform certainly cannot
take the form of a free market. It will have to introduce some system that will benefit the underdeveloped countries, to the tempo-

---

[28] *Ibid.*
[29] On this subject it is remarkable to note that the book of J. Y. CALVEZ
and J. PERRIN, mentioned above, still contains, even in the revised edition,
only a few paragraphs on economic underdevelopment and the international
aid for which it calls.
[30] See J. Y. CALVEZ: "Justice dans le commerce avec le Tiers-Monde," in
Revue de l'Action Populaire, Paris, No. 177, April, 1964, pp. 396–408;
R. SCHEYVAN: "Pourquoi l'aide aux pays sous-développés est-elle mal partie?"
La Revue Nouvelle, Tournai, July/Aug., 1964, pp. 3–19.

rary detriment of the more developed, and this will involve planning on an international scale.

The church's social doctrine will have to take all this into account during the coming years, and this will quite normally involve considering the principles and methods to be applied to this new joint international economy, i.e. an economy that is planned to an extent, and in ways which are difficult to foresee, but in which the international organizations will play an increasingly important part, in addition to the "zones of preference" that groups of nations may organize among themselves, and the agreements that they arrange separately. The increasing interest shown by the Popes in the great international organizations already points in this direction.

Duties and Rights in Planning

A. *The Acceptance of a Planned Society.* Since the creation (of the world) was not accomplished all at once, but is still being carried out progressively by God in history, man is associated in this process in his own modest way, according to his ability, within his own sphere. And within this historical process there is a kind of principle that is progressively unifying what was dispersed. Whether through competition or through fellowship, on the basis of rights or of duties, men are gradually feeling more and more linked by a common destiny, and are realizing that they are participating in building their own future. Whereas formerly each separate society sought its own destiny, today everything is combining to make them seek together for their common destiny. And whereas in former times the effort to attain a high level of civilization normally took the form of empirical groping (through trial and error), today information has been accumulated so that the way is gradually becoming clearer. God, who gave mankind control over the mineral, vegetable and animal spheres, also gave men the intellectual ability to gain control of their earthly destiny. It is for mankind to overcome the obstacles in their way and to control themselves, in the freedom that God has deliberately granted to them in his love as he patiently waits for them to do so. Thus, mankind responds to God's call both by accumulating information and experience, and by extending its activities, even if original sin does make its efforts ambivalent.

It is within this general perspective that men are called to more extensive planning of societies. Christianity as a whole, and the Roman Catholic Church in particular, cannot withdraw from the struggle. In addition to carrying out its spiritual mission among men, the church has also the indirect mission of helping to bring about the form of secular society best suited to meet the needs of men and to ensure their natural development, as well as their spiritual growth.[31]

B. *The Limits of Planning.* Although men are called to introduce more and more rationality into their societies, certain aspects of their life remain independent of rational calculation (without being irrational). This applies to certain spheres the importance of which is due precisely to the fact that they are worldwide. There is, for example, the function performed by the family in creating balanced personality. Although the family forms an integral part of the worldwide society, through its activities and its dimensions, and must be harmoniously integrated into that society, it is equally true that the family exercises a special function—that of protecting its members and developing them through the wealth of its intimate life. Now socioeconomic planning at this level destroys what is essential for the exercise of these functions, and everything that gives the family universal validity. That is why the principle of subsidiarity (which establishes a kind of ladder of confidence in the social process, and which preserves as its central concern the person, and the elementary forms of social life) must be retained as the guide to economic and social planning.

We must therefore bear in mind the inadequacy of our information, both about the elements themselves that have to be considered and about the criteria for the decisions to be taken. Here again, whatever the value of the previous studies, of the experts called in, or of the executive bodies, the principle of *subsidiarity* retains its full original validity. This is indispensable; for, as the methods and resources available increase, the danger of making mistakes increases also.

---

31 See FR. HOUTART: *Eglise et Monde*, Paris: Editions du Cerf, 1964.

C. *The Value of the Person.* The primordial value of man himself in all planning has been sufficiently stressed, and here the church merely emphasizes an essential, absolute principle. But planning is not merely a problem of dominating matter and techniques: Planning also means concerted action to develop the intellectual resources of a society.

Today this is the most serious problem, because of the tremendous technical resources now available for use by the public authorities in planning. Now that they have complete control of all the media of information, both in education and through the mass channels, men are obliged to formulate an ethic of planning much more strictly than in the past. If the principle of subsidiarity (which lays down the principle of autonomy for the intermediary social bodies) cannot, for technical reasons, be respected, the ultimate control of operations and aims must none the less remain in the hands of the individuals who constitute this society and whose welfare is the whole object of planning. It is therefore essential for planning to be controlled on democratic lines, as it becomes increasingly global and important.

There may seem to be a contradiction between the demands of technology and those of democracy, but this is only an alibi. It is the task of political science to find new forms in order to reconcile these claims, which are not really opposed. Many countries must now find new political techniques that will enable them to reconcile the demand for stability and continuity in planning with the need for basic control. On this point too the church will certainly have to draw attention, during the next few years, to certain principles or to formulate new ones.

The future development of the social doctrine of the Roman Catholic Church will therefore take the form of accepting (as a necessary technique) the economic organization of the developed countries, and especially the development of the other countries both at the national and at the international level. Planning, however, is subordinate to certain principles, such as respect for the human person, subsidiarity and democratic control—which implies the rejection of totalitarian planning, and especially of ideological planning.

10

BETWEEN THE OLD AND THE NEW WORLDS

by MASAO TAKENAKA (Japan)

SEVERAL factors contribute to the complexity and the peculiarity of the issues which arise in the process of transition from the traditional to modern society in Asia.

First of all, in contrast to what happened in the West, the process has occurred within a relatively short period in history. In the West the transition began about the time of the Reformation and covered a period of over four hundred years, in the course of which the peoples of the West have adjusted themselves to it. We record such revolutionary events as the Reformation, the industrial revolution, the Declaration of Independence, the French revolution, the enlightenment, the civil war and the proletarian revolution. Within this period religious, industrial, economic, cultural and political changes came about.

In Asia the transition from the traditional to the modern is of more recent date. In Japan modernization began at the Meiji restoration period in 1868, but the reform was mainly external, and the actual democratization of Japanese society did not begin until after the Second World War, when many Asian countries attained political independence. This historical time factor is an important element in our study, because a social change which is rapid and sudden may lead to confusion and frustration.

Second, the change has been not only sudden but simultaneous. With the declaration of political independence, the people of Asia have experienced all at once a reformation, an industrial revolution, a proletarian revolution and a French revolution. They are confronted with the problem caused by the lack of balance in the development of various fields and with the vital responsibility of establishing the right priorities among the different elements which demand change. After the Meiji period, the Japanese government gave priority to building up their national power, while limiting democratic freedom among the people. In the postwar period, the government's urgent concern was to raise the standard of living through economic expansion, while paying less attention to the cultivation of the quality of personal resources.

Third, we notice in Asia a harmonious coexistence of traditional cultures and modern technology. It evokes a sense of wonder to find, on the roof top of a supermodern industrial firm in Tokyo, a small Shinto shrine before which the employees meet every morning for a brief ceremony. Many taxi drivers in Osaka hang a Shinto talisman in their cars to ensure their safety. In an ordinary rural Japanese home it is not unusual to find a Buddhist family shrine on top of the television set. The harmonious attitude toward other religions, ideologies and ways of life has been greatly influenced and nurtured by the impact of nature, which has always been of fundamental importance in Asian life. Rather than fight against nature, the dominant attitude has been to live with and according to nature.

This harmonious attitude was extended to the realm of thought and human relations, creating an atmosphere of coexistence and tolerance. This means that in the process of transition we encounter a carry-over of the traditional element of culture into a new setting. Deep down in the minds of ordinary Japanese, for example, there is a primitive religious mentality, and their human relationships are quite often based on a feudalistic pattern. Yet they not only wear modern clothes but live in a modern organization, receiving the constant impact of advanced, supermodern technology. Thus Asia today reveals a peculiar coexistence and harmony of primitive, feudalistic, modern and supermodern elements.

Fourth, in many of the Asian countries the people experienced colonial control, by western powers and by Japan, during the Second World War. The impact of western dominance cannot easily be forgotten and removed. Having gained political independence, Asian nations live in interdependence with other nations of the world. Today this degree of interdependence has been accelerated by the impact of commercial and technological developments. The end of colonialism does not mean the isolation of the Asian countries from the rest of the world. It means the demand for a new type of interdependence and world solidarity.

Over one hundred years ago (1853) three steamships arrived for the first time at the port of Uraga, near Tokyo. Their arrival shocked the people of Japan, who were enjoying a long sleep, having cut themselves off from the rest of the world. From that time on, social change in all realms of society proceeded with great speed and soon the problem of maintaining harmony and coexistence, in a diverse cultural climate yet in an interdependent world, arose. It is in this setting that we should examine the specific issues which emerge from the process of transition from a traditional to a modern society.

From a Vertical Society to a Horizontal Community

One of the decisive trends in the process of transition is the breakdown of the feudalistic, hierarchical structure and the rise of the masses to demand their individual rights and freedom. In the early process of modernization in the West we can distinguish a strong emphasis on individualism. There, an effort was made to safeguard individual dignity as the basic unit of society. Later, however, trends in the opposite direction were discernible—stressing the fulfillment of individual desires without considering the welfare of the whole community. We recognize here the difficulty encountered in the process of modernization in the West—the trend from a vertical, feudal society to that of an atomized, disintegrated community.

In Asia the breakdown of the feudalistic society provides an opportunity to establish an interpersonal, horizontal community. But in reality there is a trend toward one of two extremes—either to individualism or to the new form of hierarchical relationship.

In 1866, Hiromichi Kozaki, a distinguished leader of the Christian church in Japan, wrote a provocative book called *Seikyo Shinron* (The New Thesis on Religion and Politics). In it he made a violent attack on Confucianism, which was the basic ethical foundation of the old society. According to Kozaki, Confucianism is a quite distinct way of governing society with the aim of bringing peace to the nations. He examined the means of achieving this end, depicting the five basic Confucian codes as these rules of government. The Confucian ethics divide society sharply into two groups, not according to functions, but to status, which demands loyalty from those who are governed and gives those who govern the right to order. Thus, the five codes state that the subject must give absolute loyalty to the emperor; the son must give filial obedience to his parents; the wife must follow the husband; the young must obey their elders; and friends must trust each other.

It was Kozaki's contention that except for that among friends, all these relationships are hierarchically defined, toward a vertical human relationship in which the lower accepts the orders of his superior and obeys his commands. Thus, the feudal structure of society is a closely organized society in which vertical relationships predominate. Kozaki diagnosed the need for a radical change in this situation and advocated the transformation of the traditional structure into an interpersonal, horizontal relationship as exemplified by the Christian faith. But in the course of modernization during the last eighty years, between the Meiji restoration of 1868 and the end of the Second World War, the trend was less toward extreme individualism than toward a resurgence of the spirit of the old, traditional society in the new dress of a modern setting. Japanese nationalism first took the form of the civil liberty movement in the early 1880's, but after the Imperial Edict of Education in

1890 it became increasingly authoritative in character. The Imperial Edict became the cornerstone of Japanese society; it took the Confucian moral teachings and adapted them in such a way as to strengthen the national power within the hierarchical structure. Japan quickly accepted western technology and industrialization, but changed little in the international orientation of life until 1945, when the absolute divinity of the emperor was first challenged. This shows that technological development does not necessarily introduce a new perspective, but that it is often used as a means of supporting a traditional, established system of values.

The Increase of Conformity

In a traditional society the people are required to give loyalty to a higher authority. It is a society which operates by commandments from the top to the lower strata. In modern Asian society, despite much discussion and inclination toward individualization, matured selfhood has been a slow and struggling process. One of the difficulties in this process of transition is that a technologically organized life demands a readiness to adjust. To use David Riesman's terminology in his book, *The Lonely Crowd,* we see an increasing trend among the people to assume an "other directed" pattern of personality. At work one must obey the production schedule; in the home, one becomes a passive recipient of the TV program. Rather than develop the power of self-determination, people become sensitive in modern society to the evaluation and stimulation of others, especially to the demand to organize. Here we see that the traditional Asian attitude of adjustment to natural environment strengthens the trend to social conformity. A harmonious attitude toward nature tends to be transformed into social relationships which strengthen attitudes of conformity.

There are three characteristic ways in which human relations develop in this situation. One is an attitude of conformity, observed in the external life of organization. Another is an extreme attitude of conflict and antagonism which is occasionally manifested at a moment of crisis as the result of an underlying dissatisfaction. A third is to criticize and talk about others without personal confrontation. There is a decisive lack of genuine personal dialogue.

Here we see the key question, whether the impact of technology increases a sense of conformity or whether it opens up opportunities to develop interpersonal horizontal relationships. In countries where the traditional culture has been strongly rooted and where the harmonious attitude toward the natural environment has been predominant, technology and organization may strengthen attitudes of conformity and adjustment. On the other hand, technology may bring about a change not only in people's external working conditions but in the human relationships of an industrial society.

For example, the development of the labor union movement may create new opportunities when it cultivates a horizontal and interpersonal society, raising the status of workers and promoting mutual dialogue among people who have different functions and specialized gifts and abilities. The labor union movement may help the workers to recover their dignity and self-identity and may bring people into a horizontal relationship wtih other components of industrial society. On the other hand, within organizations in industrial society, including labor unions, the feudalistic spirit of conformity and the harmonious attitude toward nature still survive in a way which creates a new form of vertical control and passive adjustment. Union members tend to lack a positive attitude in participating in the democratic process within the union. They would rather support an undemocratic boss because in the old society they were accustomed to be subordinate to orders from above.

Many of the social changes in Japan took place not at the grass-roots level, but from the top to the bottom by order of those who were in positions of control. The Meiji restoration of 1868 was not a revolution from below, but a restoration of the sovereignty of the emperor, who initiated reforms for the benefit of the people. Again, in the postwar setting, it was the occupation forces who introduced many revolutionary policies, such as land reform, the establishment of labor unions and the dissolution of the financial oligarchy. These reforms were directed from the office of the general headquarters of the supreme commander rather than coming from the people themselves. Many labor unions sprang up like mushrooms after rain. To members of the unions, the right to organize was given from above rather than being personally acquired after struggle. Thus the changes took place quickly, without causing much damage. But we must not forget the underlying problems of mutual adjustment. We acknowledge especially the importance of labor education and the cultivation of the workers in order to bring about healthy and responsible industrial relations.

Division and Cooperation

Technological development and scientific advance imply specialization. As science develops, the fields of discipline which investigate particular phenomena narrow. Advance in scientific investigation leads to the fragmentation and disintegration of life. We experience this today in our universities, which add an increasing number of new courses and of specialists every year. Technology is the application of scientific study to practical operations. As science develops specialized fields of study to increase technological progress, a greater division of labor inevitably takes place, which in turn necessitates a greater number of specialists with technological knowledge and competence in each particular field of operation. This leads to a disintegration of organic life, separating specialists from each other according to their respective fields.

In a traditional society other factors have tended to divide people—language, religion, caste, place of birth, education; and though people increasingly migrate from rural to urban areas, they still tend, in the cities, to form associations according to the prefecture from which they come. There is a strong sense of identification with a particular group. In the modern setting society puts much emphasis on education. People are classified according to their university rather than to their ability or qualifications. In industrial companies and large organizations associations are formed by those who graduated from the same university, for the purpose of mutual help. In many instances, a person's promotion depends on the "school family" to which he belongs. Divisions according to school families and local circles disintegrate society.

The sudden change from a feudalistic to an industrial and technological society does not give adequate time in which to develop and exercise selfhood. Instead, technology may increase the group divisions which already existed. In the industrial society the forms of divisions are admittedly different from those of the pre-industrial and feudal society, yet a similar mentality and attitude of group divisions tends to be carried over into the technological society. For example, in the past if a person were ill he was treated in hospital by a doctor and an attendant nurse. But today the treatment of the sick involves many specialists: chemists, social caseworkers, psychotherapists, machinists, computer operators, and so on. In a highly developed industrial organization the division of labor is much more highly intensified. Here we see the danger of carrying over into the modern industrial society the feudalistic group identity—widening the cleavage and division not according to a person's place of birth but according to his specialized function.

Yet at another level, technology forces people to cooperate. Technicians and engineers must work as a team. Of necessity people are brought together to cooperate, respecting each other's gifts and functions. Here we find a new opportunity to experiment, to open up a new dimension in the horizontal interpersonal relationship of people who have skills and responsibilities. Technological and industrial development requires a new type of joint human effort different from both the old paternalistic and the modern totalitarian pattern. It also differs radically from the isolated individualistic structure, since in a technical society every factory worker is involved in the process of production. Each person is essential, since the work of the group cannot be accomplished unless all contribute to the whole process.

Thus the process of transition introduces another important possibility, that of bringing a new type of solidarity and joint action into the functional interaction of people. They need to gain an understanding of the whole before they can begin their particular job. They must visualize the whole, seeing the relationship of all its parts, if they are to help create the final product. In the face of the trend toward disintegration, people long to find a foundation for a responsible human community.

Verses in the Epistle to the Ephesians which use the image of the body, have relevance here. The writer speaks neither to the conformed, nor to the isolated individual. He recognizes unity in diversity, each bringing gifts for joint action. The secret of organic life rests, not upon human resources, but on the reconciling power of Christ who "has broken down the dividing wall of hostility" (Ephesians 2 : 14). He has abolished in his flesh the old commandments and ordinances in order that he may create in himself one new man in place of two, reconciling both to God and to his neighbors. This body, the new community in Christ, helps to develop a sensitivity of partnership in solidarity: "We are to grow up in every way into him who is the head, into Christ, from whom the whole body joined and knit together by every joint with which it is supplied, when each part is working properly, makes bodily growth and upbuilds itself in love" (Ephesians 4 : 15–16). Maturity is characterized as the interrelatedness of each part in solidarity as an organic whole.[1] But it is worth remembering that the image of the body refers to the growth of the Christian community, however small it may have been, not only existed in a particular geographical and social setting, but had a mission to provide, in its everyday life, a foretaste of the coming kingdom. The image of the functioning body not only refers to the growth of a matured Christian community, but shows the pattern of the coming society, to be seen in the reality of Christian community, which is the firstfruit of the new humanity.

Toward the Provisional Telos

A man who lives during a period of transition searches for knowledge of the future. He realizes that the foundations of the

---

[1] Paul Lehman defines maturity as "the integrity in and through interrelatedness which makes it possible for each individual member of an organic whole to be himself." PAUL LEHMAN: *Ethics in a Christian Context*, 1963, p. 55.

past have been shaken and that his present existence is dissatisfying and ambiguous. He acts when he discovers something to hope for in the future. Man is a historical being living not only in the memory of the past but in anticipation of the future. A man in the midtwentieth century is not likely to think of the future in a rosy, idealistic way, as did the utopian thinkers of the eighteenth century; he is much more of a realist, if not a pessimist: he acknowledges the relativity of the present world.

In Asia, as they struggled for political independence, men and women looked toward the future with hope. Now that independence has been gained, however, apathy and uncertainty about the future have crept in. Confronted with the difficult and painful process of national development, there is a temptation to fall into social amnesia, to forget one's social responsibility and to be concerned with immediate private gain and pleasure. During the period of nationalism in Japan, the people had a sense of mission and of vocation in performing their work; national education and propaganda helped them to see a vision for the future. One must have a focus in life to understand history, and history here means personal identification in a common destiny. In times of rapid social change men and women are like travelers, leaving an old rural home and moving into the city. It is not an individual transition, but a social movement from an old to a new place. One is bound to ask seriously whither this earthly pilgrimage leads. In a time of transition people search for the meaning of the future. When the old religions and the classical ideologies are swept away, people are uncertain as to the direction of future society. One must develop a framework of the future city. In short, in times of social change, man becomes teleological. In this connection we can understand why the Communist movement and some of the new religions, like Sokagakkai, have great appeal in Japan. Despite their limitations they indicate the direction in which people should move. They present a social and "this-worldly" *telos,* something anticipated here and now as a common goal, and not the individualistic or spiritualized *telos*. It is easy to criticize the irrelevant and faulty promises contained in these quasi-religious movements, but the challenge to the Christian is to define the Christian *telos* in such times of social change as we are experiencing today. Criticizing others is not much help unless we present a positive alternative.

In Christian thinking about the future we must confess that we have been timid in considering where we are going, in relevant and realistic terms. In the eighteenth and nineteenth centuries we find several Christian social thinkers who thought of the *telos* as a realizable social structure. They were teleologists, but they were also idealists in identifying the kingdom of God with the highest social order which will be manifested in this world. They thought of the future but considered it in an idealistic way, projecting a rosy future kingdom which would come to fulfillment in the world. In spite of their diversity of thought, we find this common characteristic in the social thinkers of the eighteenth and nineteenth centuries, from Robert Owen to Walter Rauschenbusch. They anticipated the future ideal society as the kingdom of God on earth.

Against this rather worldly idealistic trend, the theological tendencies in this century are much more cautious. If, during the previous century, the predominant thinking in Christian ethics was expressed through the teleological form, the social thought of the midtwentieth century is expressed through contextual ethics. This difference is partly due to the impact of the "theology of crisis" and to the reaction against the former liberal and idealistic theology. Christian theologians have been emphasizing the moral ambiguity of men, and their ethical perplexity in modern society, in a way which helps to restore a balanced perspective. Therefore, one of the major trends in Protestant social ethics is described as "situational ethics." Instead of projecting the ideal social goal or depicting the absolute categorical commandment such as that given in the Sermon on the Mount, Protestant social thinkers consider the immediate and concrete ethical response within a particular given situation; we have become more realistic. This is relevant because, in dealing with social policies, we must think in terms, not of what is best, but of what is possible in highly complex, given situations.

Yet at the same time we cannot base ethics wholly on given social situations. If we accept contextual ethics without the constructive and positive framework of an ethical structure, we shall be in a dangerous position. Here I suggest three of the temptations or limitations to which we shall be exposed:

a. One characteristic of contextual ethics is that it tries to deal with ethical issues within their concrete context. There is no other relevant way with which, I admit, to deal with them, but it has its danger: it tends to deal with ethical responses individually, fragmentarily and to lack insight into the ethical and moral implication of the problem as a whole. We may call this the individualization trend in contextual ethics. We must guard against this temptation diligently in the Protestant church, which has strongly emphasized the strength of the individual rather than the concept of being a part of the whole. In a world, furthermore, which has become increasingly interdependent, we must break through the individualistic trend in contextual ethics. The content of the Christian gospel and the context of the present-day world urge us to think more seriously of the reality of world interdependence.

b. Then there is the conservative element in contextual ethics. We appreciate the concreteness and the realistic emphasis gained by recent developments in Christian ethics, but there is a temptation to be caught up in the dilemma of a given situation, adapting ourselves to it rather than developing creatively a new framework to replace the old foundation. In being realistic we are inclined to cynical judgment, protesting against man's sinfulness, finiteness and moral ambiguity. We need to recover a prophetic insight, in order not only to analyze a situation but to see its construction with relevance to the future. A prophet not only judges, but sees a vision—the vision of deliverance from captivity and of entering the "new Jerusalem."

c. Third, we must be aware of the element of subjectivism in contextual ethics. By taking a given situation seriously, contextual ethics leads us to make relevant personal decisions in concrete realities. This does not mean that we can make any decision primarily on the basis of the given situation. Ethical choices are made not only in the light of a realistic understanding of the situation, but also in that of the ultimate concern. In times of social change, Christians must interpret the social situations and make decisions in the light of the biblical drama of redemption. Instead of proclaiming an ideal society created by human ability, we should discern the signs of the times in the light of God's design in the world. We have been given, in the coming of Jesus Christ, the vision of the final goal of history. In this event we affirm the victory of the redeeming power of God over principalities and powers. Through the testimony of the Bible we have received the vision and promise of the new city which will come at the end of history. Living between two eras, Christians always look to the future. They are not idealists or dreamers who talk of the future in an irrelevant way. No one has a definite blueprint for the future society, but Christians possess a power in the gospel which provides a provisional *telos* in the light of the ultimate *telos*. This provisional *telos* must be thought of in terms not of an individual's purpose but of a common goal. The Bible expresses this thought in the image of a common life, the city of God. "Behold, the dwelling of God is with men. He will dwell with them, and they shall be his people, and God himself will be with them; he will wipe away every tear from their eyes, and death shall be no more, neither shall there be mourning nor crying for pain any more, for the former things have passed away" (Revelation 21 : 3–4).

In our ecumenical thinking, therefore, on church and society, we are entering a new stage. Between Oxford, 1937, and Amsterdam, 1948, the emphasis of Christian teachings was on the social issues of that period, yet the common framework of thinking was not clearly expressed. At Amsterdam, the concept of responsible society came into existence and provided a basic perspective. Someone has referred to the concept of responsible society as the middle axiom, presenting a general guide in the light of Christian perspectives. Since Evanston, 1954, in meeting the challenges of the revolutionary world, we have developed the study on the common Christian responsibility toward the areas of rapid social change.

It has helped Christians to gain a practical understanding of the changing world and to make relevant decisions. We are now at another stage—that of the provisional social *telos*. As we build up definite knowledge of the changing world and begin to interpret and analyze the actual situation, we need to think together about the common provisional direction and pattern of future society in the light of the biblical revelation. We may not necessarily think of the kind of society required for the year 3000, but we should direct our attention to thinking out of the provisional social goal which we want, not only in our own national and local community, but in our interdependent world.

Search for the Ground of Hope

In the period of transition from the old to the modern society, people are confronted with three social issues, uncertainty, rebellion and indifference.

Since the traditional norm is not applicable in a new society, people become uncertain as to the foundation of moral life. In the feudalistic period, the Confucian teaching and the Buddhistic attitude to life provided the basic framework of society. In the nationalistic period, the moral teaching as described in the Emperor's edict on education was the basis for the national way of life. But today, there is widespread ambiguity in defining the center of moral life. In this period of transition confusion and uncertainty prevail. A small group may take a negative and critical attitude, rebelling against the existing order and institutions. Dissatisfied and frustrated, their reactions are negative, and they do not play their part in developing a common framework of realistic participation in the modern world. Social injustice should certainly be met by critical protest, but there is a lack of the constructive realism that is required if we are to grapple with the development of a new society with the cooperation of different interest groups.

Perhaps the most widespread attitude is that of indifference to the affairs of society, both because people are not accustomed to participate constructively in a complex social situation and because of the impact of mass media. People are concerned with immediate individual interests and tend to forget their common social responsibilities. We forget our common humanity and put our individual private interests first. A worker, let us say, tries to get more overtime for himself in competition with his fellow worker, but is indifferent to his responsibility in the coming union election. Or a student, in a highly competitive system of entrance examinations, forgets to think of the ultimate question of the meaning of life; he is interested only in getting a better grade than his classmates in the next examination. Or a lawyer is deeply concerned with a local political deal in his Rotary Club, but forgets his role as a lawyer in the improvement of the inadequate minimum-wage law of his city. Or a churchman is occupied with installing a new stained-glass window memorial, but forgets his role in the racial struggle in his own community.

In the complex jungle of modern society, there is a tendency to apathy and resignation. It expresses itself in various ways. In Thailand a common saying is *"Maipen rai,"* "Never mind"; in Indonesia people often say *"Tida magapa,"* "Ask not why"; in Japan, *"Shikataga nai,"* "There is no other way," expresses a feeling of resignation. It is not the heroic reformer with idealistic vision to make sweeping changes that we need, but a vital spiritual force to awaken men and women from their social amnesia. We need the power of anamnesis, a re-awareness of self-hood in the human community and the recognition of one's responsibility in our interdependent world.

Marxists have charged religion with being "the opiate of the people." We should not ignore or cover up this charge. In history certain religions have quieted the conscience of the oppressed, but it is unfair to historic reality if we do not point out that this is only half the picture. There have been a number of occasions when religion was not an opiate but the driving force of a new civilization. The Christian gospel does not individualize man; it stimulates him to see his personal responsibility toward his neighbors in the community, not because he has something to give them, but because he has encountered the eternal God who became man to share the burden of all men. The Christian faith does not lead man to retire behind an individual religious wall, but sends him out into society, where the horizontal relationship is acute. The gospel proclaims that God became man to overcome man's sin and death by participating in man's suffering and struggle. When the people of God accept this vision of the gospel, they become the creative and driving force in history, functioning as the salt of the earth, the mustard seed in the field and the leaven in the bread. Man has irreplaceable and irreducible hope in Jesus Christ. It is the hope with which one can continually present a Christian witness in the midst of our struggling world. This hope is based on the historic event: God became man in order that man may become true man.

II

THE IDEOLOGICAL FACTOR
IN THE WEST

by ANDRÉ DUMAS (France)

Myth, Order and Ideology

THERE are two characteristics of our society today: on the one hand, it is increasingly possible to analyze it economically, geographically and historically—that is, to examine the forces which explain and determine man as far as his external liberty is concerned; on the other hand, society can be ordered in accordance with the findings of the "ideologists"—that is, it can be oriented in accordance with men's inward allegiance to and interpretation of history. Ideas are thus pursued as if they were only the secondary (and often mystifying) results of the material realities from which they spring, and at the same time *exalted* as if, by obtaining a global understanding and commitment, man could at last participate actively in molding the society of the future. This is an age in which we are very skeptical about ideals, but at the same time we avidly swallow compelling ideas. We object to idealism because it presupposes the existence of absolute models which do not exist in fact, dividing human life into a law that is not applied and a fact that is not justified. Idealism differs from prophecy in that it presupposes a permanent divorce between values and history. The criterion of idealism is separation, its aim is purity, its nostalgia is for the unrealizable, and its setting is the bad conscience. However, one must not draw the conclusion that contemporary anti-idealism is tantamount to pure pragmatism. On the contrary, scientific social analysis today aims at discovering a new collective "cogito" which will provide, on the basis of experimental evidence, the meaning of the whole and in which the individual will be a part. Thus, Karl Mannheim writes, the social observer seeks "to submit the whole structure of his conscience and his thought to a total sociological analysis." [1] The ideological function has become the cement which holds together the changing societies of our time.

In the primitive societies myths were used in order to explain, unite and regenerate the social reality when it was in danger of becoming obscure or dispersed, or exhausting itself as it was separated more and more from its origins. In the classical societies an order existed that was both cosmological and theological, which human society had to reproduce, thus preserving it from wastage and excess. But contemporary societies are no longer concerned about their mythical origins. Critical science has reduced them to the level of legends. Nor do our societies believe in an unchangeable classical order which would indicate man's rightful place and task. Formerly the universe was regarded as finite, reflecting its order in man. Today we seek in man's own mind for order, in order to project it onto an infinite universe. Deprived of original myths and guides-to-the-universe, our contemporary societies nevertheless need a worldwide image to inform them about the direction and convergence of their respective projects. Between Descartes and Hegel, it was possible to believe that the human mind could do without any world view apart from the mechanical reconstitution of the universe solely by the power of scientific hypothesis. That was the age of reflection which paid little attention to others or society. It was the time when the human mind worked in creative solitude, in a setting that had no soul and no life in which the "engineering" power of the human technician had free play. Man felt no need to substitute ordering ideologies for the Aristotelian view of the world, which had been shattered at the

---

[1] KARL MANNHEIM: *"Idéologie et Utopie,"* p. 74, French translation, Rivière, Paris, 1956.

beginning of the seventeenth century by physics and reflective philosophy. The ideological vacuum did not last long. The social indifference manifested by minds as different as Pascal and Descartes was succeeded, from the beginning of the eighteenth century (in a picturesque and impulsive way) and from the beginning of the nineteenth century (in a scientific and systematic way) by the renaissance of worldwide conceptions. The ideologies superseded the original myths and the cosmic order, after the brief interim of intellectual individualism.

These contemporary ideologies are more interested in the birth of a future than in returning to origins, or in preserving stability. In them history plays an eminently positive role; whereas in the mythical universe history is losing force all the time, and in the classic universe it is an accidental setting, a temptation both to the soul (perdition) and to the mind (distraction). The contemporary ideologies do not have this pejorative view of history. Even the atheist ideologies regard history as the biblical truth of the time which is running toward an eschatological consummation; history is therefore awaiting its consummation; it is not in terror of its own fragility. The future will reveal the lack of variety in the present. The purpose and meaning of history are to be found in the future, not in the past nor in some transcendent explanation. It is a paradox that this biblical idea of the-transcendent-that-is-coming (as opposed to "the-transcendent-that-was-in-the-past" or to "the-transcendent-which-exists-outside-this-world") has received greater prominence in the secularized ideologies of the contemporary world than in the classic view of Christendom, which has too often confirmed Nietzsche's opinion that "Christianity is a Platonism for the people." For this alone the ideologies merit positive appreciation by Christians. They do not claim ideals whose perfection dominates existing social forces; they present themselves in terms of forces which are already at work in history, forces which are moving toward an end that will deliver history from its ambiguity, by revealing the mystery which it unconsciously conceals within it. The ideologies, therefore, are not objects of thought, they are methods of thought. They would like merely to express the facts which have

become a collective explanation and will. Unlike the myths, therefore, the ideologies are based on a scientific interpretation; and
unlike the classical ontologies (which gave precedence to *being* and
nature before consciousness) the ideologies are based on a human
awareness which has power to organize. Here one already sees how
difficult it will be to define their status, because they want to participate both in the objectivity of science and in the subjectivity of
the human enterprise. Owing to their desire to draw upon both
sources, the ideologies will be menaced, on the one hand, by the
determinism of the certified facts and, on the other hand, by the
freedom of choice. The ideologies therefore present a tremendous
problem: *who* is entitled to interpret world history, if that history
contains the germ of an evolution which gives it meaning? Placing
themselves on the same plane as faith in a divine purpose within
and for history, the ideologies will present a tremendous challenge
to that faith.

Second, the ideologies are markedly collective in character. They
are contemporary with the rise of the masses. They appeared when
solitary reflectiveness (inaugurated by the seventeenth century) ex-
ploded through its encounter with the vast revolutionary movements whereby history took possession of the individual consciousness in France, in the U.S.S.R., in China and in Cuba in 1789,
1917, 1949 and 1959. Here again one can trace the thought of
the Bible, which speaks collectively of "the people," of "the church
of God," which never isolates the individual from his environment
(of which he is always the firstfruit or the survival), and never
thinks of the individual as indifferent or isolated. By giving positive
meaning to the masses, therefore, the ideologies consider "the
crowd" as the real potential of nations. The ideologies do not believe that collective awareness crushes the individual; they believe
that it develops the personality. Classical Christianity has always
regarded this teaching about the masses with suspicion, and has
always stressed the pejorative sense of the word implied in Saint
Augustine's "massa peccati"—the "menial lump" mentioned in Romans 9 : 21, which, however, in Romans 11 : 16 becomes "holy"
throughout. The contemporary ideologies are conceived in order

to find a positive meaning in the modern existence of the masses, crowded increasingly into the urban agglomerations, harnessed to mass production, forced into mass consumption and influenced by the mass communications. Here ideology is opposed to the two usual consequences of the mass: the tyranny of incommunicable, charismatic power, or the defense of the wishes of the individual. Indeed, an ideology may lose strength in two ways: either when authoritarianism is absolute, or when private life gains definite ascendancy over public life. But neither of these situations has much chance of developing in our contemporary societies, despite the repeated affirmations that the ideologies are on the decline; it would be truer to say that they are being modified. Admittedly, our societies do not favor absolute power to the extent of becoming disinterested in the methods by which the masses identify themselves with their projects. The extension of the word "democratic" to all countries (socialistic or capitalistic, countries with one-party government or with several parties, industrial or traditional countries, monarchies or parliamentary countries) is a universal sign of this concession to the will of the masses to assert itself and assume power.

Moreover, the growing importance of joint decisions shows that no contemporary society can allow its citizens to revert to the position of the isolated pioneer, nor even of the free artisan. If necessary, it is private happiness which plays the role of an ideological stimulus; but the ideology (whether tacit or avowed) will always be there in order to coordinate the adherence of society to the general aims.

The ideological function seems, therefore, to be a constant in contemporary societies. It springs from the desire to let the masses participate in creating their own future, at a time when that future is no longer dictated either by convincing myths or by a respected order. The ideologists play the difficult role fulfilled, in ancient times, by the priests and, in more recent times, by philosophers. It is their task to explain the latent meaning within the history that is to be made. They have to explain the social symbols which are sometimes in danger of becoming devouring idols. In fact, they must propose a mobilization of the collective energies, and their proposal may always be a mistake or—what is even more serious—a lie. The ideological function seems inevitable and essential in order to strengthen the social fabric, to avoid the tyranny of monopoly, or withdrawal into the private sphere; and therefore the exercise of this function in contemporary societies is a dangerous occupation.

Ideologies, which are at the same time the products of social conditioning and an awakening in view of commitments in thought and action, thus constitute the main challenges to the Christian faith in the contemporary societies—as the myths were in the societies of antiquity, and as the philosophies were in the classical societies. The ideologies bear a strange resemblance to religious faith because, like faith, they are growing up, moving toward the collective future of history, guiding it toward a central point which may be a mystery or a meaning, and asking man to help, through his own consecration, to hasten the time when the ideological scheme will become an idealized experience. There was far less resemblance between the archaic myths, or the theories of the philosophers, and the substance of faith, than is apparent in history. But this very similarity means that the ideologies are formidable competitors with faith. Do they not manifest a constant tendency not merely to question faith but to replace it, at a time when the evidence of de-Christianization coincides with the speeding-up of history and with the rise of the masses? With their similarity to religious faith, the ideologies often try to replace the very content of faith, either in the extreme form of total ideologies—like Marxism—or in the diluted form of an ideological ethos.

I shall examine these two forms one after the other before dealing with the relations between the Christian faith and the ideological function in contemporary societies.

Ideology and Marxism

Ideology is a comparatively recent word. It was popularized through a work by Antoine Destutt de Tracy, published between

1803 and 1815 and entitled "Eléments d'idéologie," which was consulted by Marx in 1844. Following the tradition of Locke and Condillac, Destutt de Tracy studied the formation of ideas, regarding them like plants which grow up in man's logical nature. Ideology classifies ideas in relation to their characteristics and in relation to their etymology. The ideologists therefore believe that a sensualistic naturalism and a rational optimism can be taught as the bases of liberty. In their view ideology has an essentially positive meaning. It is rooted in man's rational nature and provides a sound basis for his action in history. It is the abstract and collective expression of the observations carried out concerning the functioning of the human mind.[2]

Very soon, however, the word "ideology" assumed a pejorative meaning. Napoleon, who was attacked by the ideologists, cast the word in their teeth as an insult. In his view it denoted idle, subversive speculations, inventions divorced from reality which really concealed a thirst for power. "It is to ideology, that sinister metaphysic, that all the misfortunes of France must be attributed," he stated to the Conseil d'État in 1812. Most important of all, ideology is connected with another tradition in philosophy far older than that of Locke or Condillac—namely, the tradition of Bacon. According to Bacon, science is constantly menaced by ideas (idols). Bacon draws a distinction between the "idola tribus," illusions inherent in the human mind, the "idola specus," errors peculiar to individuals, the "idola fori," false concepts derived from current language, and the "idola theatri," the speculations of the philosophers. Ideology thus denotes the speculative idolatry which impedes true scientific knowledge. In the eighteenth century these misleading idols were called "prejudices." The Age of Enlightenment served to unmask them and to disclose the interests which lay beneath them. Even before Marx encountered it, therefore, ideology had acquired a pejorative sense, for two reasons: Napo-

---

[2] See ANDRÉ LALANDE: *Vocabulaire de la Philosophie,* I, 336, 4me édition, Paris, 1938.
CHARLES WACKENHEIM: *La faillité de la réligion d'après Karl Marx,* p. 271, Puf, Paris, 1963.
H. BARTH: *Wahrheit und Ideologie.*

leonic power had accused it of being an abstraction; and the critical, material tradition of Helvetius and Holbach had branded it as a delusion and an oppression.

Marx was aware of both these attacks on ideology. He proceeded to take up his own battle against the idealism of Kant and especially Hegel, whom he accused of putting the cart before the horse, taking effects for causes by locating in the *transcendent,* the metaphysical and in the realm of ideas the basis for explaining economy and need, which can be explained only in what is *immanent.* Ideology was to become the typical example of mystifying, roundabout thinking. Ideological thinking meant inconsistency, secondhand thinking which claimed to stimulate reality whereas in fact it merely reflected it in order to conceal it. Stendhal also attacked the ideologists because they wanted to classify ideas apart from the human consciousness: "An ideological treatise is an insolence," he wrote. "You don't think that my reasoning is good?" From a different point of view Marx also attacked ideology for its insolent, incapable externality, which claimed to explain and justify history without reference to political economy.

In his first works, Marx did not use the word ideology. He speaks of theories characteristic of the imaginary ideas which the ruling classes use to clothe and conceal their real interests. I quote a single passage which appeared in the "Gazette Rhénane" in May, 1842: "As the real position of these gentlemen in the modern state does not correspond in any way to the idea that they have of their own position, as they live in a world that is *outside the real world,* so that their *imagination* takes the place of their heads and their hearts, since they find no satisfaction in practice they are forced to turn to theory, but to *the theory of the transcendent,* namely *religion.* This . . . becomes more or less consciously only a cloak of holiness concealing aspirations which are extremely secular and quite imaginary. . . . To the requirements of practice they oppose a mystical-religious theory which is the pure product of their own imagination; to what is humanly reasonable they oppose sacred entities superior to man; and to the true sanctuary of ideas they oppose points of view which are vulgar, arbitrary and impious." [3]

The "theories" (which Marx was soon to call "ideologies") are therefore the fantastic product (partly deliberate, partly unconscious) of a *contradiction* between what is real and its idealistic justification in the minds of those who profit by it, but refuse to evaluate it in terms of the reality of their own needs. Theories are like Noah's cloak thrown over the needs of this life by people who are walking backwards toward an imaginary life "beyond."

In this passage written in 1842, however, Marx still speaks of "the sacred sanctuary of ideas" and opposes it positively to the utilitarian vulgarity of the theories. In the best tradition of eighteenth-century France and of German idealism, he martials the "humanly reasonable" ideas against the suprahuman entities. The great turning point toward historic materialism had not yet been taken. At that time Marx would still have been glad to be called a humanistic idealist, inspired by Hegel's "phenomenology of the mind" in his fight against conservative supranaturalism.

It was in 1845 that Marxism became the science of the materialist approach to history, when Marx replaced the word "theory" by the word "ideology" in his famous work *"L'idéologie allemande —Critique de la philosophie allemande la plus récente dans ses représentants Feuerbach, B. Bauer et Stirner et du socialisme allemand dans ses divers prophètes."* [4] "Ideology" is the pathology of human knowledge which strays away from the real processes of life (the development of productive energy, relationships within production, the division of labor) and finally opposes human ideas to the conditions of human society. The ideologist thus reflects the maladjustment of man. The people who are really producing wealth no longer enjoy the product of their work. The workers no longer regard the social force as their own power, but as a foreign force which enslaves them. Ideology conceals the economic and material origin of this enslavement; it even justifies this enslavement at three levels, which are dealt with in Marx's later writings: the level of money (the economic fetish which interposes a screen between the

---

[3] MEGA I, 1, pp. 198–199.
[4] First published in full in 1932.

producer and the consumer), the level of the state (the political fetish which interposes a screen between the citizen and the self-administration of his communal life), and the level of religion (the metaphysical fetish which interposes a screen between man and his own possibilities). Man is thus prevented by the illusory ideologies from perceiving the real production on which his own position depends and which creates a good environment for him, if he knows how to realize it.

Furthermore, Marx does not deny that this real productivity also includes ideas which thus escape the condemnation of the ideologies. Marxism will always protest that it is not a purely economic theory, as one might be led to think from the famous polemical phrase: "It is not conscience which determines life, it is life which determines conscience." [5] Indeed life, if it is summed up in the processes of production, explicitly includes in those processes the material products, and also "the principles, ideas and categories," which correspond to human social relations, because (like those relations) they are "the transient outcome of history." [6] It would therefore be wrong to exclude from human nature man's capacity to produce ideas, which are destined in their turn to influence society. Engels reacted against this materialistic view, which defaces the whole of human reality. He recognized the power of ideas and their reactions; at the same time he tried not to deny the materialistic assumptions of Marxist theory. "The reflection of all the real struggles in the minds of those who participated in them —political, legal and philosophical theories, religious concepts and their development into systems of dogma—also influence the course of the historic struggles. . . . An ideological point of view reacts in its turn upon the economic basis and may modify it to a certain extent." [7]

We now have the *two different concepts of ideology* contained in Marxism, which make it so difficult to analyze:

[5] MEGA I, 5, p. 15.
[6] MEGA I, 6, pp. 179–180.
[7] Letters to Joseph Bloch and Conrad Schmidt: "Etudes philosophiques," pp. 128 and 135, *éditions sociales*, Paris.

I. First, the function of ideology is criticized in class societies. There, ideology is the reflection of the interests of the dominant class, protecting the privileges of material and spiritual production. Ideology covers up the economic divergences, whereby one class makes use of the ethical universality of ideas in order to camouflage its own selfish interests. A classless society should therefore be able to do without any arsenal of ideology, because in a classless society man can clearly perceive where he is going. The function of ideology should be eliminated in a classless society, together with its three classical products—money, the state and religion. The ideological mystification of a divided society should be superseded by a creative infrastructure in a classless society. Thus the immanence of work would replace the transcendence of ideas. Philosophy would be put into practice and carried into effect by the proletariat. In the Manifesto, Marx clearly affirms that in any case communism could not present itself as a new ideology: "The theoretical concepts of the Communists are not based on ideas or principles invented or discovered by these or those reformers. They are merely the general expressions of the actual conditions within an existing class-struggle, a movement of history which is taking place before our very eyes." By abolishing class divisions in society, Marxism ought therefore to abolish the ideological products of the false mentality—the hypostatized, mystifying projections of real life.

II. However, Marxism presents itself as an essential, true ideology. The Communist parties in power attribute a decisive function to the ideological struggle. Ideology is therefore no longer the inverted reflection of the real world (as Marx originally regarded it); it is the instrument whereby the proletariat awakens to its unifying role in history. It is the responsibility of the Communist party to promote this awakening by raising the ideological level of the masses. There is a change here in the essential meaning of the word "ideology"; it is no longer a mystifying reflection. It is becoming the description of aims to be attained on the communal road toward essential freedom. Marxism justifies the maintenance of the ideological function in the societies which are moving toward communism, by explaining that ideology is no longer used there to disguise individual interests, which are opposed to the main stream of economic development, because the infrastructure of private interest has been suppressed. Within the interaction between basis and superstructure (as Engels expresses it) ideology does not reflect the basis inversely: it helps it to develop its potentialities more and more. The basic antagonism between ideology and reality disappears, giving place to an emulation which tends toward concord. It is only a tendency, for since Communist society has not yet fully realized its theoretical objectives, it still needs ideological stimulus. Theory still has precedence over practice, but there is no longer any contradiction between the idea and the real. Since ideology now reflects the real basis of society, it participates in its truth, while anticipating its experience. "In this function theory becomes ideology again, not in the form of false conscience, but as a deliberate distance and dissociation from, even opposition to, repressive reality. By this very fact, ideology becomes a political factor of the first importance. For the Communist states the struggle on the ideological front becomes a struggle for survival." [8]

This justification for maintaining ideology in a society which is theoretically moving toward the suppression of "screens" and mediations between man and his self-transformation through work presents difficult problems. In actual fact the proletariat should abolish the temporary function of ideology by transforming reality. In actual fact ideology has not been eliminated, any more than the state. It has become stronger the longer Communist society lasts. This compels one to ask: "Instead of being the temporary corrective of an evolving society, has not ideology merely become an instrument of coercion in the hands of those who hold the political power?" "Just because Marxist analysis reveals economic discrepancies and ideological camouflage, is it not completely disarmed when this camouflage is used by a state which theoretically fully expresses the needs of all?" One must believe in the perma-

[8] HERBERT MARCUSE: *Le Marxisme soviétique*, p. 170, Gallimard (French translation).

nent value of the proletariat, as the agent and instrument which carries out the immanent meaning of universal history, in order to be immune from all doubt concerning the nature of the proletarian state, and the fundamental impossibility of that state becoming in its turn an ideology which oppresses the individual worker.

Where can Marxism find the guarantee that its own ideology will not also reflect the interests, if not of a class at any rate of a country which is unique, despite its claims to universality? And how can it guarantee that as it advances into the future, the Communist party may not become divorced from the realities of the force of production, thus divorcing theory from practice in the same way as it accuses the class societies of doing? By what signs can one recognize the disappearance of ideology in favor of the productive relationship between man and his instruments? In what sense is this disappearance linked with the disappearance of the state, of money and of religion? Is it a consequence of their disappearance, the final vestige of the class society? Or should ideology disappear before the state, money and religion, thus manifesting that the new society is sufficiently clear about itself to dispense with authoritarian teaching carried out by strengthening the Communist party?

This evolution of the function of ideology within Marxism reveals two points:

1. As a method, Marxism is an aspiration to harmonize word and action (as in the biblical concept of God's Word). This harmony is destroyed by idealism, which creates a divorce between the ideal and reality. To paraphrase Marx's famous phrase about religion, Marxism (as an anti-ideological method) is the expression of man's real distress due to being separated from himself, and his protest against that distress.

2. As an achievement, Marxism is a movement in which the transcendent is replaced by the future. In Marxism, ethics disappear in history, and freedom becomes comprehension of historical necessity. The persistence of the ideological struggle is an indication that the Communist "Parousia" is delayed. But then, if the

end of history is replaced by an indefinite dialectic of progress in history, ideology serves the purpose of measuring the distance between the aims and the reality. This re-establishes a transcendence situated in the future which (like everything transcendent) in its turn becomes an unattainable goal, that is, an ideal.

After having promised the end of ideological mediation, therefore, Marxism becomes merely one of the prospects of the industrial society. It has changed from a complete ideology into an ideological ethos, which is so characteristic of the situation in the West today.

The Ideological Ethos of the West

Karl Mannheim draws a distinction between ideology and utopia, defining the former as the conservative justification of the *status quo* and the latter as a creative outlook which transcends the social reality and wants to change it. In his view, ideology is the formation of a system interested in benefiting power; whereas utopia is an invitation to stop regarding the form of that power as inevitable. In this sense ideology would not constitute a real alternative, but would always be an idealization either of the present or of the future, an idealization which would consolidate the existing power. The utopia which reveals itself as different from the present and from its logical future, would arouse the aspirations of the masses to a possible change of the structures. After the decline of the ideologies, is it possible that the contemporary world will return to the utopias?

The question is a serious one, for the ideologies (including the most totalitarian of them—Marxism) have not realized their ambition to change the quality of history. In the advanced industrial societies of the West the ideologies have reduced their global promises to the dimensions of a quantitative improvement of society. The political parties no longer mobilize the masses to take decisions on radical alternatives. They have become families which survive by virtue of people's attachment to a certain tradition and the electoral machinery which seeks to enlist the support of people by taking care not to frighten them. To a large extent, therefore, the ideological programs belong to the past. Their present electoral strategy consists in trying to capture the votes of the *center*—the decisive voice in the affluent society of the West, which has no major collective ideology.

Unlike a total ideology, an ideological ethos recognizes its own inability to establish a reality which is perfectly coherent. As Jeanne Hersch writes, in a total ideology "instead of being proposed to everyone as an endless task, the cohesion of plans for living becomes the affair of a body of doctrine, through which it explains itself and through which it is carried out." [9] In an ideological ethos the overall aim is still to nationalize and direct the social struggle; but the objections involved in the project are recognized at the same time as the project itself. What was a struggle for radical liberation develops into an adaptation to fresh obstacles and a reflection on the contradictions that exist within the great ideological movements. There are manifestations of such adaptations and reflections in the West today. I shall proceed to analyze them on the basis of their principal motivations.

1. *The first ideology of the industrial societies is economic growth.* The slice of cake to be distributed to each person must be increased; the pitiless technical competition, national and international, must be maintained; more leisure must be offered—rather than liberation in work—in order to counteract the bad effects of modern work. Thus a pragmatic socialization takes shape which absorbs the isolated elements that lag behind. This "productivist" ideology combines national power with private prosperity. It tries to avoid the anarchy of personal profit and also the apathy of an overcentralized bureaucracy. It makes use of the methods of flexible or concerted planning. It becomes the common good of the industrial societies because, in face of the menace of worldwide nuclear warfare, their political régimes have decided to transpose their doctrinal competition to the level of their economic expansion. The race for the moon has superseded the crusading spirit.

---

[9] JEANNE HERSCH: *Idéologie et Réalités,* p. 14, Paris, 1956.

This change is a good one, for the pragmatic pursuit of greater affluence is less destructive than the terrorism of superior thinking.

However, there are serious internal and external limits to the ideology of growth. First, growth creates disparities and inequalities, which are on the increase. There is a growing disparity between those who produce the output and those who have to beg for a few crumbs. On the worldwide level, growth is widening the gulf between the industrial countries and the underdeveloped countries. Within the industrial countries the gap is widening between the skilled workers and the unskilled; this gap is less apparent, but it is widening just as much. Expansion does not create homogeneity; rather it produces tensions which are very difficult to overcome, because they seem to be due to rational causes. The disparity between the different standards of living creates bitterness and violence among the underprivileged. And there is no worldwide demonstration or denunciation on their behalf, like the protest made by Marxism against private capitalism on behalf of the industrial proletariat. The weaker sectors are vegetating. Confronted by the ideology of growth they feel incapable of establishing their right to humanity except on the fact of their poverty. They are the lame horses of industrial society, and bear no resemblance to the "reserve army" of industry, as Engels called the unemployed workers of the nineteenth century. They do not constitute a labor force, for they cannot work. They see themselves not as a potential majority but as a forgotten minority, until the day when, in certain situations, their mass exclusion from the fruits of expansion makes them attack the affluent societies. Their stagnation, in strong contrast with the rapid progress in the other sectors, is the outer limit of "productivist" ideology—the living obstacle to its universal application.

Moreover, growth is an *indefinite* objective. It does not constitute a value in itself, as competition may have been in a system of free enterprise, or justice in socialism. Admittedly the planners for growth like to recognize its formal side. Whether they are Communists or neo-capitalists, they associate other criteria with expansion: the degree of social participation, the priority of creation over consumption, the priority of public solidarity over private interest, the priority of international aid over national egoism. But these ulterior values added on to the original objective of growth, with its different incitements, are in grave danger of remaining theoretical. They are desirable, optional correctives, not objectives assigned and desired by the collectivity. They are the moral luxury permitted by economic growth, not a basic program. This is clear from the difficulty experienced in trying to integrate collective utopias into the "productivist" societies, as soon as state compulsion slackens in favor of private affluence.

The ideology of growth is therefore a contradictory phenomenon. On the one hand, it is the realization of the economic and political plans which preceded it. Its aim is to abolish the poverty which is due to scarcity, and to promote freedom which is rendered possible through abundance and choice. On the other hand, it takes away all justification from the people who happen to be excluded from growth, not as the result of exploitation but owing to bad luck at the start. And growth has no qualitative aim. It is the rule of means which have no collective ends. Having partially solved the question of needs, its lack of any meaning apart from material prosperity is all the more apparent. To quote Karl Mannheim again, growth is an ideology which conserves technical power without stimulating society to utopian aims.

2. *The second ideology of western societies is security*. The hazards of life are diminished through provision and foresight. Society tries to become its own providence, deliberately planning certain characteristics for the future. This increase in the degree of awareness and collective organization is clearly an advance in social thought. By extending the field of action, society widens its responsibilities. In this way our societies are trying to substitute prevention for cure, competence for improvization, and education for dissatisfaction. This security represents a high degree of respect for human personality, by safeguarding people against the machinations of the "manager" and protecting them within a network of institutions. The more definite and calculable this security becomes, the more certain and reliable this policy becomes, and

less and less arbitrary. It is less brilliant, but also more serviceable. Instead of deploring the phenomenon of technocracy, we should pay tribute to it for the fact that human government benefits from a good administration of affairs.

Security is also a paradoxical phenomenon. It is the major claim made by industrial societies, but it does not supply them with an equivalent amount of affection. Two deep needs seem to be in conflict here: on the one hand, *the daily* round of little disciplines which are indispensable to the functioning of modern social security; and, on the other hand, the need for *adventure,* the myth of movement and "getting away from it all" fed by the press, culture and personal desires. There is a tension between this continual practice of strict adjustment and the dream of carefree spontaneity. In our industrial societies this tension expresses itself especially among young people; they have to force themselves to enter the system of skilled workers, and at the same time they are longing for a life that is extravagantly rich in affection. They imagine that they are living a life full of poetry, whereas in reality they are destined merely for security. But it is not only the young people who feel this tension. The whole culture in the social-security societies manifests this thirst for what is interesting, unpredictable and uncontrollable. The security of the imagination is undermined by novels, plays and films. On the other hand, in the societies which offer no economic security, the chaos of experience is transfigured into a controlled, legitimate contemplation by the classic arts. When society provides for all real needs, the artist becomes unrealistic or surrealistic. He turns from the concrete to the abstract, from harmony to discord, from the security of what he knows to the insecurity of what he invents.

Social security, the constant ideology of our societies, is thus accompanied by a deliberate inward insecurity. The public life organized by man bores him as a private person. It does nothing to feed his imagination. The western world (which increasingly includes Soviet society) is not solving the tension between efficiency and affectivity. That is why the industrial societies are so affluent materially and at the same time so frustrating psychologically. The ideology of security does not automatically bring happiness. There is a paradox here, manifest especially in the outbursts of youth and in modern art, but it exists everywhere and it prevents the ideology of security from resulting in a utopia of hope. That is why the advanced industrial societies no longer venture to extol social hope to the same extent as their technical progress.

3. *Lastly, the contemporary ideologies are internationalized.* Expansion and security are universal phenomena. Not only do the social techniques and models tend to be similar everywhere, but so do the young people and the different cultures. Internationalism, which was formerly the utopia and the ideology of the great revolutionary movements, has become a fact in contemporary society. Marxism finds a strange confirmation: the mode of production is becoming uniform, even if politics are different. The divergence is more and more taking place between the North and the South, and less and less between East and West. Internationalism is a phenomenon which levels out the ideological differences and creates similar standards of living everywhere.

However, this internationalism is paradoxical also. The special forms of nationalism are springing up again on every hand, and not only as expressions of chauvinist egoism. The people and the nations belonging to the common universe of technology are afraid to go forward toward a future that has no past, toward a project that has no memory, in other words, a civilization that has no culture. Our time may thus be said to be experimenting in interdependence and celebrating independence; on the one hand, it is moving toward a world market and, on the other hand, it is tending to establish national or continental conclaves. The ideology of internationalism does not result in an international utopia. The image of the world is therefore much more confused than at the time when nationalism and internationalism constituted two clearly opposed views.

Thus the ideological climates of the West seem to be complex phenomena in which one project conflicts with another, in which the aims cast a shadow: growth creates disparity and insignificance security creates the longing for adventure; internationalism revives loyalty to the special traditions of the past. The West has no total ideology affirming the radical need for liberty, as Marxism had. This explains the relativization of the ideological ethos in a society which nevertheless aspires to an awareness of its collective future. Paradoxically we are experiencing the exact opposite of utopian socialism which preceded the Marxist régime, and which believed in its aims without having the means. We have the means, but we have lost the aims. Partially realized, socialist ideology has become a technique of indefinite growth, of progressive security and definite internationalism. But it lacks the collective will which animated socialist utopianism. Instead of denouncing the worship of ideology, we must therefore revive people's belief in utopias, if we want to tackle our situation in the West.

Christian Faith and Ideology

Faith is not an ideology—that is, the expression of a social group with its own causes and its own interests. Faith is a response to a call which comes from elsewhere; it is an act which does not express a situation, but which replies to a call through obedience. An ideology is a rational system of collective needs. On the other hand, faith is a personal commitment, a venture at a turning point in history. For instance, Abraham's faith was not an ideology corresponding to the transient needs of the Children of Israel at that time. It was a personal decision taken by the "father of that people" (Ab-ham). Faith is the acceptance of a vocation; it is not the deduction of an interpretation. Faith and ideology, therefore, are not on the same level of knowledge and action. This can be seen more clearly if one compares their final stages: faith never turns into sight; it is always eschatological, otherwise it would no longer be faith. Ideology, on the contrary, has to manifest itself in collective expressions, otherwise it would have to be classified among the abstract categories of the ideal.

A clear distinction must therefore be drawn between *faith* (which is a personal response and an eschatological expectation) and *ideology* (which is a collective symbolization and a history program). However, they must not be systematically opposed to one another. They are rather two spheres which should preserve each other; for the secular ideologies warn faith not to merge with the spiritual armament of a particular group (social, national or cultural), not to deteriorate into a Christian ideology side by side with the other social ideologies. When faith becomes confused in this way with the collective stimulus of a human group, it loses its savor, its universality, its risk and its promise. It is then obliged to play the role of a competitor, and this alienates the members of the other groups from it. It then replaces the kingdom by Christian civilization, the gospel by the social principles of Christianity, the Holy Spirit by spiritual values, and vocation by planning.

Parallel with this, faith warns the ideologies not to set themselves up as faiths to be worshiped, involving personal obedience and promises of eschatological transformation. The ideologies must remain methods of rational interpretation and historic change. When an ideology yields to the temptation to become a faith, it replaces analyses with the *credo,* its principles by a *message,* its aim by a *vocation,* and its impersonal method by *the cult of personality.* An ideology then becomes corrupt, because it is attempting to be a challenge instead of an explanation.

An ideology therefore represents the degradation of faith into the abstract; and faith represents the personalized degradation of ideology. However, it is not so easy to distinguish between faith and ideology in actual life. The function of ideology is part of our contemporary societies. It acts as a running-belt between the aims of society and the masses. Its role is positive, if it symbolizes a collective project of which it has become actively aware. Its role is negative, however, if the symbol becomes an idol, a schema imposed by power, a collective unawareness serving a false aim. It is dfficult to discern between these two aspects of the ideological function. We often have illusions about its positive side, or else we only perceive its dangers. Both aspects do exist, both in the total ideologies and in the ideological climates. We must therefore be constantly on our guard, and this means supporting symbols as well as criticizing idols. The Christian faith is not opposed to ideologies, but to *idols*. Like Marxism, the Christian faith aspires to act as it speaks, both collectively and personally. In order to do this it supports itself, not on an idealized sublimation of needs, but on a concrete continuation of the incarnation. The Christian faith is faith not in the idea, nor in what is real, but in God's act in human history, in the commitment of God's action in the evolution of the world.

COMMUNITY—CHRISTIAN
AND SECULAR

by CHARLES C. WEST (U. S. A.)

WHAT is the basis of human community? This question is not
raised by people who are secure in their stable cultures and philosophies. Ideologists out to transform the world into the image of
their ideal put it only as a foil for a certain answer. But the characteristic of our time is that this question is being asked, search-
ingly, sincerely, not only by the Christian contributors to this volume, but by secular and religious men, by politicians, scientists
and philosophers in every part of the world, in a tone which shows
that none feels that he knows the answer.

The question is not new to the ecumenical movement. The experience of ecumenism has in fact been the questioning, the breaking and the experimental renewal of the communities of the church,
as they face, in missions, the work of God with a non-Christian
world; in ethics and evangelism, the destructive impact of the
word of God on traditional Christendom; and even in "faith and
order" the force of a biblical rediscovery of the church over against
the existing churches. The World Council of Churches indeed lives
by the grace which comes to Christians when they honestly face
the uncertainty, the problematic nature, of their own communities
or ideologies.

What is new in our time is that during the past generation a
large part of the world has begun to take part in a secular form

of this experience. Ancient cultures are seeking in their national independence, a self-identity they once thought they had. Ideological movements (notably communism, but also the humanist secularism of the western world) find that the social realities with which they must cope call their basic assumptions more and more in question. Religions of all kinds are being forced by events into that self-questioning which Jews and Christians have faced from the beginning because of the God they serve. The behavioral sciences underline the experience of all of us that the very communities in which our being takes shape—family, neighborhood, parish, class—are shifting, relative units made and broken by larger social forces, not structures of a permanent order. Communities, cultures and ideologies, even where we cling to them or try to make them anew, are no longer the source of our certainty and security. They have become tasks in an uncertain world.

This process, and our recognition of it, we know as secularization. It moves toward a state of human relations in which no religion or ideology dominates, and where no common sense of the timeless order of reality prevails. Is this a real possibility for modern man? Does this condition inevitably give rise to a flight toward religion, or a philosophy of secularism which imposes a humanist world view and an unlimited confidence in man on the world? Is it possible for man to live with the relativity which a fully secular society brings with it?

This writer believes in this possibility. He does so because he is a Christian, and finds the secular attitude to be required by a faithful response to God's revelation in history. But he hopes to demonstrate also to non-Christians that secularization is not the practice of self-deception by unstable men and cultures, but the real state of affairs in society today, a state which is full both of dangers and promises for the future, and within which our responsibility for our fellow human beings is given to us.

The Process

We start with a historical definition. The word "secular," with its variations "secularism" and "secularization," is relatively new as a general term in our western languages. Derived from the Latin word "seculum," meaning "age" or by derivation "this age or generation," its meaning until the nineteenth century was highly specific. Today, in the vocabulary of the natural sciences, it still refers to a long, indefinite period of time which is, however, not recurrent or periodical, as for example "the secular cooling of the earth." In cultural history it was used for centuries to designate those clergy whose ministry was in the "world" as distinct from those who were part of monastic orders. The implication was clearly that the structure and order of the church itself, expressed especially in its monastic life, was not temporal but eternal, whereas the secular realm would pass away. The structure of the medieval synthesis, brought to completion in Thomas Aquinas but deep-rooted in the popular consciousness as well, was not, however, dualistic, but hierarchical. The secular realm was not evil. It was given a certain value and autonomy at its level. It was the realm of temporal political power, of labor and trade, of the appetites in their place, of the natural virtues and the natural law. It was the realm where man seeks his proper ends with the help of his unaided reason controlling his passions. But it was, in principle, a lower realm, the realm of nature not of grace, the realm where reason demands its completion by revelation and where goodness is subordinate to the higher virtues of faith with their structure in the church.

Into this relatively stable world view broke the dynamic process of secularization. The word seems first to have come into use when church lands were turned over to secular princes in the Treaty of Westphalia in 1648. The reality however was already at work, as not only property, but positions of political power, expressions of art and culture, fields of knowledge, and even human ideals and values were gradually removed from the dominance of the church and the sacred structure of ideas and culture it represented. Its expressions were manifold. Already in the late Middle Ages William of Ockham attacked the concepts of substance, being, and first mover as categories for understanding nature, and opened the way for later natural science's tendency to think in terms of functional operations. Galileo, himself a believing Christian, sought the right to declare as true a theory of the movement of the earth which his observations suggested and his imagination conceived, even though the entire religious as well as physical world view of his time, was threatened by this breakthrough.[1] The artists of the Renaissance broke through their religious subject matter to express increasingly the vitalities of secular existence in all its variety. Machiavelli, sometimes called the first social scientist, analyzed the political forces of his day to give advice to his prince without regard for any larger structures of philosophy, ethics or religion or for any goal save the unification of Italy. Hugo Grotius, spurred on by the terrible example of the wars of religion, felt it his proper service of God to develop a system of natural law in ethics which would be valid *etsi, per impossibile, Deus non daretur,* for it would be evidently true to all reasonable men, whatever their dogmatic persuasion.

All these examples have one common feature. They did not represent efforts to combat Catholic Christianity with another world view. They were simply movements toward autonomy in various spheres of thought and life. In most instances Christian faith accompanied, if it did not inspire, them. They were not aware of leading revolution, nor of setting up great new systems of truth. They were trying to solve the relative problems of thought and life which they saw before them, to express the reality they knew. The inherent dynamic of this process is to call in question not only the world view of medieval Christendom, or other forms of Christianized culture, but any sweeping ideology from any source, which

---

[1] Galileo was, as VON WEISZÄCKER points out, fighting for a theory which he could not yet prove (*The Relevance of Science,* pp. 104–107). His theory, however, was not a new world view, but an explanation of a certain sequence of natural events. Galileo took no responsibility for the philosophical, religious and social consequences of his scientific theory. He demanded the right to be free as a scientist not to do so.

tries to organize all of life and thought into one system of meaning and order. This is the process we are a part of today.

The Ideology

In religious circles resistance to this process has been continuous, subtle and varied. Our entire understanding has been clouded however, and our very reaction to the word "secular" misled, by the rise of a massive wave of humanistic ideology which in recent years has taken to itself the very name "secularism."

Secularism differs fundamentally from the process of secularization. It is, in fact, one form of resistance to it. As a specific philosophy it is associated with the nineteenth-century free-thinker, G. J. Holyoake. Holyoake described his philosophy as a system of ethical principles based on four foundations: (a) primary emphasis on the material and cultural improvement of man; (b) respect for and search for all truth, from whatever source, which can be tested in experience as leading to human betterment (Holyoake believed that theological dogmas were both irrelevant and dangerous for this search for truth, since they were proclaimed *a priori* and limited freedom of investigation and expression); (c) concern for this world and its improvement and not with another (investigation of a possible kingdom of God or eternal realm could be left to those interested); (d) an independent, rational morality which did not base itself on faith in divine commandments.

This is a typical rather than a unique expression of principles. Holyoake was reacting, like many other humanists, against the church of his time. He was sharing that strange combination of radical epistemological relativism with complete optimism about the goodness and rationality of human nature which characterized the utilitarianism of Bentham and Mill. He was echoing Auguste Comte's positivism without the latter's elaborate religion of humanity. He was reflecting, in short, a world view which has pervaded recent centuries and has presented itself as a living alternative, and successor, to the Christian faith. It has many names of which secularism is only one. But its beliefs can be roughly described, on the lines of Romano Guardini,[2] under three heads:

1. Belief in the objective reality and normative value of nature, "the immediately given, the wholeness of things before man does anything about it, the embodiment of all energy, matter, essence and law—the binding norm for all perceiving and creating, of that which is right, healthy and perfect."

2. Belief in man, his reason, his feelings, his individual freedom, his unlimited development and power. Humanism has its antecedents in the secularizing process; there too the shift takes place from God and his order to man and his experience as the natural starting point and testing ground for human thought and action. Nicholas Berdyaev for example maintains that the spirit of the Renaissance showed a natural tendency to humanist faith:

This divorce from the spiritual depth in which man's forces had been stored and to which they had been inwardly bound, is accompanied not only by their liberation but their passage from the depth to the periphery and the surface of human life, from medieval religious to secular culture; and it implies the transference of the centre of gravity from the divine depth to purely human creation.[3]

3. Belief in culture, that is, belief in the process whereby man creates the values and conditions by which he lives. "In regarding the world as 'nature'," writes Guardini, "man posits it in himself; in understanding himself as 'personality' he makes himself lord over his own existence; in the will to 'culture', he undertakes to build its form (Dasein) as his own creation." [4] Culture then, like

---

[2] Das Ende der Neuzeit, Würzburg, Werkbund Verlag, 1950. Eng. Tr. The End of Our Time (Buras, Oates). Guardini is not responsible for all the use we make of his categories.

[3] The Meaning of History, p. 131. EMIL BRUNNER: Christianity and Civilization, and PAUL TILLICH: "The World Situation" in The Christian Answer, H. P. van Dusen, ed., support this general conviction that the movement away from the medieval religious world view must be understood in terms of an alternative faith—in man and his possibilities—and that secularization, in the sense of this essay, does not exist. HENDRIK KRAEMER: World Cultures and World Religions, also inclines to this view.

[4] Op. cit., p. 50.

nature and personality, becomes something mysterious and indefinable, a religious symbol of secularism.

Anglo-Saxon secularism has expressed the same faith somewhat differently. Adam Smith and the nineteenth-century utilitarians who followed him phrased it in terms of a view of history. The private efforts of individual human beings, each to enlarge his own happiness and profit, would lead to an ever greater development of the welfare of the human race, for the desires which lead toward harmony and cooperation predominate in human nature. Even the chilling evolutionary theory of the survival of the fittest through conflict was adapted to this optimism. Pragmatism, indeed, provided a better vehicle for this faith than did idealism, as John Dewey has demonstrated, because it placed fewer preconceived limits on what man would discover and create by his cultural experimentation. Man was free to affirm his individual ambition, for the natural checks and balances of his own nature and society would mold them to the good of the whole. He need no longer ask the question of the good in itself, for in his own self-assertion in interaction with others he would create the values which constitute this good. Similarly man was free to be a specialist and an empiricist in his investigation of the world. He need no longer ask the question of truth in itself, because all that he would discover would be a portion of this truth. Faith in man's cultural creativity and the reality it would bring forth replaced faith in God's providence and redemption of the world.

Hence the ideology of secularism, which the Jerusalem meeting of the International Missionary Council in 1928 rightly placed alongside Buddhism, Hinduism and Islam as one of the world's great religions. It deserves the epithet "secular" only in the sense which Holyoake defines: It is concerned with this world and not with another. It is, in the Quaker philosopher Rufus Jones' words at Jerusalem, "a way and an interpretation of life that include only the natural order of things and that do not find God or a realm of spiritual reality essential for life or thought." But it is also a structure of belief about nature, man and history in this world which says far more than this. It is a faith about the processes of nature and the possibilities of man which glorifies them both. It endows this world, the *seculum* in its historical development, with absolute and self-evident meaning and value.

Within the context of this faith, secularism is not inherently hostile to religion as such. As the expression of the human spirit reaching beyond itself toward wider and more complete structures of meaning, religion can have its due place in the secularist's view of life. The secularist objects to man's being confronted by a reality which enters his history from outside human capacities. He objects to dogmas other than his own. But religion, and even God, understood as the depth of human reason and experience or a predicate of the human consciousness, and as affirmation of the world in terms of it, is quite possible for him.

The curious result has been, in the postwar world, the growth of an alliance between secularism and religion; it would be more accurate to say, perhaps, a resurgence of religion, both Christian and non-Christian, on secularist premises. This resurgence has been long in preparation. Its roots are in the eighteenth-century enlightenment's concept of "natural religion," as reverence for and consciousness of God, nature, morality and human goodness common to all men, and expressed differently in different ages and cultures. David Hume annihilated the enlightenment's form of this religion, in his *Dialogue,* but he left the nineteenth century with the question: Where, then is religion based in the human consciousness? This question became the basis of the philosophy of religion from Kant and Schleiermacher to the present day. Many such philosophers have been subtle apologists for a Christian world view. Schleiermacher, for one, demonstrated the superiority of Christianity as the highest religion and developed a whole trinitarian dogmatics from the logic of the human feeling of "absolute dependence." They were all concerned to combat the secularist ideology with a reasoned philosophy which would give more place to specifically Christian values. But in their argument they accepted the basic secularist premise from the beginning: That man is the measure, through his capacity for religious experience and understanding, and that any truths asserted about God must be verified by reference to this capacity. Theology, then, was enclosed in religion, and religion was understood as one department of human life, one expression of human consciousness.

It was one step from here to the advocacy of religion, not because its propositions or beliefs are true, but because they are useful, and even necessary, for the stability of the social order and the flowering of culture. But secularist religion is not limited to Christendom today. It expresses the essential ambiguity of the resurgence of non-Christian religions as well. The late Professor K. M. Panikkar spoke for a large number of his fellow Indians when he analyzed the radical reforms which are needed in legislation and social custom in order to humanize his society and then asked, "What would remain to identify the Hindus as a race? Surely the Hindu religion and the samskaras associated with it, a purified and invigorated social order based on religion.[5] It was foolish, he argued in another book,[6] for Christian missionaries to imagine that they could change the religion of Indians or of any other Asians, for religion is precisely that which distinguishes a culture, which is its root and the basic expression of its self-consciousness. The relation of a nation to its eternal ground and meaning is expressed there. Religion is, in short, for Panikkar, the servant of the nation's and the culture's self-assertion. It is measured by its social usefulness to this end.

Once again, this illustration is typical, not exceptional. The principle, worldwide, is clear. There is no inherent opposition between religion, as such, and secularism, because religion can easily be explained and professed in a secularist framework.

The Uncertain Trumpet

In the long run secularism is a conservative force. It did not seem so in the beginning, for secularists made themselves the

---

[5] *Hindu Society at the Crossroads,* Asian Publishing House, London, 1961, 3rd Ed.

[6] *Asia and Western Dominance,* Oxford, 1957. Only the first edition contains the analysis of Christian missions in detail which for Christians is the chief value of the book.

spokesmen of the laws of nature and of the emancipation of man. It was secularist ideology which seemed to find the new discoveries in science and the new horizons of society meaningful and hopeful, when church and theology appeared to be holding the floodgates closed. But appearances are deceiving. The floodgates of change were opened by forces beyond the control and comprehension of either churchman or humanist. The world view we have described above took the form of many different philosophies as new problems arose in the secular world. But always these were efforts to control the flood of events, to bring order out of chaotic phenomena, to see meaning in the whole on the basis of faith in the goodness and the unlimited capacities of man. They did not follow knowledge wherever it led; they were forever setting up dikes to redirect the flow of its possibly dangerous conclusions. They did not allow secular events to take their course: they tried to form them into one great historical channel of human development toward harmonious community, and to banish from reality what did not fit.

Nowhere is this more clear than in the way in which both the idea and the reality of revolution developed. The reality is older in modern times than the idea. The prototype of all our later understanding is the "Copernican revolution" in science; a total reversal of perspective on the external world and on the place of man in it. Machiavelli initiated a revolution in political and ethical thought in similar fashion. Revolution takes place when men break fundamentally with the values and perspectives of the past, when they no longer feel themselves to be within that reality or indeed whenever they are in fact outside it regardless of their feelings. Revolution is the seeking of truth and standards for action in the future, not in the past, which results from this break.

The curious fact, however, which has attended revolutionary change is that its most radical agents have been unaware of their own agency. Copernicus was a profound conservative in spirit who propounded his theory of the heliocentric movement of the planets as an interesting mathematical hypothesis. Machiavelli dreamed of a united Italy which might one day recover the civic discipline of the ancient Roman Republic. The first modern use of the term "revolution" designated the restoration of the Stuart monarchy in England in 1660. The "glorious revolution" of 1688 was understood as completing what had at the earlier restoration been incompletely done. Life had been turned back to its preordained order.

It was the secularist philosophy of the French enlightenment which first grasped the reality of revolutionary change with an idea: the idea of progress toward the perfectibility of man, of the liberation of human reason from the fetters which bound it so that it might reach out toward the unbounded horizons of human achievement. The architects of the French revolution were not afraid of destroying the order of the past because they believed in the imminent dawning of a new age whose name would be freedom and whose laws would be the eternal laws of nature, the Supreme Being and the divinely rational heart of man.

It is a matter of history that this ideology could not contain the revolution it had itself promoted. Its own believers instituted the reign of terror. Some of its fondest ideas—Rousseau's general will, for example, or Helvetius' view that characters could be made by education—turned out to have demonic implications which dismayed the faithful and sometimes the philosophers themselves. The French revolution became a *torrent revolutionnaire* which moved with a force of its own, sweeping actors and victims with it. History became a problem in itself. In the words of Hannah Arendt: "The point of the matter is that all those who throughout the nineteenth century and deep into the twentieth followed in the footsteps of the French revolution, saw themselves not merely as successors of the men of the French revolution but as agents of history and historical necessity, with the obvious and yet paradoxical result that instead of freedom necessity became the chief category of political and revolutionary thought.[7]

The philosophy of history, then—the discernment of a meaningful pattern in historical necessity—became the last device of secularist ideology for bringing revolution under control. Hegel is

---

[7] *On Revolution,* Viking Press, New York, 1963, p. 46.

known to us as the philosopher whose massive *tour de force* put together a philosophy of being and history, of reason, fact and value, after the philosophy of David Hume and the events of the French revolution would seem to have separated them forever. It was he who explained the forces of historical necessity in such a way that they were made to contribute after all to the good of the whole society, just as the human spirit was shown its relation to the world spirit even in the midst of apparent alienation. He did this, however, at the cost of one basic step beyond secularism, which was to prove the downfall of conservative religious metaphysics: He embodied a continuing revolution in his very concept of knowledge and being. For Hegel, man can know the truth only as he struggles to realize himself against obstacles. The same is true of nations and cultures. "Spiritualization"—the conquest of every object and its absorption into the self—is the destiny of men and nations. Through it the world spirit, or God, realizes himself in our human spirits and the alienation between them is overcome. This means in practice that truth is a function of struggle, and being is the relation established as its outcome.

Karl Marx was in this latter sense a Hegelian, who destroyed Hegel's secularism with Hegel's own methodology. Marx inscribed on his banner that neither truth nor morality exists except as a reflection of the class struggle through which man expresses his relation to the forces of production. Marx and the Communists are in this sense the most genuinely secular, and therefore anti-secularist, of social scientists. They glory in their adherence to a revolutionary cause the relation of which to any system of truth or goodness outside its own strategy is meaningless and irrelevant. They deny any doctrine of man or any concept of nature in order to concentrate on the way in which they intend to remake both. They challenge all other ideologies, not in order to argue theory but to prove themselves in practice as more effective in forming the events of human history.

Yet Marxism is still, as everyone knows, an ideology based on a faith. It believes in the unlimited capacities of postrevolutionary man as a collective or generic being. It reckons with the dialectic movements of history as Christians reckon with God. Its concept of science and of the scientific method clothe it in the jargon of empirical objectivity. In many societies of great social injustice its analysis seems closest to human need and hope. But wherever the question of strategy and tactics arises, to achieve the revolution or to maintain it, the basic secularism of this faith reveals itself. Not the laws of history of the movement of the proletariat, but the program and power of the Communist party become the absolute. Not man as he emerges in the new society, but man as he will be molded by controlled social conditions is the object of adoration. Not reality with its revolutionary dynamic, but an ideal essentially achieved and waiting only to be realized progressively in practice, becomes the object of "scientific" understanding. Marxism, which began as a summons away from mystifying ideas to real social existence and which promised to follow the revolution wherever it would lead, has become one more structure of ideas by which men seek to impose their own meaning on history and to keep the revolution from getting out of hand.

This is the fate of secularism in all its forms, religious or atheistic. Beginning as a philosophical rationale of change, it ends by being itself a bulwark against changes the complexity of which its theory can no longer understand. Beginning as an emancipation of man from dogma, it ends by trying to bind man by an ever more futile repetition of its own dogmas. Lest the point be missed: this is just as true of Catholic Christian democracy, of British utilitarian common sense, of the American way of life, of Pan-African nationalism, of resurgent Islam, Buddhism or Hinduism as it is of Marxism. Human events themselves render philosophies of culture and history obsolete. The variety of human knowledge casts doubt on the theories which would knit it all together. A more acute sense of the human situation itself explodes our various doctrines of man. This is a process of which we are all a part, however much we may resist it.

Secularization

An earlier ecumenical study has defined this process as "the withdrawal of areas of life and thought from religious—and finally also from metaphysical—control, and the attempt to understand and live in these areas in the terms which they alone offer." [8] Such a definition has the advantage of coupling religious and secular world views and defining secularization as a movement away from both. But it hardly catches the drama which the word "life" implies, as familiar certainties are blotted out in the hurricane of events which has blown up in the last generation. It is the human crisis which concerns us mainly here. Let us look at it more closely.

1. Secularization is a process whereby men and societies have lost the sense of living in a totally coherent world the basic elements of which can be grasped by the human mind or by religious beliefs and practices. The word "empirical" suggests itself to describe this attitude, but it is deceptive. The spoiling of a beautiful theory by a single recalcitrant fact does not describe the way in which scientific investigation operates. Rather, it is in the realm of theory itself that total coherence has been lost. In the field of physics this has been dramatically illustrated by the disappearance of the mechanical model of the universe in favor of mathematical formulae of which no model can be made. But it is equally the case in economics, where the integrated theories which once undergirded capitalism or predicted its destruction have been replaced by a variety of functional models; in sociology, and not least in politics, where the great ideologies which at the end of the Second

---

[8] This definition was first offered as a tentative working proposition in a background paper for a consultation on "The Meaning of the Secular" for university teachers at the Ecumenical Institute, Bossey, Sept., 1959. It was again reflected in the report of this consultation, which is available from the Ecumenical Institute (Château de Bossey, Céligny, Switzerland). The discussion on the subject was continued in a European conference of the World's Student Christian Federation in Graz, Austria, 1962, and in its staff meeting in Jan., 1963. The papers from these meetings are published in *The Student World* (13, rue Calvin, Geneva, Switzerland), No. 1, 1963. See especially STEVEN MACKIE: "European Christians and the Secular Debate," pp. 4ff.

World War competed for the task of rebuilding the world have one and all lost their power to convince even the people under their influence of the power and truth of their basic ideas. Doubt about a coherent world has eroded not only religious institutions, but Communist, Social Democratic and Christian Democratic parties, labor movements, patriotic associations and countless other movements as well.

2. This in itself could be a healthy reaction, a return to concrete human realities from the abstractions which have bedeviled them. But beneath it lies a crisis, the crisis of being itself. Secularization is the process whereby men and societies have learned, more sharply than ever before, the relativity of human knowledge and ethics to the standpoint of the knower and the conditions of his investigation, or the character of his action. This was the insight of Hegel and Marx, though it goes back to David Hume. The world is known only by interaction with a collective or individual agent; and the resulting knowledge, or value, is never detachable from that relation. Once again physics offers the most dramatic illustration: as the objective reality of physical substance dissolves in sometimes contradictory pictures (the wave and quantum theories of light) and the experimenter finds it less and less possible to discover that which the conditions of his experiment themselves do not help to create, the physicist magnifies human control over an unknowable reality to frightening and exhilarating proportions. The ontology of physics becomes ever more problematical; its functionality increases every day. So also with social existence. Ancient structures of the common life, cultural, economic, political and familial in one, often rooted in a profound and ageless sense of relation to divinity, suddenly lose their power to give security and meaning to human community. As industry moves in, trade moves more rapidly and persons are forced to work, often alone, with those of other cultures, the ontological question loses its relevance also in the social sphere, and the question of function takes its place. Nature and society alike become, in the words of Guardini, "a complex interaction of relations and functions which can only be grasped by mathematical symbols, and which are based

on something which can no longer be given a name." [9] Secularization is the experience—the critical experience—of losing contact with being, of no longer being able to grasp the structure of reality as it is in itself, and at the same time being caught up in a changing network of relations and functions wherein lies greater power for good and evil than was dreamed of by our ancestors.

3. Secularization involves, as a by-product of this functional direction, a movement toward specialization, in thought and life. By a curious paradox the organ of universalism in man's spirit—his ideology and religion, his sense of continuity with the being of all things—has been rendered obsolete by the reality of universal history into which mankind has been swept. It is demanded of modern man not that he explore some realm of being, but that he master a field which has a functional value. The language of this field is related to its functionality; the psychologist, the sociologist, the physiologist and the neurologist all study some function of man, but none feels it necessary to have a doctrine of man as a whole. Functional collaboration among them may be wise at times, but no overall theory need embrace them. But what works well in the realm of thought becomes a crisis for human existence. For secularized man is himself a bundle of specializations—that of his place of work, of his family life, of his circle of friends and perhaps of his church or other group which claims a portion of his loyalty and time. The relevant confrontations with reality other than himself take place in these local, particular contexts, in the persons and conditions he meets there.

4. Secularized man, then, is integrated not by the structures of the world in which he lives but—if at all—by his sense of what it means to be a person in this network of relationship, and what it means to be responsible for the function and the power which lie in his hands. His is a terrifying freedom from which there is no escape in shifting the burden of his responsibility into some god or nation or philosophy of nature and history. As a nuclear physicist or a biochemist, he cannot beguile himself with confi-

---

[9] *Op. cit.,* p. 77.

dence in the inevitable beneficence of scientific discoveries for man. As an industrialist amid automation he cannot escape with theories of economic progress his responsibility for the growing mass of unemployed semiskilled workers which his policies help produce. As an African politician he cannot draw comfort in private from his public ideology of a developing nation catching up with Europe and America. As an American politician he becomes dangerous to his country and the world when he sincerely believes in "total victory" over the enemies of his way of life.

The list could be extended indefinitely. Responsibility for the control of the power he himself has produced, for the fateful consequences of his own accomplishments in a world where metaphysical dreams no longer convince and where no superior power makes things right, is the hallmark of secularized man.

This is a dangerous and exposed position. Many of the greatest thinkers of our time regard it as an unstable one, a stage in the dramatic process of social decay which seeks to exclude the divine structure of reality which gave it birth only to end by setting up sacred absolutes of its own which are all the more rigid for being unrecognized as such. Mircea Eliade speaks of "raw religion," that urge to divinize portions of the world that is present in every man and culture. Paul Tillich speaks optimistically of extreme autonomy of man preparing the way for a new breakthrough of theonomy. But Roger Mehl describes the trend more ominously:

We discover in the midst of secularized society a process of resacralization. Some turn back to the church as a sacred structure, some turn to secular religions. . . . They make no clear distinction between the sacred and the profane. They bring the sacred down to earth in a false incarnation which results in a self-deification of man.[10]

The flight to secular religion is furthermore only one of the dangers which beset us in this condition. Nihilism in its various forms threatens equally from the other side. Technology can become an

---

[10] Summary of Professor Mehl's remarks in the report of the conference of the Ecumenical Institute on *The Meaning of the Secular, op. cit.,* Appendix, p. 7. See also "La sécularisation de la cité" in *Le problème de la civilisation chrétienne,* Presses Universitaires de France, 1958.

end in itself for those fascinated by its processes, regardless of its human effects. The Sophists of ancient Greece who sold the art of argument to the highest bidder have their counterparts today in the physicists, chemists, biologists and engineers who limit their horizon by the project in which they are engaged; in the economists and financiers whose ideas or policies are at the disposal of the particular interest that hires them; and in the technicians of politics and of advertising who manipulate the human mind for their clients. Power can be its own rationale in a world where "realists" reckon with no universal power which limits and judges their own. Human beings can be misused and their humanness destroyed not only by fanatic idealists, but also by cynics who recognize no objective values in society or structure to human nature. If Orwell's *1984* symbolizes the one type, Skinner's *Walden II* might stand for the other.

This is the demonology of secularization. But there remains one descriptive word to be said. Man without religion and metaphysics, man the problem solver alone with his responsibility for a world which he has made, remains a human being. There is implicit in the secular attitude an open reciprocal relation of man with man in the pursuit of truth and the solution of problems. There is an acceptance of the relativity of every man's point of view and interest and therefore of the inevitability of conflict and compromise. There is a search for the form of humanity not in an ideal or a doctrine, but in the give-and-take of human relations. He may say with sober relativism, "We need not hope in order to act, nor need we succeed in order to persevere," [11] but he is seeking nevertheless the substance of a reality which will claim his allegiance, and to which the future belongs, in the business of daily human life.

Christians in the Seculum

We have described secularization as a movement away from religious world views in theory and away from the dominance of

---

[11] CARL J. FRIEDRICH: *Transcendent Justice,* Duke University Press, Durham, N.C., 1964, p. 116.

religious institutions in practice. This means, in large parts of the world, a movement away from Christianity and the authority of the church. Those historians have been largely right who have described it as a drama of Christendom, imported in an advanced state of development into cultures which had never known the dichotomy of religious and secular before. But now we must say more than this. Theologically perceived, the proclamation of the Christian gospel is responsible for the dynamic of secularization, and is its first agent. This is so, even when those who carry it have no idea of producing these consequences, because the process begins with the history of the Hebrew people—with the calling of Moses and the revelation at Sinai—and is fulfilled in the incarnation of Jesus Christ and is expressed by the sanctifying work of the Holy Spirit in the church. To put it bluntly, the secularized state of human mind and society can be creative and is full of hope because it is the state into which God calls his people through their relation with him, and in which he sustains them by his grace. It is the attitude toward structures of thought and the common life which is most appropriate to the history and promise of that relationship. It is a quality of faith in believers and, where faith is not present, it is a condition in which, precisely for lack of any social and metaphysical obstructions, the word of God can be heard most clearly. Let us examine this thesis more closely.

Secularization begins with biblical history. The Dutch philosopher Cornelis van Peursen suggests two forms of man's relation to objective reality which precede it: (a) the mythical, wherein man feels himself continuous with the nature and society around him, deriving his very sense of self from his participation in their forms; (b) the ontological, in which being is objective and accessible in its timeless substance to the human reason.[12] Arend van Leeuwen combines them both, on the basis of a comparative study of Hindu, Chinese and early Mesopotamian civilization, into what he calls the "ontocratic pattern." [13] It is pre-biblical, but it is also modern, a

[12] "Man and Reality—The History of Human Thought" in *The Student World,* No. 1, 1963, pp. 13f.
[13] AREND VAN LEEUWEN: *Christianity in World History,* Edinburgh House Press, London, 1964, Chap. IV.

temptation and a tendency in primitive culture and modern social science.

From this baseline the biblical history departed, toward a totally new orientation to reality. The story of this is now familiar to biblical scholars and cannot be told here in full.[14] We can only indicate its direction.

1. Man's efforts to lay hold of a structure of being which he himself would control, by grasping it with his mind (metaphysics) or by securing it with ceremonies and experiences (religion) were overturned by the way God revealed himself. One could illustrate almost at random from the Bible. When God first spoke to Abram there was no evidence of mystic illumination or of rational insight into eternal order; rather the content of the address was command, "Go out from your kindred, from your father's house, to the land which I will show you," and promise, "And I will make of you a great nation—and in you shall all the families of the earth be blessed" (Genesis 12 : 1–2). The God who made himself known to Moses introduced himself historically: "I am the God of your father . . ." and specifically refused to answer the question about his name, except in historical terms (Exodus 3 : 14–17).

2. As with the being of God, so also with nature and history, reflected in the human activities of economics and science, politics and culture. The biblical basis of human knowledge and action in all these spheres is the relation which God establishes with his people, known as covenant. The biblical covenant is first a personal relation. The reality it reflects is that of the personal claim of another on us as free and responsible agents. But it is also a relation between God and a community of believers through which his relation to the whole human world is expressed; and it is a dynamic, active relation which expresses itself in events to which structures of society and the stuff of the material world are instrumental.

Once again the biblical history is the story of human attempts

---

14 See, for example, MARTIN BUBER: *The Prophetic Faith;* J. PEDERSEN: *Israel;* G. ERNEST WRIGHT: *The Old Testament Against Its Environment,* et al. A good summary of the argument is found in VAN LEEUWEN: *op. cit.* Chaps. 2 & 3.

to capture this relationship in sacred structures of political or natural order, and of God's judgment on the structures which re-establish the community of faith in a properly secularized world. We take three examples which still play a role in our life today.

(a) It is well known that the basic principles and prescriptions of human behavior known as the law play a large part in biblical, as in later Jewish and Christian, history. The laws in the Old Testament, as the prescriptions for Christian behavior in the Pauline letters of the New Testament, are of various kinds. They have borrowed heavily from the codes of surrounding peoples. In some cases they represent improvements on those codes, in others they reinforce the best available morality of the time. In any event they were modified and even reversed from time to time as historical conditions in the covenant relation between God and his people changed the response required. Ceremonial laws commanded at the time of the Exodus became an offense to the eighth century prophets, as did commandments in modified form for the postexilic Jews. The Ten Commandments were drastically modified by Jesus; in some cases, as with the law against killing, adultery and covetousness they were given a new dimension; in others, as with the Sabbath commandment and that on honoring parents, they were sharply corrected. The moral law, in the Bible, was basically those teachings (*torah*) which expressed for a time and place, the quality of relation which God had given with his covenant and which is made finally clear in Jesus Christ.

In short, biblical history secularizes the law. It also records revolts against this secularization. The Book of Deuteronomy records a legal reform whereby the people of Judah hoped to make themselves acceptable to God, only to be told by Jeremiah, "They have healed the hurt of my people slightly saying 'peace, peace,' when there is no peace" (6 : 14). The law which Paul rejected was of the same character. His "All things are lawful for me, but not all things are expedient" (I Corinthians 5 : 12) expresses exactly the congruence of biblical and modern secular attitudes. Law is, and should be, the servant of expediency.

(b) The biblical story also secularizes nature. It places creation—the physical world—in the context of the covenant relation and does not try to understand it apart from that relation. The history of God with his people has a setting, and this setting is created nature. But the movement of history, not the structure of the setting, is central to reality. Physical creation even participates in this history; its timeless or cyclical character, so far as it exists, is unimportant. The physical world, in other words, does not have its meaning in itself. There are no spirits at work in it which can help or harm mankind. It is the creation of God alone and is the object of his manipulation.

(c) The biblical history secularizes the forms of the community of believers itself. This has been the hardest lesson of all for believers to learn. The people of Israel did not believe the prophets who prophesied the victory of their enemies because God, in their minds, was bound to his temple and to the prosperity and security of the people he had chosen. Even the disciples throughout the life of Jesus were thinking in terms of the kingdom of God as a sacred order which he would bring in: "grant us to sit, one at your right hand and one at your left, in your glory" (Mark 10 : 37). And Paul was at constant odds with the sacralists to whom he himself brought the gospel: "already you are filled! Already you have become kings! And would that you did reign, so that we might share the rule with you!" (I Corinthians 4 : 8). Over against all this the covenant shows itself to be an ever-changing relation, the constancy of which lies in the character of God and not in the structure of the community.

The church is the community which cannot escape knowing all this, and which is called first to apply it to its own life. It lives by its participation in the death and resurrection of Christ in the Lord's Supper (Holy Communion, Eucharist). Its worship is a hearing and a responding to the word of God preached in its midst. These two acts give to the church itself a functional, secular existence. Because of them the church lives by rediscovering itself as judged and renewed by the work of Christ, by the transformation—potentially the transformation of the world—which goes on in its midst.

Secular Theology

This sets the terms of the theological task in modern society. We close with some suggestions on its content and direction.

1. We are left by the whole history we have described with the question of the reality of God. We say "reality" rather than "being," "essence" or "nature" in a deliberate effort to avoid the kind of thinking we have hitherto called metaphysical. We mean by it that long tradition of deductive system building based on the first principles of thought and being, which is associated with the names of Aristotle and Plato, with the Greek Church Fathers and with Thomas Aquinas, with Descartes, Spinoza and Leibniz, and subjected to basic criticism by Kant. The secular mind and biblical revelation are at one in rejecting the way of thinking which this system building requires, and the understanding of reality which is associated with it. Neither God nor his creation reveal to the human mind the structure of their essential being, for the very idea of such a structure or essence is a product of the human mind and therefore the instrument of man's desire to make his own ways sacred or absolute. The metaphysical task in the secular context then must be differently conceived—as the task of clarifying and relating ideas about man's situation within the limits of a particular position and bias in human history. Its point of reference will not be an ultimate structure of being but the dynamic relations of this history and the responses it brings forth.[15]

We know the reality of God only in and through his acts in history, his covenant relation with man, his calling, judging, forgiving, reconciling and saving acts toward society, centrally expressed in the life, death, resurrection and coming again of Jesus Christ. Through these acts and in this relation we know him to be free sovereign Lord over creation, man and history. The words we use to describe him—just, merciful, loving and the like—are not definitions, but themselves expressions of our relation, and

---

[15] I am grateful to Mr. Ian Ramsey for the reminder that such a metaphysical task is possible. Cf. also S. N. HAMPSHIRE: "Metaphysical Systems" in *The Nature of Metaphysics*, D. F. Pears, ed., London, 1958.

pointers to a reality which transcends our comprehension. Nevertheless, we know God as truly and wholly present with us, not partially removed into a mystical absolute. "God is who he is in the deed of his revelation," writes Karl Barth.[16]

This reality is differently perceived from most objects of human knowledge. He who acknowledges it lives within it. It lays claim on his actions; he understands himself and his world as part of this history. It is not a doctrine the truth of which he demonstrates, but a relation which he explores with his mind and expresses with his responsible life. For him "the will of God is what God does in all that nature and men do. It is the universal that contains, transforms, includes and fashions every particular." [17] He does not comprehend it or control it fom God's perspective. He reckons with and depends on it as God's gift.

This is conventionally known as the response of faith. It is not, however, optional for secular man. In his specialized fields of activity, in the variety of his human relations, in the use of the power in his hands and in his free responsibility the question cannot be avoided: What is the character of the reality with which I will reckon here? It is first a practical question. It is answered in the way money is spent—in families or in the budgets of nations. It is answered in the way machines are built and handled, and in the direction of research. It is answered in the way of a man with a woman, in lifelong marriage or passing relation. It may well be that most of us at this level are practical polytheists. Our realities clash and jostle, and we acknowledge them all. But it is the most responsible secular man whom this satisfies least, for he is left with the question of the integrity of his human responsibility itself.

There is a law in me or in my mind, the law of my integrity; and there are many laws in my members, the laws of response to many systems of action about me. In my responsiveness and responsibility to the many I am irresponsible to the One beyond the many; I am irresponsible as a self, however responsible the natural, the political,

---

[16] KARL BARTH: *Kirchliche Dogmatik*, II/i, p. 203.
[17] H. R. NIEBUHR: *The Responsible Self*, Harper & Row, New York, 1963, p. 164.

the domestic, the biological complexes in me may be in relation to the systems of nature, or to the closed societies of nation, church, family or profession, or to the closed society of life itself.[18]

The problem of reality in secular terms is the problem of the one Other to whom I as a whole human being am responsible, in and through the actions I perform and the other responsibilities I bear.

2. We are left with the question, then, of the secular reality of man. Toward this the whole foregoing discussion points. "The being of man is the history," writes Karl Barth, "in which one of God's creatures is elected and called by God, is included in his self-responsibility before God, and in which he shows himself qualified for this call and task." [19] The reference is of course to Jesus Christ. It would be incomprehensible were we to think of God, Christ or man as substances with attributes. In fact, however, it expresses the heart of the dynamic relation of all three. Christ, says Bonhoeffer, is "the man-for-other-men." This is his character. It describes the innermost quality which his acts and relations revealed. As such he revealed also the decision of God to be for man, epitomized the meaning of all the full-bodied terms—holiness, righteousness, mercy, loving-kindness—with which the Old Testament had tried to express this relation. Man then is defined —given his existence, calling and destiny—by his relation to the action of this God in Christ. In this action the whole world is included in its secularity and man is turned toward it as servant and witness by virtue of being "in Christ."

Man exists, then, as Christian faith sees it, in a field of personal relationships at the center of which is Jesus Christ. He is constituted in his very being by his actions and responses in that field. From him we derive our power to be human and our ever-changing understanding, in specific relations, of what it means. Through his work God negates the power of our inhumanity, releases us from fear of ourselves and frees us to shoulder responsibility and take

---

[18] *Ibid.*, p. 138.
[19] *Op. cit.*, III/2, p. 64.

action which serves our neighbor, even when we incur guilt thereby. Because Christ is there, man is not an individual, nor part of the masses, nor the creature of a race or culture, nor the citizen of a nation, but a person in these various contexts, free for the responsibilities they carry because he is free from defining himself in terms of them.

3. The question of an authentically secular society receives thereby a theological answer. Society—the political and economic structures of the common life and the cultural habits and values which give it a sense of unity—is a creative task given to man, not a structure to be received. It is a Christian responsibility to help the secular world to remain truly secular when it itself is tempted to lose confidence in itself and to give way to new ideologies or myths.

The church participates with every secular society in its search for justice and freedom for all its people. As this involves social analysis, political action and formulation of the particular hope of that people, it may mean many an ideological risk. But the church and its theology have the task of reminding such a society that its focus is the true need of man, that its function is the cultivation and development of personal relations among its members in free and experimental interaction. They have the task of warning the commonwealth whenever human beings are in danger of being sacrificed to institutions, projects or ideas. They have the task of confronting such a society through the church's own life and thought with the vision of what man is, the purpose for which he lives, in Jesus Christ, and with the continual self-criticism and reform which this involves. The final point will attempt to spell out one illustration of what this implies.

4. In no area of society are the problems of responsible action more baffling or the situation more dangerous than in the sphere of national and international politics. This is partly because power which can destroy the world is located here, but also because it has been so incompletely secularized. Many political ideologies have lost their convincing power; indeed we owe the precarious peace of coexistence to the fact that this is so. But mythology, especially of

the secular religion of nationalism, persists even among those who no longer believe it, and political decisions are made which reflect illusions more than reality. The present writer is an American. What he says will inevitably reflect that country's experience. But it may still be of some more general value to pose the question from one setting: What is a Christian's responsibility for his country's policy?

First, he is called to act as a solvent of the nation's remaining ideological illusions. When several years ago George F. Kennan propounded the thesis that foreign policy must be based frankly on a nation's self-interest, and not on moral principle, he was speaking as a responsible Christian. When a nation sets up its own national morality—even its concepts of freedom, justice and peace —as a universal standard by which to measure others, this self-justification becomes the heart of disobedience to God. In fact, a nation is, like its citizens, a self-interested body, whose insight into the truth about world order and whose morals in working for it, are highly relative. It lives in a world of other such nations with which it must interact. The Christian is called to prepare the nation to see the judgment and calling of God in the give-and-take of world affairs, in the defeats as well as the victories of its policies. As a secular institution the nation is not absolute. Loyalty to it must be critical and qualified, in order that it may better serve its proper limited purposes, as one expression of responsible community among men.

Second, the Christian is deeply involved in the responsibility which his nation has for using what power is at its command to serve human need. From this responsibility there is no withdrawal without unfaithfulness to God and to one's fellowman. Having said this, however, let us be clear that there is a radical difference between a nation's self-interested use of power and the use of it which God intends. The power of foreign aid and trade is a major example. Christians are in the position therefore of continually seeking to help the nation to reinterpret its self-interest in terms more inclusive of the needs and interests of others, and at the same time holding up the mirror of Christ to all self-interest as a judgment and a stimulus to the imagination. The nation will always argue that its most creative and altruistic policies are consistent with its self-interest. The church lives from the conquest of its self-interest by the power of Christ, on which the peace of the world depends. By the continual operation of this tension the policies of the nation are made fruitful.

Third, the Christian, fully involved with his nation's capacity to make war—in this case possibly nuclear war—bears witness to the nation of the relativity of all conflict to the purpose of reconciliation. No nation is righteous enough to seek an unconditional surrender. No cause is just enough to excuse any means of conflict to fight it. Because Christ has brought peace to all men there are no absolute conflicts or enmities. There are also no absolute governments. It may be that a nation must fight at times for people— its own or others. But then the welfare of the people must be the test of the battle and of the terms on which it ends.

Finally, the Christian recognizes that political power, like all power, has its limits. It can coerce, but rarely heal. It can set limits to human behavior, but rarely win people's allegiance. It can put down rebellions, but it cannot—at least American power cannot—produce a social revolution. Secular reality in politics includes the moment when the most creative political action is to renounce power and to bear witness in defenseless service to the human relations one seeks to establish. There are times—and there are nations which have lived through them—when the only wise political act is to suffer injustice and oppression not in hate but in forgiveness and inner freedom, out of which a new relationship may grow. Here also the pattern of secular reality is the pattern of the Man-for-other-men. Secular men in any situation can see the human logic of this. But that this pattern contains hope, that the future belongs to the reality we find in this man, is a truth for which there is no proof, there is only witness. This is perhaps the irreducible Christian contribution to the integrity of the secular community—to live within it ourselves, in all its incoherent functionality, in all its appalling responsibility for power and for powerlessness, in all its search for particular forms of humanness, as men who see by faith a promise here which is based on analyses of social trends, but which comes to all of us from without. If we live by the reality of this future we shall be secular men but we shall not be conformed to "the world," for we shall be looking at it from the angle of its meaning and direction given by that acting reality whom we call God. By the never-ceasing operation of this tension in all who believe, the secular life of the world is made fruitful.

DATE DUE

DATE DUE			
FE 9'70			
MY 11 '71			
APR 1 4 1972			
MAR 7 1973			
DEC 1 2 1973			
GAYLORD			PRINTED IN U.S.A